PLANET EARTH

KNOW IT ALL!

MOIRA BUTTERFIELD AND PAT JACOBS

Cavendish
Square

New York

Published in 2016 by Cavendish Square Publishing, LLC
243 5th Avenue, Suite 136, New York, NY 10016

Website: cavendishsq.com

This publication represents the opinions and views of the author based on his or her personal experience, knowledge, and research. The information in this book serves as a general guide only. The author and publisher have used their best efforts in preparing this book and disclaim liability rising directly or indirectly from the use and application of this book.

CPSIA Compliance Information: Batch #CW16CSQ

All websites were available and accurate when this book was sent to press.

Cataloging-in-Publication Data

Butterfield, Moira.
Planet Earth / by Moira Butterfield and Pat Jacobs.
p. cm. — (Know it all)
Includes index.
ISBN 978-1-5026-0888-8 (hardcover) ISBN 978-1-5026-0886-4 (paperback) ISBN 978-1-5026-0889-5 (ebook)
1. Earth sciences — Juvenile literature. 2. Earth (Planet) — Juvenile literature. I. Butterfield, Moira, 1960-. II.
Title.
QB631.4 B88 2016
550—d23

Project managed and commissioned by Dynamo Limited
Consultants: Sally Morgan, Dr. Patricia Macnair, Brian Williams, Carey Scott, Dr. Mike Goldsmith.
Authors: Moira Butterfield and Pat Jacobs
Editor / Picture Researcher: Dynamo Limited
Design: Dynamo Limited

KEY – tl top left, tc top center, tr top right, cl center left, c center, cr center
right, bl bottom left, bc bottom center, br bottom right.
All photographs and illustrations in this book © Shutterstock except: Fisherss/Shutterstock.com, cover;
iStockphoto.com 42cr, 43tr, 5826tr; X-ray: 40tl10tl, 40tr 10tr Donald Walter (South Carolina State University)/
Paul Scowen and Brian Moore (Arizona State University), 40bl 10bl J. P. Harrington & K. J. Borkowski (U.
Maryland), 40c 10c The Hubble Heritage Team/AURA/STScI, 40r 10r JPL-Caltech/CXO/WIYN/Harvard-
Smithsonian CfA; Science Photo Library 35cl 5cl Gary Hincks, 44tl 12tl Claus Lunau, 46tl 14tl Gary Hincks, 49tc
17tc PlanetObserver.

Printed in the United States of America

Table of Contents

🌐 Inside the Earth

The ground on which we stand is only the thin outer crust of planet Earth, like the skin on an apple. There are deeper layers that are much thicker and far hotter.

The Earth's core

The Earth's core has an inner and outer layer. The outer part is about 1,400 miles (2,260 kilometers) thick. It is a mixture of very hot liquid iron and nickel metal. The inner core is thought to be a solid ball of iron and nickel about 1,400 miles (2,260 km) across. Scientists have worked out the size and makeup of the core by measuring seismic waves, a type of energy generated by earthquakes. These waves of energy pass all the way through the Earth, and their measurements change as they go through different materials.

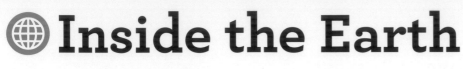

Peridotite, the main type of rock that makes up the oceanic crust

Rock on top

The Earth's outer layer is made of oceanic crust and continental crust. Oceanic crust is found under the seas and makes up around 60 percent of the Earth's surface. It is an average 12.5 miles (20 km) deep and is made mainly of a type of rock called peridotite. The continental crust is the part of the Earth's surface that is land. It is on average 18.5 to 25 miles (30 to 40 km) deep and is made of granite and basalt rock.

Deeper and hotter

Underneath the crust there is a much thicker rocky layer called the mantle. It is thought to be about 1,800 miles (2,900 km) deep and makes up around two-thirds of the Earth's mass. We still do not know exactly what the mantle is like all the way through, but we know that the temperature of the rock must get very hot.

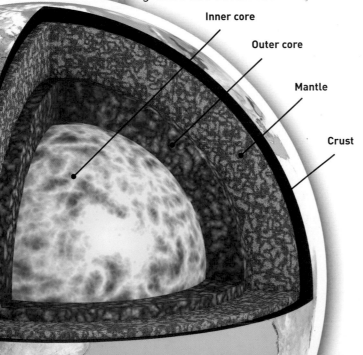

Inner core

Outer core

Mantle

Crust

💡 Know it all!

● Diamonds come from the Earth's mantle layer. They come up to the surface during volcanic eruptions.

● Scientists have managed to drill nearly as far as the mantle, but not quite. They hope to be able to reach it by around 2020.

The Earth's Surface

The Earth's crust isn't one smooth layer. It is broken into pieces that fit together like a giant jigsaw puzzle.

Moving plates

The pieces that make up the surface are called tectonic plates (the word "tectonic" means "building" in Latin). On top of the plates there is land and ocean. Underneath them is the red-hot rock of the mantle layer. The plates float on the mantle layer, moving around very slowly. There are several very large plates and lots of smaller ones. The edges where they meet are called plate boundaries.

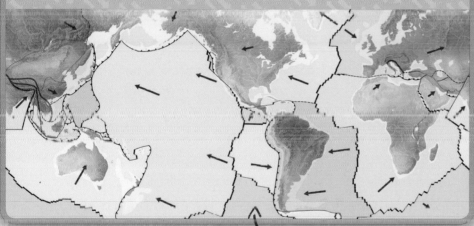

A map of the world's tectonic plates. The arrows show the way they are slowly moving.

Red-hot rock currents

Molten rocks flow in currents through the mantle layer beneath the plates, rather like sea currents in the world's oceans. It is this constant movement that moves the plates on the surface above.

New crust

New crust is being made all the time in huge cracks called mid-ocean ridges. These are found along the edges between plates on the ocean floor. A mid-ocean ridge is a long, underwater mountain range, split by a deep valley. Down in the chasm, molten magma bubbles up from below and cools into solid rock, making the new crust.

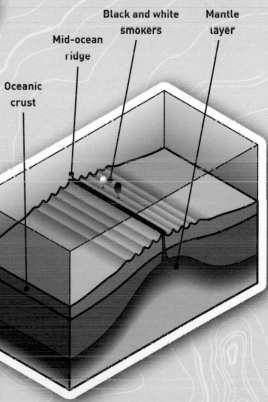

Oceanic crust

Mid-ocean ridge

Black and white smokers

Mantle layer

Hot shots!

SMOKERS!

Super-hot seawater, heated by volcanic rock deep in the ocean crust, spews out of cracks in the ocean bed. As it flows out, the minerals it contains turn the water white or black, like a chimney pouring out smoke.

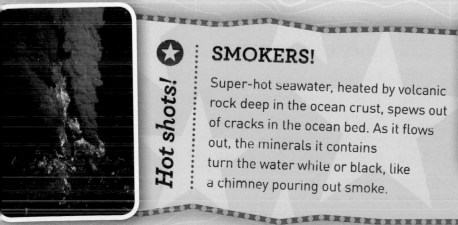

Moving Plates

As the Earth's plates move they carry the land and ocean floor with them, changing the shape of the planet's surface.

Colliding

When two plates collide the Earth's crust buckles and folds, pushing up long lines of mountains called ranges. The Himalayas were born this way around forty-five million years ago, when the Indian subcontinent smashed into Asia. Sometimes when plates collide one plate slides under the other and hot magma bubbles up between the plates, creating a line of volcanoes. The Andes in South America were created this way.

Moving apart

When plates move apart they create giant splits and molten rock bubbles up from below. In the oceans this creates mid-ocean ridges. On land it creates long basins called rift valleys, such as the Great Rift Valley that runs for 3,728 miles (6,000 km) from Syria to Mozambique.

Mount Ama Dablam in the Himalayas, Nepal. The Himalayas were pushed up by two colliding plates.

Know it all!

● The world's plates are given names. Six of the biggest plates are named after the world's continents.

● Some of the world's largest freshwater lakes are found in the rift valleys of the world, which are created by plates moving apart.

★ ROLLED-UP ROCK

Hot shots!

This rock has been folded by the movement of the Earth's crust. You can see the fold shapes in each layer of the rock.

The San Andreas Fault lies beneath this Californian landscape.

Earthquake zones

When plates slide past each other they create so much strain that earthquakes occur. For instance, in California, two plates are sliding past each other along a line called the San Andreas Fault. Scientists monitor the area all the time to try to predict when the plates might trigger an earthquake.

The Continents

The Earth's continents move around with the plates beneath them. The movement is slower than the growth of a human fingernail, and it has taken millions of years for the continents to reach where they are today.

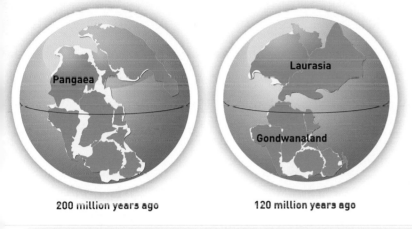

200 million years ago

120 million years ago

One becomes two

The continents were once one big supercontinent called Pangaea, surrounded by a vast ocean called Panthalassa. Pangaea started to break up around 200 million years ago, and by about 120 million years ago there were two continents—Laurasia and Gondwanaland. Before Pangaea there were probably other supercontinents that broke up and rejoined during the Earth's long history.

Our continents appear

Gradually Laurasia broke into North America, Europe, and Asia. Gondwanaland broke up to become Africa, South America, Antarctica, Australasia, and India (shown below). The continents are still moving very slowly today. For instance, North America moves away from Europe at a rate of about 0.8 inches (2 cm) a year.

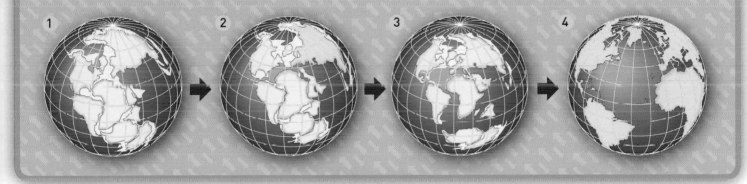

How do we know?

Fossils of plants and animals provide evidence of the continents breaking up. For instance, the island of Spitzbergen is now in the chilly Arctic Ocean, but we know it has drifted north over time because it contains fossils of plants that could only have survived in the warm, tropical climate of the equator. Meanwhile fossils of matching dinosaur species have been found in areas as far apart as Africa, India, and Australia.

Icy Spitzbergen was once a warm, tropical place.

Know it all!

● The eastern coast of South America and the western coast of Africa were once joined. Take a look at their modern shapes and you will see that they could fit together like jigsaw puzzle pieces.

🌐 The Earth's Rocks

There are three types of rock on the Earth. They are given the names igneous, sedimentary, and metamorphic.

Obsidian is a shiny, black igneous rock. It was used to make this Aztec ceremonial knife.

Igneous rock

Igneous rocks are formed when hot, molten material bubbles up from the mantle beneath the Earth's crust, then cools and hardens. Pumice, granite, and obsidian are all examples of igneous rock, but they do not look the same because they cooled at different rates. Granite cooled very slowly but obsidian cooled quickly.

Sedimentary rocks

Sedimentary rocks are mostly formed underwater. They are made up of layers of different material that have been squashed down and hardened. The layers could be mud, sand, gravel, clay, or even dead plants and animals that have dropped to the seabed. Limestone, sandstone, and shale are all examples of sedimentary rocks.

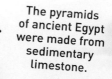

The pyramids of ancient Egypt were made from sedimentary limestone.

Marble is a type of metamorphic rock. It is highly prized for its beauty and is used to decorate buildings.

Metamorphic rock

Metamorphic rocks are formed deep beneath the Earth's crust, when igneous or sedimentary rock gets changed by heat or pressure. The rock breaks down and changes shape to become a new rock type. Examples of metamorphic rock include marble (once limestone), slate (once shale), and quartzite (once sandstone).

Riches Underground

Some of our most important sources of power—oil, coal, and gas—all come from beneath the Earth's surface.

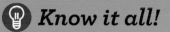
Coal is mined from underground.

Oil is often found under the sea and pumped up using oil platforms.

Natural gas is burned to create heat.

Coal from trees

Coal is formed from trees and ferns that grew around three hundred million years ago, when the Earth was a steamy, swampy place. When the trees and other plants died, they sank to the bottom of the swamps and were gradually squeezed under rocks until they lost all their liquid and turned into coal.

All about oil

Oil is made from the bodies of primitive, single-celled organisms that lived millions of years ago. When these organisms died they sank to the seabed, making layers that slowly squeezed down until they eventually turned into oil. Oil is extracted from underground by drilling and pumping.

Natural gas

Natural gas comes from animal and plant bodies that decomposed (rotted) around one hundred million years ago. It is found deep underground in rocks and is brought to the surface to use as fuel. It has no color or smell. Energy companies add a "rotten egg" smell to it so that gas leaks can be detected.

The Earth's Metals

Metals come from the Earth's rocks. There are lots of different types. Some metals are very good at conducting (passing on) electricity and heat. Some are particularly useful for making structures, and some are very strong.

Molten steel in a furnace

A bar of rhodium, the world's most expensive metal

Metal mining

Rock that contains metal is called ore. Ore is mined from underground. Then the metal is separated out from the rock using chemicals, water, or a heating process called smelting. For instance, iron is smelted from iron ore. Iron can also be mixed with other materials, such as coal, to make strong steel. This is done in a blast furnace, where the iron is heated until it melts and then mixed with other materials. A metal that is mixed with other materials is called an alloy.

Most valuable metals

Gold, platinum, and palladium are examples of rare, precious metals. The most valuable metal of all is rhodium, a type of platinum that is very difficult to extract and is found only in parts of South Africa, North America, and Russia. It is used in jewelry and in some car exhaust systems.

An ancient Greek silver coin from around 128 BCE

Ancient metal-working

Early humans worked out how to mine metal and create alloys such as bronze (a mixture of copper and tin) to make objects. One of the earliest mines is the Lion Cave in Swaziland, where people mined a type of iron called hematite from around 40,000 BCE. They ground it up to make a red paint used for wall paintings. Metal-working also made it possible for people to make the first coins.

💡 Facts & figures

WORLD'S BIGGEST PRODUCERS:

Copper – Chile
Gold – China
Silver – Mexico
Iron ore – China
Rhodium – South Africa
Steel – China
Tin – China

🌐 Precious Stones

Gems form as crystals in rock and vary in color, shape, and size. Because they are rare and beautiful they have been prized for centuries.

Rough, uncut diamonds

Precious or semiprecious?

Gems are put into categories, depending on how clear and beautiful they look and how rare and hard they are. Diamond is the hardest natural substance on Earth, but other gems, such as opals for example, are much softer and more easily damaged. The category called "precious" contains diamonds, rubies, sapphires, and emeralds—the most expensive, highly prized gems.

Raw emeralds embedded in rock

Color and size matter

Diamonds are found in a type of igneous rock called kimberlite, which is mined as ore and then processed to find the diamonds inside. The color of a diamond can vary a lot and affects its value. It may be clear or tinted blue, red, yellow, pink, or even black due to the minerals it contains. Colored diamonds occur once in every one hundred thousand diamonds found, so they are the most expensive. The word "carat" refers to a diamond's size. The bigger the diamond, the more carats it has.

Gems from rock

When igneous rock bubbles up as magma from underground it cools and crystallizes. Amethysts, emeralds, garnets, and diamonds are all igneous rock crystals. Gems are found in sedimentary rock, too, when it has been made from layers of igneous rock particles squashed together. Jasper and opal both come from this source. Metamorphic rock is the place to look for rubies and sapphires.

A Russian diamond "pipe" mine, dug on the site of an extinct volcano.

💡 Know it all!

WHERE TO LOOK:

● Rubies are much rarer than diamonds. The finest ones come from Myanmar (Burma).

● The best sapphires come from Myanmar, Kashmir, and Montana.

● The finest emeralds come from Colombia.

● The best opals come from Australia.

 Volcanoes

Volcanoes are formed when magma (hot liquid rock) bubbles up from beneath the Earth's crust, usually when two plates push against each other or pull apart.

How volcanoes form

Pressure builds up underground and pushes magma up from a chamber beneath the surface. It bubbles out of a crack in the ground as lava. Ash, rocks, and lava cool and build up a cone shape with a crater in the center. Sometimes the lava seeps out through side vents, called dikes.

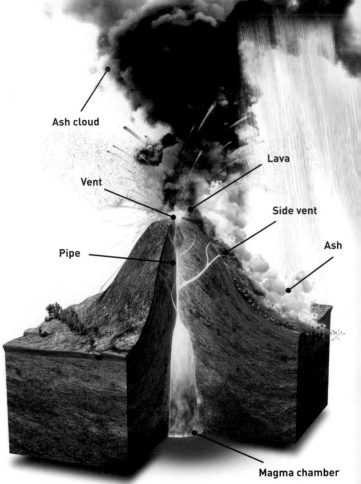

Ash cloud

Vent

Lava

Side vent

Ash

Pipe

Magma chamber

An eruption

It is impossible to predict exactly how a volcano might erupt. Some pour out thick lava that flows slowly in fiery rivers. Others make noisy explosions and throw out large lumps of molten rock, called volcanic bombs. The biggest eruptions are gigantic explosions that throw out huge clouds of deadly gas as well as lava.

Mount Vesuvius, an active volcano in Italy

Active or not?

Volcanoes that are erupting are called "active." Volcanoes that might erupt in the future are "dormant," and volcanoes that have stopped erupting completely are called "extinct." Famous active volcanoes include Mount Fuji in Japan and Mount Vesuvius in Italy. In 79 CE Vesuvius famously erupted and buried the Roman towns of Herculaneum and Pompeii, killing many people.

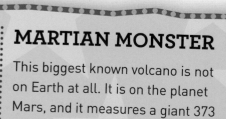

Hot shots!

★ MARTIAN MONSTER

This biggest known volcano is not on Earth at all. It is on the planet Mars, and it measures a giant 373 miles (600 km) wide.

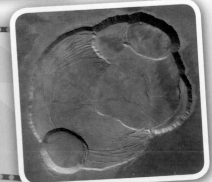

💡 *Know it all!*

● Crushed volcanic stone is used in toothpaste, makeup, bath cleaner, and road surfacing material.

● Between fifty and seventy volcanoes erupt each year, mostly under the ocean.

🌐 Geysers and Hot Springs

Hot springs and geysers are found in volcanic areas of the world where hot underground rocks are near the surface.

Why geysers are so steamy

Geysers and hot springs occur when underground water is heated by hot rocks beneath the Earth's surface. The boiling water rises up through cracks in the ground. Hot springs are warm pools, whereas geysers are regular spouts of steamy, boiling water. They occur when water builds up underground and then gets pushed up by pressure. After they spout they die down for a while until the pressure builds up again.

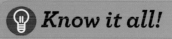

💡 Know it all!

● Hot water from geysers is used to heat homes and offices in Reykjavik, Iceland's capital.

● Hot springs have long been associated with healing. For centuries, people have bathed in them to cure illnesses such as skin complaints.

● The ancient Romans thought that hot springs were entrances to the underworld, a magical realm where gods and goddesses lived.

Snow monkeys love to relax in the hot springs of Nagano, Japan.

A geyser in Iceland

Ledges around the hot springs at Pamukkale, Turkey

Greatest geysers

Yellowstone National Park in Wyoming is the area with the greatest number of geysers in the world. It has around five hundred, half the world's total. Steamboat Geyser, the highest spouting geyser in the world, is here. Its steaming water jet shoots up once or twice a year and can reach heights of up to 394 feet (120 m). Old Faithful is Yellowstone Park's most famous geyser. It erupts every ninety-one minutes and even has its own webcam.

Hot spring shapes

Geyser and hot spring water contains mineral salts—material that has dissolved in the water from rocks underground. When the water reaches the surface and cools, the salts are deposited and harden to form beautiful shapes. Over time they can build up to form basins and ledges.

⊕Earthquakes

Earthquakes cause the ground to shake and occur when there is a sudden movement in the Earth's crust. They happen in areas where two of the Earth's plates meet under the ground.

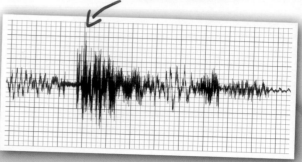

A seismograph readout. The longer the line, the bigger the shock wave.

Earthquakes (shown as red dots) closely follow the borders of the Earth's plates (grey lines).

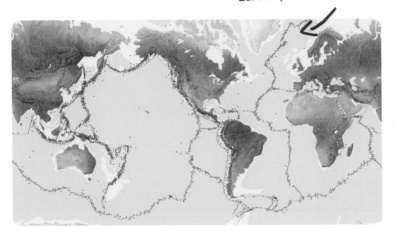

Measuring earthquakes

Instruments called seismographs measure earthquakes. A seismograph detects the shock waves produced and displays a line that records how strong each wave is.

Earthquake areas

Most earthquakes occur around the edges of the Pacific Ocean or in mountainous areas such as the Himalayas. It is here that the plates under the Earth's surface are pushing or sliding the most. Scientists monitor these areas to try to predict earthquakes, measuring for possible warning signs—such as minor tremors that might build up to a larger event.

💡 Facts & figures

THE RICHTER SCALE

The Richter scale has ten numbers representing the energy produced by an earthquake. Each number represents ten times more energy than the previous number.

Scale	Effects	Frequency
0-2.0	Not felt	8,000 a day approx.
2.0-2.9	Not felt but recorded	1,000 a day approx.
3.0-3.9	Felt but no damage	49,000 a year approx.
4.0-4.9	Felt slightly indoors	6,200 a year approx.
5.0-5.9	Weak buildings might fall	800 a year approx.
6.0-6.9	Destructive up to 100 miles (160 km) away	120 a year approx.
7.0-7.9	Severe damage in large area	18 a year approx.
8.0-8.9	Severe damage over 620 miles (1,000 km)	1 a year approx.
9.0-9.9	Devastation up to 6,200 miles (10,000 km)	1 in 120 years approx.
10.0	Has never been recorded	

🌐 Mountains

Mountains are giant masses of rock at least 2,000 feet (600 m) high. They cover about a quarter of the Earth's surface and are usually found in groups called ranges.

A dome mountain in the Adirondacks.

Mount Everest in the Himalayas, a range of fold mountains. The Alps and Andes are fold mountains, too.

A fault-block mountain in the Sierra Nevada. Trees grow only on the lower slopes of high mountains such as this.

Mountain building

The world's tallest mountain ranges were built when two of the Earth's plates collided with each other, slowly pushing up the Earth's surface. The process of mountain building takes millions of years and is still going on today. The highest mountain range of all, the Himalayas, first began to form about seventy million years ago and is still rising by about 0.4 inches (1 cm) every year.

Mountain shapes

Mountains are different shapes, depending on how they formed. Fold mountains are created when rock folds upward, like a piece of paper crumpling up in folds. Fault-block mountains form when giant blocks of rock are pushed up. Dome mountains are pushed up by magma bulging up from below, and plateau mountains are made when a wide section of flat land is pushed up.

Mountain profile

At the bottom of a mountain there might be trees, but at some point it becomes impossible for them to grow. The place where they stop is called the tree line. Above it only tough plants such as mosses can grow. Higher still, no plants survive and there is often snow all year round. The line between where snow melts in summer and stays put all year round is called the snow line.

Glaciers

A glacier is a huge, incredibly heavy mass of ice that moves down a mountainside as a giant ice river.

The front edge of the Perito Moreno glacier in Patagonia, Argentina

Facts & figures

The giant Franz Josef glacier in New Zealand, snaking like a river across the landscape

Where to find glaciers

Glaciers are found on every continent of the world, but most occur in the far north and south—in the Arctic and Antarctica. The world's biggest glacier, the Lambert glacier in Antarctica, is a gigantic 250 miles (400 km) long, 62 miles (100 km) wide and around 8,200 feet (2,500 m) deep. Glaciers move at different rates, depending on their size, but can move up to 65 to 100 feet (20 to 30 m) a day.

The birth of icebergs

Most icebergs are formed when chunks of ice break off a glacier and fall into the sea. The birth of an iceberg is called calving. Roughly ten thousand to fifteen thousand icebergs calve each year. Icebergs formed from glaciers tend to be narrow and spiky-looking. Icebergs that break off the giant ice sheets found in the polar regions are flat.

Carving out the land

As a glacier travels it carves out the land, forming a wide U-shaped valley. As the glacier grinds forward, nothing can stop it. It pushes rocks aside, eventually dumping them a long way from where they were first found. If the climate changes and a glacier melts, the landscape left behind is recognizable by the valley shape and by the areas of dumped rocks, called moraines.

Hot shots!

★ **INSIDE A GLACIER**

There are icy caves and water channels deep inside a glacier. This blue ice cave is an example. At any time the ice could crack, so it is not a safe place to explore.

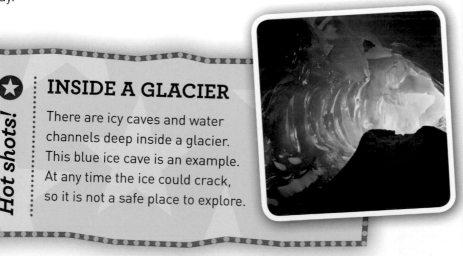

Rivers

Some rivers begin high up in mountains, where snow collects and melts. Some rivers begin where underground springs bubble up to the surface. All rivers run downhill, carrying fresh water to the sea.

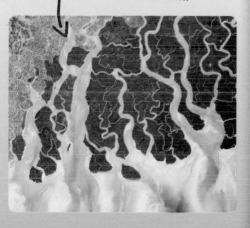

The Ganges Delta. The land between the water channels is made from river sediment.

River erosion

A river gradually erodes (wears down) the land it crosses. It slowly carves a V-shaped valley as it travels, wearing down rock and earth and carrying the particles in its waters. One of the best examples of a river changing the landscape is the Grand Canyon in Arizona. It has taken around seventeen million years for the Colorado River to carve the canyon from rock.

The Colorado River has carved the Grand Canyon up to 6,000 feet (1,800 m) deep.

Creating new land

A river slows down as it gets nearer to the sea and the ground becomes flatter. When a river slows the particles of earth and rock it is carrying drop to the bottom as sediment, creating mudflats and islands. Sometimes these spread out at the river's mouth in a wide area called a delta. The Ganges and the Brahmaputra Rivers meet in India and Bangladesh to form the world's largest delta, stretching over an area of 40,540 square miles (105,000 square kilometers).

The world's waterfalls

If a river reaches a very hard band of rock, it will wear down the softer rock on the other side and end up plunging down as a waterfall. The world's highest waterfall is the Salto Angel Falls in Venezuela, which plunges 2,650 feet (807 m) over a cliff. One of the world's largest falls is Victoria Falls on the African Zambezi River. Over time the Zambezi has carved out a channel around 3,304 feet (1,007 m) wide.

Victoria Falls, on the border between Zambia and Zimbabwe

Facts & figures

TOP FIVE RIVERS IN ORDER OF LENGTH (APPROX.):

1. Nile River, Africa: 4,160 miles (6,695 km)
2. Amazon River, South America: 4,000 miles (6,400 km)
3. Yangtze River, Asia: 3,900 miles (6,280 km)
4. Mississippi River, North America: 3,710 miles (5,870 km)
5. Ob River, Russia: 3,440 miles (5,537 km)

A River's Journey

Rivers do not look or behave in the same way throughout their journey from their source to the sea. They change shape and speed through three phases, called courses.

A river's upper course

The first part of a river is its upper course, when it flows fast downhill. It may gather water from other mountain streams as it rushes downward, sometimes racing through narrow gaps or bubbling over shallow rocks, creating fierce rapids. Strong-swimming fish and clinging plants live in this part of the river.

Fierce rapids in a river's upper course

A river's middle course

In its middle section a river flows along a gentler slope. It travels more slowly and goes around bends called meanders, rather than rushing through gaps. As the river cuts across the land it may leave shelves on either side called river terraces. Lots of fish and plant species live in the more peaceful waters of the middle course.

A river's lower course

In its lower course a river slows down and gets wider. The earth and rock fragments it has picked up on its journey are now worn down to tiny particles, which may pile up to form mudflats and banks. Waterbirds like to nest in this course, where there are likely to be lots of plants.

River terraces and meanders in a river's middle course

A waterbird wading on the mudbanks at the mouth of a river

 Coastlines

A coastline is the area where the land meets the ocean. The Earth's coastlines vary. One stretch might have sloping sandy beaches while another section might have steep cliffs.

Shaped by the sea

The sea shapes the coastline in different ways. If there is a crack in a cliff, seawater will get into it and gradually hollow it out over time to make a cave. Sometimes waves will pound either side of a headland until they wear away an arch through the middle. How quickly the sea reshapes a cliff depends on whether it is made from soft or hard rock.

On the beach

The sea gathers up loose stones as it wears away the coastline. The waves grind the stones into tiny particles and they are dropped onto the shore, creating beaches. Beaches are different colors, depending on what the sand is made of. It might contain yellow rock particles, white shell fragments, pink coral pieces, or even black volcanic lava.

Estuaries

Where a river meets the sea there may be a flat, muddy plain called an estuary. The sea washes over the mud, creating salty mudflats. In tropical areas there are sometimes giant swamps filled with mangrove trees (above), the only trees able to survive in salty water.

Some coastal shapes made by the sea

Headland

Arch

Stack

Stump

Beach

Where in the world?

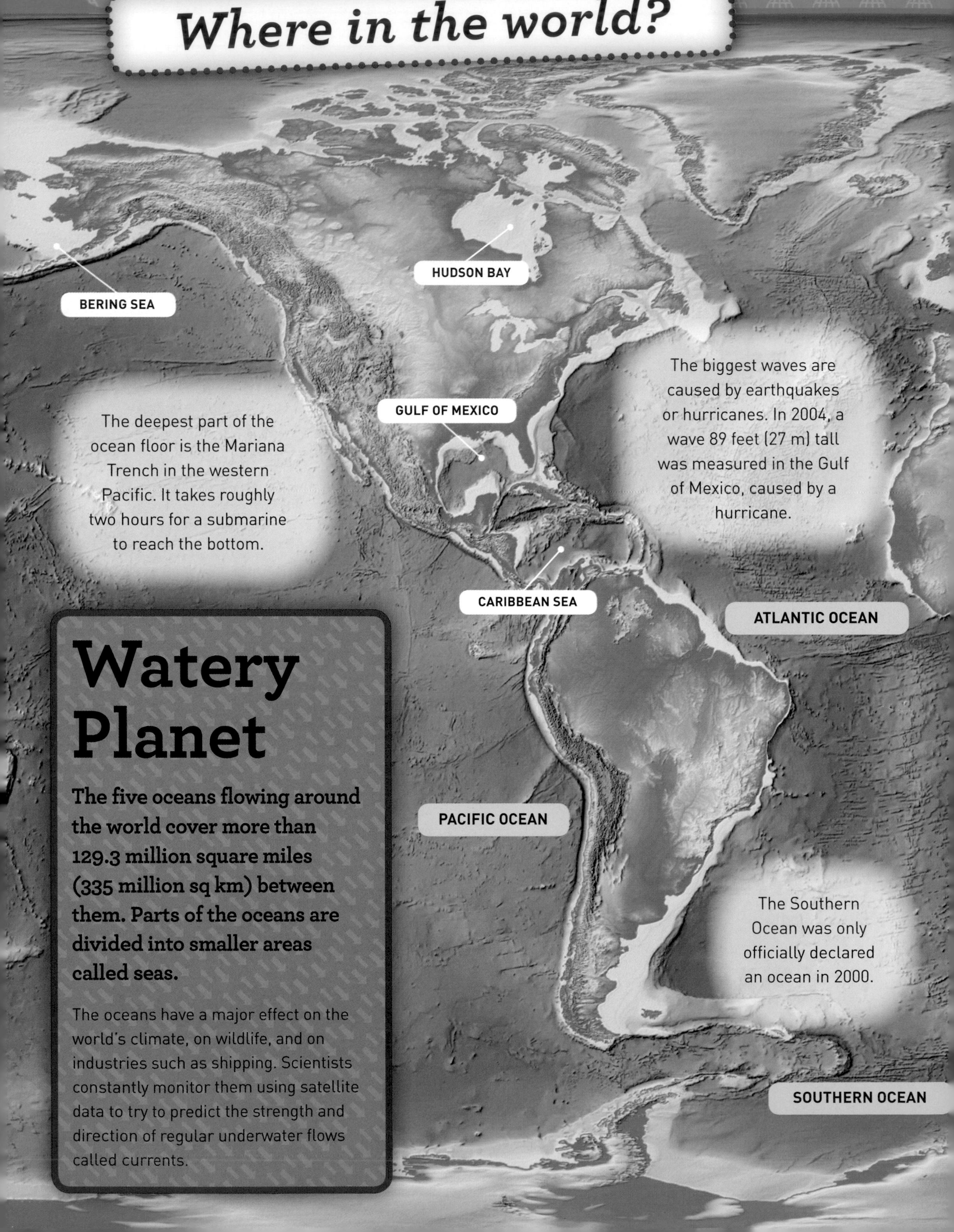

BERING SEA

HUDSON BAY

GULF OF MEXICO

CARIBBEAN SEA

ATLANTIC OCEAN

PACIFIC OCEAN

SOUTHERN OCEAN

The deepest part of the ocean floor is the Mariana Trench in the western Pacific. It takes roughly two hours for a submarine to reach the bottom.

The biggest waves are caused by earthquakes or hurricanes. In 2004, a wave 89 feet (27 m) tall was measured in the Gulf of Mexico, caused by a hurricane.

The Southern Ocean was only officially declared an ocean in 2000.

Watery Planet

The five oceans flowing around the world cover more than 129.3 million square miles (335 million sq km) between them. Parts of the oceans are divided into smaller areas called seas.

The oceans have a major effect on the world's climate, on wildlife, and on industries such as shipping. Scientists constantly monitor them using satellite data to try to predict the strength and direction of regular underwater flows called currents.

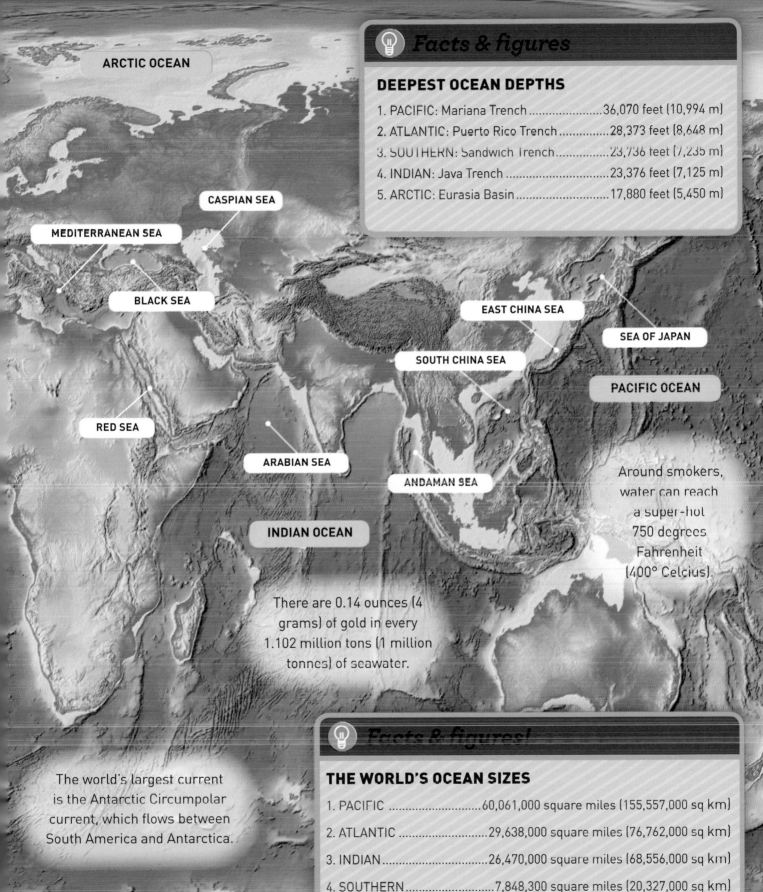

ARCTIC OCEAN

CASPIAN SEA

MEDITERRANEAN SEA

BLACK SEA

EAST CHINA SEA

SEA OF JAPAN

SOUTH CHINA SEA

RED SEA

PACIFIC OCEAN

ARABIAN SEA

ANDAMAN SEA

INDIAN OCEAN

Around smokers, water can reach a super-hot 750 degrees Fahrenheit (400° Celcius).

There are 0.14 ounces (4 grams) of gold in every 1.102 million tons (1 million tonnes) of seawater.

The world's largest current is the Antarctic Circumpolar current, which flows between South America and Antarctica.

Facts & figures

DEEPEST OCEAN DEPTHS

1. PACIFIC: Mariana Trench ....36,070 feet (10,994 m)
2. ATLANTIC: Puerto Rico Trench ....28,373 feet (8,648 m)
3. SOUTHERN: Sandwich Trench...............23,736 feet (7,235 m)
4. INDIAN: Java Trench ....23,376 feet (7,125 m)
5. ARCTIC: Eurasia Basin...........................17,880 feet (5,450 m)

Facts & figures!

THE WORLD'S OCEAN SIZES

1. PACIFIC ....60,061,000 square miles (155,557,000 sq km)
2. ATLANTIC ....29,638,000 square miles (76,762,000 sq km)
3. INDIAN ....26,470,000 square miles (68,556,000 sq km)
4. SOUTHERN.........................7,848,300 square miles (20,327,000 sq km)
5. ARCTIC...................................5,427,000 square miles (14,056,000 sq km)

Earth's Land Biomes

We divide the Earth into different regions called biomes. Each biome has a different climate and range of plant and animal life.

It rains most days in rain forest regions.

Some deserts are sandy landscapes. Some are rocky.

Grasslands stretch for many miles, with very few trees or shrubs.

Forests far and wide

Forest covers about a third of the Earth's land surface. Across the far north of the planet there is a huge belt of evergreen forest called the taiga. Further south there are temperate forests, where most of the trees lose their leaves in winter. Tropical rain forests grow around the equator, where the climate is warm and moist.

The toughest biomes

About a fifth of the Earth's land is desert, where there is little or no rain. A desert's dry climate makes it a tough place for animals and plants to survive. The tundra biome in the far north is also a very difficult location for animals and plants. The ground is always frozen just below the surface, and there isn't enough soil for trees to grow there.

Grasslands of the world

Grasslands cover about 40 percent of the Earth's land. Here it is too dry for forests to grow but there is enough rain for grasses to survive. In North America the grasslands are called prairies. In central Asia they are called the Steppe, and in South America they are called the Pampas. Grassland in hot, tropical areas is given the name "savanna."

Climate

The climate of a place is the pattern of weather it has from year to year. Climate varies across the world.

Main climates

There are four major world climates. The far north and south have a polar climate, which is always very cold. Slightly further toward the equator the climate is temperate, with warm, dry summers and mild winters. Moving closer toward the equator the climate becomes subtropical—warm with dry and rainy seasons. Around the equator itself the climate is tropical—always very warm with rainfall every day.

Forests of deciduous trees grow in areas where the climate is temperate.

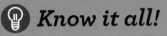

Know it all!

● Vostock, Antarctica, is the coldest place on Earth, with temperatures colder than a home freezer.

● Dallol, Ethiopia, is the hottest place on Earth with an average temperature of 94°F (34.4°C).

● Siberia, in Russia, has the world's biggest temperature range, between -94°F (–70°C) and 98°F (36.7°C).

● The driest place on Earth is the Atacama Desert in Chile, where in some areas rain has never been recorded.

The far north and south of the world are always icy cold.

Why are climates different?

Around the equator, the sun's rays hit the Earth straight on. But the rays hit the poles at an angle and have to travel through more of the Earth's atmosphere to reach them. Less heat reaches those areas. Because of this, the farther a region is from the equator, the colder its climate will be.

Special climates

Some places have their own microclimate, a particular type of weather and temperature different to their surroundings. Big cities often have a warmer climate than the surrounding land, for instance, because their concrete buildings absorb the sun's heat during the day and radiate the heat at night, warming the air.

A big city often has a climate that is slightly warmer than its surroundings.

The Seasons

The seasons of spring, summer, fall, and winter come to different parts of the Earth at different times of the year.

The Earth's orbit

The seasons are caused by the Earth's orbit. For a few months each year one hemisphere (half of the Earth) is tilted toward the sun and gets strong rays, while the other half is tilted away from the sun and gets weak rays. Then the Earth turns and the position reverses.

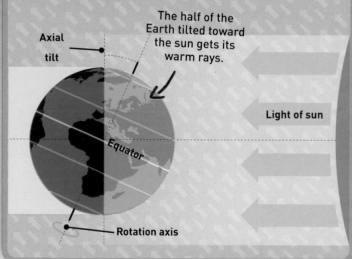

Axial tilt

The half of the Earth tilted toward the sun gets its warm rays.

Light of sun

Equator

Rotation axis

The Northern Hemisphere experiences winter while the Southern Hemisphere experiences summer.

The seasons change

As the Earth moves on its orbit, the sun's rays grow strong or weak across each hemisphere, and the seasons change. When it is summer in one hemisphere it is winter in the other. In fall and spring the two hemispheres are an equal distance from the sun.

Freezing or sweltering summer?

The seasons are not all the same in different areas of the world. In Antarctica, which never gets the sun's rays strongly, the temperature stays below freezing even in summer. The farther you get from the chilly far north and south, the warmer summers become.

Hot shots! ⭐

HAVE A HOT CHRISTMAS

In the Northern Hemisphere the December festival of Christmas season is associated with wintery ice and snow. In the Southern Hemisphere December is during summer and Santa Claus is more likely to be spotted on the beach!

Wet and Dry Seasons

The areas around the equator, known as the Tropics, do not have fall, winter, spring, and summer. Instead they have wet or dry seasons.

Animals must do their best to find water holes during the dry season.

Waiting for rains

The dry season lasts longer than the wet season, and only a few inches of rain falls during many months. Waterholes and rivers dry up, and plants and animals must try to survive as best they can until the rains arrive. In the Southern Hemisphere the dry season lasts roughly from April to September. In the Northern Hemisphere it lasts from about October to March.

Wildebeest migrate across the Mara River in Tanzania

Monsoons

Some tropical areas are in the path of rain-carrying winds called monsoons that bring very heavy rainfalls. West Africa, Asia, Australia, and parts of the southwestern US experience monsoons. Almost half of the world's population lives in areas affected by the monsoons. Too much or too little monsoon rain can mean failed crops and disastrous famine or floods.

A flooded market in Varanasi, India, during the monsoon season

Finding water

The wet and dry seasons on the African savanna lead to the biggest animal migrations (journeys) on Earth. During the wet season hundreds of thousands of plant-eating animals move around in herds to find the lush plants and waterholes created by the rains, and hunting animals follow them. When the wet season ends the herds move elsewhere to find food.

🌐 The Sky Above Us

The Earth is surrounded by a blanket of gases called the atmosphere.

Sky layers

The atmosphere has five main layers.

1. The **exosphere** exists between the altitude of 310 and 5,000 miles (500 and 8,000 km) high. Weather satellites orbit up here.

2. The **thermosphere** sits between 50 and 310 miles (80 and 500 km). The temperature is highest at the top.

3. The **mesosphere** is between 31 and 50 miles (50 and 80 km) in altitude. Unmanned balloons reach this layer.

4. The **stratosphere** is between 11.2 and 31 miles (18 and 50 km) in altitude and is a cold layer. Aircraft fly here to avoid rough weather below.

5. The **troposphere** reaches 10 miles (16 km) in altitude and contains nearly all the planet's water vapor. Earth's weather develops in this layer.

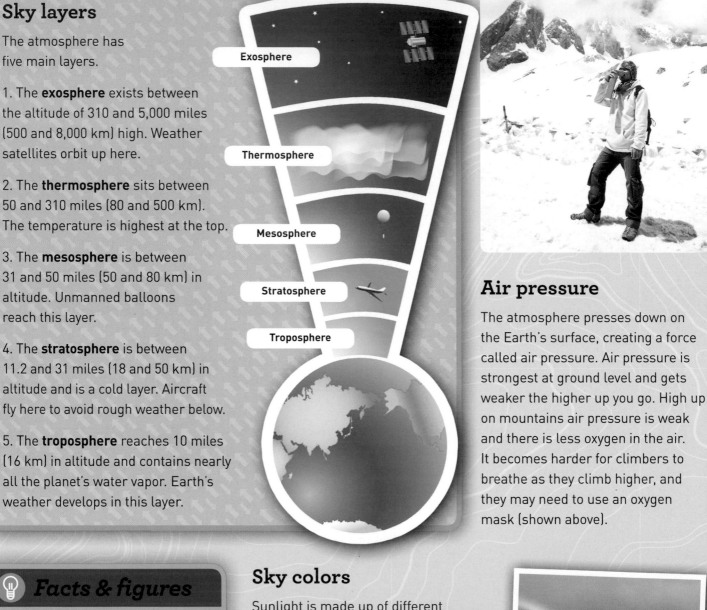

Exosphere

Thermosphere

Mesosphere

Stratosphere

Troposphere

Air pressure

The atmosphere presses down on the Earth's surface, creating a force called air pressure. Air pressure is strongest at ground level and gets weaker the higher up you go. High up on mountains air pressure is weak and there is less oxygen in the air. It becomes harder for climbers to breathe as they climb higher, and they may need to use an oxygen mask (shown above).

💡 *Facts & figures*

THE ATMOSPHERE IS MADE UP OF THESE GASES:

78.09% nitrogen

20.95% oxygen

0.93% argon

0.03% carbon dioxide, helium, hydrogen, methane, krypton, neon, ozone, xenon, water vapor

Sky colors

Sunlight is made up of different colored light waves. You can see all the visible colors in a rainbow—red, orange, yellow, green, blue, indigo, and violet. When the sun's rays reach the Earth's atmosphere the blue light waves scatter in all directions, making the sky look blue. Reddish skies occur when the blue light waves are blocked by dust particles in the air and only red light gets through.

Why We Have Weather

The temperature of the Earth's atmosphere and the amount of water vapor in it are always changing. This causes weather.

The water cycle

The sun heats the world's oceans and rivers. It makes water evaporate (become an invisible gas or vapor) and rise upward. As the vapor gets higher it gets colder and turns back into water droplets, which gather around specks of dust in the air. Billions of droplets together make a cloud, and eventually they fall as rain.

Water evaporates and falls as rain again and again, in a circular pattern called the water cycle.

Snow, hail, and fog

When water droplets get very cold they turn into ice crystals and fall to the ground as snow. Alternatively they might become hailstones—icy pellets (shown above) that are buffeted around inside tall storm clouds, growing bigger until they are heavy enough to fall. When the ground is cold and the air above it is warmer, water vapor in the air sometimes turns into a cloud of water droplets called fog.

The world's winds

The sun's rays are reflected off the Earth's surface and warm the air above. The warm air rises, and cold air flows into the space below it. This movement of air is wind. Some winds appear and disappear from day to day, and some blow constantly in regular patterns around the Earth, caused by warm air rising above the equator and cold air flowing inward from the polar regions.

Giant wind turbines generate electricity as they turn in the breeze.

Hot shots!

★

A PERFECT FLAKE

A snowflake is made up of snow crystals that are stuck together. Every flake is thought to have a slightly different pattern of crystals, so no two flakes look the same under a microscope.

Glossary

Air pressure The force of air pressing on a surface over a certain area.

Atmosphere A blanket of gases surrounding the Earth.

Biome A region of the Earth, defined by its climate and range of plants and animals.

Climate The pattern of weather and temperature that a region has every year.

Crust The Earth's outer layer.

Current A regular direction of flow.

Delta A wide rivermouth, dotted with mudflats and islands, where a river meets the sea.

Dike A side exit in a volcano, where red-hot magma seeps up to the Earth's surface.

Dome mountains Mountains pushed up by volcanic material bubbling up from below the Earth's surface.

Earthquake A release of pressure between two of the Earth's plates that are pushing against each other, sending waves of energy through the Earth.

Equator The imaginary line around the middle of the Earth.

Erosion The gradual wearing down of land by forces such as rivers, oceans, glaciers, and weather.

Estuary A flat, muddy plain where a river meets the sea.

Fault-block mountains Mountains created when giant blocks of rock are pushed up due to pressure between two of the Earth's plates.

Fault A giant crack in the rocks of the Earth's crust, caused by two of the Earth's plates pushing up against each other or sliding past each other.

Fold mountains Mountains created when rock folds upward, due to the pressure between two of the Earth's plates.

Gems Crystals that form in rocks. Rare and beautiful gems are used to make jewelry.

Geyser A regular spout of steaming-hot water that shoots up from under the ground.

Glacier A huge mass of ice that is so heavy it moves down a mountainside as a giant ice river.

Grassland An area where it is too dry for many trees to grow but there is enough rain for a carpet of grasses to survive.

Hemisphere The southern or northern half of the Earth.

Hurricane A powerful storm that brings lashing rain and winds of up to 200 miles per hour (320 km/h).

Igneous rock A type of rock formed from molten material that has bubbled up from under the Earth's surface and then cooled.

Kimberlite A type of igneous rock. It is the only type of rock that contains diamonds.

Magma Underground rock that has become so hot it has melted.

Mantle A thick layer of very hot rock underneath the Earth.

Meander A bend in a river.

Metamorphic rock A type of rock created from igneous or sedimentary rocks that have been broken up and changed by heat or pressure.

Microclimate A particular type of climate in a small area, different to the area around it.

Mid-ocean ridge A range of underwater mountains created by a huge crack between two of the Earth's plates.

Mineral salts Material that has dissolved into water from underground rocks.

Monsoon Regular, heavy rainfall brought by seasonal winds.

Moraine An area of rocks dumped by a glacier.

Ore Rock that contains metal.

Pangaea A vast supercontinent that once contained all the Earth's land.

Plateau mountains Mountains created when a wide section of flat land is pushed up by pressure between two of the Earth's plates.

Polar ice cap The permanently frozen far north or south of the world.

Rain forest A thick forest that grows in tropical regions of the world where there is daily rainfall.

Rhodium The most valuable metal on Earth.

Richter scale A scale used to represent the energy produced by an earthquake.

Rift valley A giant, flat-bottomed valley created when two of the Earth's plates move apart.

Sedimentary rock A type of rock made up of different layers of small particles that have been squashed down and hardened.

Seismic waves A type of energy generated by earthquakes.

Seismograph An instrument that measures the size of the shock waves produced by an earthquake.

Smelting A heating process used to separate metal from rock.

Subtropical A warm, dry climate with rainy seasons.

Taiga A huge belt of evergreen forest stretching across the far north of the Earth.

Tectonic plates Giant moving pieces of the Earth's outer crust. They fit together like a jigsaw puzzle.

Temperate A climate of warm, dry summers and mild winters.

Tree line The point on a mountainside above which trees can no longer survive, due to low temperatures and a lack of soil.

Tropical A climate that is always very warm, with frequent rainfall.

Tropics The areas around the equator.

Tundra Lands in the far north, which are permanently frozen a few inches below the ground.

Further Information

BOOKS

Chancellor, Deborah. *Discover Science: Planet Earth*. New York: Kingfisher, 2014.

Gullo, Arthur. *Volcano*. Power of Nature. New York: Cavendish Square Publishing, 2015,

Miller, Petra. *Earthquakes*. Power of Nature. New York: Cavendish Square Publishing, 2015.

Palmer, Douglas, Robert Dinwiddie, John Farndon, Michael Allaby, David Burnie, Clint Twist, Martin Walters, and Tony Waltham. *Earth*. 2nd Edition. New York: DK, 2013.

WEBSITES

Discovery.com's Planet Earth

www.discovery.com/tv-shows/planet-earth/
Watch the Discovery Channel's programs on our planet on the ground, under the sea, and in the air.

Nova Planet Earth

www.pbs.org/wgbh/nova/earth/
Public television presents excellent content on the Earth in video, slideshow, and printed form.

Index

Merry Christmas!
Happy New Year '85
May we continue to cook
in a grand style together?
Love,
Bonnie

Hi Guys —
Merry Christmas & Happy New Year
('85)   ('86)
May you both have a great time in the
new year and both find much happiness!!
lots of love
Ray

FOODS OF LONG ISLAND

FOODS OF

A NEWSDAY COOKBOOK   HARRY N. ABRAMS, INC., PUBLISHERS, NEW YORK

LONG ISLAND

BY PEGGY KATALINICH   PHOTOGRAPHS BY J. MICHAEL DOMBROSKI

To Jerry, for his good taste

The author wishes to thank Bloomingdale's, Garden City; Fortunoff, Westbury; Rosalind Light, Cedarhurst; and The Snow Goose, Northport, for their generous help in loaning props for photographs.

Project Managers: ERIC HIMMEL, PAMELA HARWOOD
Editor: RUTH PELTASON
Designer: JUDITH HENRY

Library of Congress Cataloging in Publication Data
Katalinich, Peggy. Foods of Long Island.
"A Newsday book."
Includes index.
1. Cookery—New York (State)—Long Island. 2. Farm produce—New York (State)—Long Island. 3. Seafood—New York (State)—Long Island. 4. Long Island (N.Y.)—Social life and customs. I. Dombroski, J. Michael. II. Title.
TX715.K188 1985   641.59747′21   85–1245
ISBN 0–8109–1261–9

Illustrations copyright© 1985 *Newsday*

Printed and bound in Japan

Contents

Introduction

I knew I was hooked when farmer Ed Latham reached down to the stalks of asparagus poking through the bare spring soil and cut them off at ground level. It was the best gift he could give me, with the advice that I cook them before sundown to fully appreciate fresh, truly fresh, sweet asparagus.

Standing there that crisp May afternoon, surrounded by the farmers of Long Island, and the baymen, too, who head out before dawn to dig for clams or the fishermen who haul up their nets as the sun breaks over Gardiners Island, made me a convert to these people and their lives. I was impressed by their pride, their insistence on fresh food, and their belief in the quality of their products. From ducks to soft clams, and from cauliflower to raspberries, I tasted the best and the freshest of Long Island, and above all, I came to admire greatly the producers of such wonderful bounty.

I had no idea when I started out to write a cookbook for *Newsday* that I would become such a fierce chauvinist, so defensive of the producers on this 120-mile-long island flanked by the Atlantic Ocean and Long Island Sound. Let any restaurateur try to pass off Michigan duck as superior and he has a fight on his hands. Our lobster needs to make no apologies, and, please, we do have the best clams and oysters. Even in an off year when there is too much rain in the spring, the Long Island strawberry looks and tastes far better, to my loyal taste buds, than the West Coast import.

As *Newsday*'s food editor for the past five years, I was given the task of shaping a cookbook that would reflect the rich diversity of Long Island. There were dozens of approaches, but focusing on the people who produce the luscious, high quality ingredients seemed right to me. Like many Long Islanders, I didn't know what it took to grow the gorgeous vegetables that flood the farm stands in late summer; I just knew that I liked them. So, determined to tell the story of the producers as well as to provide recipes for using what they grew or caught, I spent the summer of 1984 on boats and walking through fields,

Twin Pond Farms, Riverhead

watching oysters being dredged, and broccoli being harvested.

Even though I am a transplant from the Midwest—a suburb of Milwaukee, Wisconsin, to be exact—I do not come armed with a farm background, unless a few days at Aunt Mavis's house with eleven acres and a couple of cows count. And while I was food editor at *The Minneapolis Star* for 4½ years, my staff writers covered the business of farming while I took cooking lessons in Italy and Paris.

This project was my chance, then, to get out of the kitchen and down on the farm. Luckily, the farmers and fishermen responded to the idea of this book. At first, they were surprised and a bit skeptical that I wanted to tell their story. Once I convinced them that I loved Long Island cauliflower, that in season it tasted almost sweet, they opened up and told me why. They talked about the cool fall nights and warm days that let their cauliflower develop the best flavor.

When I wasn't getting up at 4 A.M. to make the fishing boat by 5, I was touring duck hatcheries to watch chicks scratch their way out of their shells. Perhaps, more than anything else, my admiration for the farmers and fishermen soared. They work hard, much harder than I ever imagined. They got a laugh when I told them I pay good cash dollars to work out at a health club; all I needed to do, they said, was spend a week or two with them to get in shape.

Even as I stood in the summer heat, scratching notes in my pad while watching a farmer transplant fledgling herb plants, I started hearing what was to become a recurring theme: concern for the future. Owners of second homes on Long Island have discovered what the farmers always knew: this is a pretty splendid place to be. The pressure to build on farmland is tremendous and much of it is already in the hands of speculators.

The loss of Long Island cropland or shoreline to development is a tragedy. I'm selfish, perhaps, but I don't want to give up the food grown here; it's just too good. The scallops are the best you'll ever taste, the duck meat has a sweetness I don't find easily duplicated. I hope a way is found to balance the needs of the summer people with the needs of the farmers and fishermen; I know there's a better way than random, unbridled development.

I want Will Bennett to keep turning out tender soft clams that melt in your mouth. I want Vinnie Daley to keep hauling in littlenecks for the restaurateurs who care about quality. I want Bob Van Nostrand to keep devoting an acre to fresh herbs. For as every good cook knows, the quality of the raw ingredients is one of the most important parts in turning out a delicious meal.

Selecting recipes for this book, then, was easy since I had such high quality products to work with and a wide range to choose from. The only criterion for inclusion was that one of the ingredients be local. That meant I could include baked desserts because Long Island produces eggs, and there could be a small meat chapter as a few farmers still raise pigs and some cattle. The emphasis, though, is naturally and properly on fish and shellfish, duck, vegetables, and fruit.

Many of the recipes are from the *Newsday* food files—from staff writers Marie Bianco and Sylvia Carter, and readers. Since I enjoy developing recipes, I took lobsters from a day out on the Sound and created a few dishes, or duck from a visit to a farm and perfected the quintessential roast. There are a few restaurateurs on Long Island who specialize in all things local, so I went to them for recipes as well.

I looked for recipes that did not require an advanced degree in sauce making; though some are challenging, the majority are designed for today's life-style, simple with a touch of sophistication. As you use the book, you will come to recognize the primary contributors. Marie Bianco's recipes reflect her Italian background, nearly always featuring a clove of garlic and a sprig of basil. When there's a stick of butter, some bacon and potatoes, you can see the hand of Sylvia Carter. Jules Bond, who wrote a column for four years called the *Long Island Kitchen*, shows his European background, a blend of simplified classic cuisine with local ingredients. All of the contributors are listed in the appendix.

In using these recipes, remember that fresh, in-season fare is virtually always best. When you have time to make fresh stock or homemade mayonnaise, do so; but don't hesitate to make a recipe simply because you don't have duck stock on hand. Substitutions are allowed. Herbs are always used in their dried form, unless a fresh sprig of basil or parsley is called for. Of course, if your garden overfloweth, use a fresh herb instead. Generally, you should use three times as much of a fresh herb as dried.

Because the food scene is constantly changing, don't take the statistics in the following essays as gospel; they are accurate as of this writing.

I hope you enjoy reading and using this book as much as I have enjoyed producing it. I hope J. Michael Dombroski's photographs can make you feel as if you are there, on the farm, or in the boat. And I hope you will be pleased by the quality of Long Island ingredients and ask for them in your local market. One way to ensure the future is to create the demand that can only be supplied by this slender island and its dedicated farmers and fishermen.

PEGGY KATALINICH
Long Island

All About the Land

If there is a unifying theme among the amazingly diverse farmers of Long Island it is their steadfast belief in the superiority of things locally grown. Ducks. Cauliflower. Cucumbers. Sweet corn. And they take much pride in the variety this soil can support—Jerusalem artichokes, raspberries, eggplant, tomatoes, peaches.

"I'll tell you I'm no world traveler," says Tony Tiska, a potato farmer in Bridgehampton. "I've been to the Caribbean and up into New England, Canada to the West Coast. And I'll tell you I really haven't run into a place that produces as many varieties as Long Island. It is really incredible. We have peaches and a range of apples and pears, strawberries. It is incredible what this area will produce."

Potatoes still fill the largest portion of the 40,000 acres under cultivation at 15,000 acres. The remaining acres produce cauliflower, cabbage (including Chinese cabbage), sweet corn, snap beans, peppers, cucumbers, spinach, onions, tomatoes, squash, pumpkins, melons, fennel, shallots, kale, dandelions, asparagus, beets, chard, eggplant, lettuce, and leeks. There are slightly over 1,000 acres of grapes, 500 peaches, 330 apples, 300 strawberries, and 50 raspberries. In addition, about 4,000,000 ducks grow up each year on the East End, along with several thousand chickens, geese, and turkeys.

For each local product, of course, there are fierce off-Island competitors, armed with cheaper land and, in some cases, longer growing seasons that can combine to undercut local prices.

"The Midwest farms are closer to the grain belt," says Mark Miloski who runs a poultry farm with his father Will in Calverton, "so they can get grain a lot cheaper. But you can't beat a Long Island duck. I had a Midwestern duck and it was terrible, I couldn't even eat it. I guess I'm partial to Long Island. It has the perfect climate to raise poultry and vegetables, especially in the fall when you get that cold weather. Everything raises better when you get that little chill. Fish taste better in cold weather. Animals taste better in cold weather, vegetables like cauliflower and cabbage need the cold."

In 1984, about eight hundred farmers were in business, taking advantage of those qualities that traditionally have made Long Island agriculture successful and diverse. "It's our climate and water supply, a long growing season with lots of sunshine," says Ron Leuthardt, executive secretary of Long Island Farm Bureau. "One of the reasons we are so diversified within a relatively small area geographically is that we have two different shorelines and two significant bodies of water providing us with microclimates that are quite different." These microclimates, in turn, are suitable for a variety of crops, even different varieties within a single crop. "Another reason our agriculture has been able to become so intensive is readily available water for irrigation." The soil is not particularly fertile, he says, but it responds extremely well to irrigation, fertilization, and management of pests.

"We can grow anything, really," says Lyle Wells who with his wife, Susan, farms seventy acres in Riverhead Town. "In terms of what's grown in the U.S. we have tremendous variety. Quality? It all depends on the grower; when he wants to, he can put out top quality."

The income from such variety and quality puts Suffolk County first in New York state; the Cooperative Extension Service estimates that the gross income is $92 million a year, and farm stands and pick-your-own operations could push the income over $100 million.

But the 15,000 acres now planted in potatoes represent quite a drop from 42,700 in 1960, and there's every indication that the numbers will continue their downward spiral as farmers give in to the attractive prices real estate developers are willing to pay. The number of ducks is also down from 6.5 million in the 1960s and 1970s, as producers fall prey to rising costs and expensive pollution controls. In the past thirty years, more than 60,000 acres of farmland have been converted into residential development or abandoned because the soil is marginal.

"Riverhead Town and all of Long Island and all of the country I suppose has changed," says Nathaniel A. Talmage, a longtime farmer in Riverhead. "I suppose it has changed just as any other industrial business has changed in years. Potatoes have always been the big crop, but in the last twenty years that

Ray Halsey, Water Mill

has changed. Idaho has come in the picture. Cauliflower is still an important crop but nowhere near the volume it was twenty or thirty years ago. There have been many other changes partly due to the labor, the inability to get folks to do the kind of labor associated with crops like lima beans and peas, snap beans and strawberries."

Stepping in as farmers leave are sod farmers— on about 3,000 acres—and the nursery and flower industry, thriving with about 4,000 acres and 350 commercial wholesale flower operations. More horses than ever before are kept for riding (there are well over 3,000 horses in Suffolk) and there are 41 thoroughbred farms. Another new industry to take advantage of the prime soil are grape growers.

"Potatoes were good for this area," says Pete Corwith, a potato farmer in Bridgehampton. "The soil is well-drained and we have an adequate amount of rainfall. We're close to the market. But it's becoming increasingly difficult to raise the crop and control the beetles." Taxes are high, the farmers believe,

compounding the natural challenges of bringing in a crop.

And then there are the houses popping up in fields, the second homes of city dwellers who want to escape to the country. Except that in the country there are noisy tractors that run at five in the morning, and insecticide sprays that drift onto decks and into cocktail parties. "If you want us to stay out here and keep producing food that's fresh, don't come out here and build a house," says Wells. "You can't have both. There has been an influx of people coming out here and the first thing they do is complain about the farming. 'You're spraying too late at night, your irrigation pumps are running...' My tractors are running most of the time until 10:30, 12:00 at night. To change that I couldn't really run a farm economically."

Such is the mixed blessing that comes with the surge of money into the towns from tourists—the ready market for summer produce and the realization that any farmer with 100 acres who wants to sell

Cauliflower farmer John Brezny, Riverhead

could be a millionaire. "I have mixed feelings about the development; since land is so valuable it takes away the concern somewhat of growing older, of not having enough money to survive on," adds Corwith.

The high cost of land, though, makes it almost impossible for any new farmers to get into the business. If farmland is going for $12,000 an acre, a farmer can't buy it and grow potatoes on it, according to Tiska. "I can sell one acre of land here and make more than I can in farming 250 acres of potatoes. If that was your land, what would you do?" asks Tiska.

State, county, and town governments have stepped in with programs designed to protect farmland. In 1971, New York State passed a law that would allow the creation of agricultural districts, giving farmers a tax break and forbidding local governments from enacting ordinances that would limit farming practices beyond health and safety. Then in 1974, Suffolk County initiated a program to buy development rights. The farmer gets cash upfront for

the value of these rights while he keeps ownership and the right to farm the land. The farmer can sell it only for agricultural use. By 1984, nearly five thousand acres have been safeguarded, but a start that could keep families who have been farming on the East End since the 1600s still down on the farm.

"My ancestors settled here in 1640," says Ray Halsey, who farms in Water Mill and owns a farm stand, The Green Thumb. There are dozens of Halseys, though, on the South Fork. "We're all eleventh or twelfth generation from the founder and we're so far separated, we hardly consider ourselves cousins." Many in the extended family have stayed in farming in one way or another; Ray has specialized in a mix of vegetables which is his way of carving out a specialty niche and staving off developers. "My dad was the youngest of five brothers, so he ended up with no land at all. He started work as a gardener, then got into chickens as a sideline. He began buying land back and got started in potatoes."

When Ray and his brother Abram started farming in the late 1930s and early 1940s, cauliflower, cabbage, and lima beans proved unprofitable so they turned solely to potatoes. His brother dropped out, but Ray stayed with it, trying a vegetable stand to get additional revenue. It was a brilliant move; the stand succeeded, he dropped potatoes, and now farms about 160 acres of vegetables, with a payroll in summer of nearly thirty people. "If any customer mentioned anything new or we read about anything new, we'd try it. We couldn't always raise it the first year or two, but you just keep working until you figure it out," says Halsey. He's perfected sixteen or seventeen different kinds of lettuce, arugula, a range of herbs including French tarragon and coriander, blackberries, purple beans, yellow peppers, Italian and Japanese eggplants along with the standard tomatoes, cucumbers, and cabbage. "I like a challenge of something new," Halsey says.

Ed Latham, by the Halsey standard, is new on the scene, with his grandmother's family settling in Orient in 1806, and the Lathams following shortly after. He still lives in the family house, built in 1840. "In those days the average farm in Orient was thirty acres; some were a lot smaller," says Latham. "They had horses and cows, it was a family farm. They raised some potatoes, some sprouts, pasture, grew corn for feed and some cash crops. When I first started way back, potatoes were the thing to plant. But I lost money like everybody else. One year you'd make money, then for four or five years, you'd work for nothing. So about the time that the changeover from hand harvesting to mechanical harvesting came in, I just couldn't see it; it meant going into hock for $50,000 or $100,000."

Instead, he went into mixed vegetable farming, developing contracts with a supermarket chain in Boston to take much of his crop and buying up enough land to allow his son Dan to join him in a farm corporation. They farm 440 acres, renting about 260 of those acres. "We are large enough now in four crops so that if one of them makes money, we make the season," says Latham.

Bob Van Nostrand has a small fraction of the land of the Lathams in the village, two miles down the road from them; his specialty is his smallness, producing just what he can retail at city farmers' markets. "I control the whole thing from the seed to the person who's going to actually eat it," says Van Nostrand. "There's a certain satisfaction in that and not just shipping it off to the commercial market. For the small grower like myself, this is more or less inev-

itable; you can't produce efficiently enough to sell on the wholesale basis." He rents ten of his eighteen acres to another farmer for green beans, leaving just enough for his wife and himself to handle. During the years he made a living from his machine tool business in Huntington, the land kept calling to him and for the last thirteen years he's been a full-time farmer. "The Van Nostrand family has been on Long Island since 1636, but my father didn't farm; by the time he was eighteen or twenty he developed horse asthma and couldn't stay on the farm. Horses were all they had then," Van Nostrand says.

Van Nostrand has a few chickens producing incredibly fresh, large eggs. "You crack one of these eggs in the pan—the yolk stands right up, it's beautiful," says Van Nostrand. Eggs are an obvious product for Sal Iacono in East Hampton, one of the few poultry farmers in Suffolk. And here, too, it's tough to close the lid on the carton. "We say the chickens bend over backwards to please, literally," he likes to tease. His chickens are killed right on the premises, in front of any customer who should care to look. "Some people don't like to see it but then if we didn't do it they'd wonder, 'Are these chickens really fresh?' They see us out in the yard, they see us doing the whole process," says Iacono.

The process starts for Iacono when he buys day-old chicks, then raises them on "pretty much natural feed," allowing them free run until they are killed at six weeks. "I like chicken baked in the oven, cooked with lemon juice and maybe a little oregano and salt." No store-bought chicken for him: "I'd rather eat cornflakes."

It's that taste for a fresh product that keeps his customers coming back, says Miloski. Like a few other farmers, Miloski gears up for the holidays by producing turkeys. "We buy them from a hatchery, they're so small we can fit 1,500 turkeys in an Oldsmobile 98," he says. Geese, ducks, and chickens are relatively easy to raise, but he has to keep his eye on turkeys. "They're dumb. When the rain comes off the roof, if you leave them out too long, they get wet and raise their heads up. The water comes down and they drown themselves."

While Long Island was never a big dairy area, from the hundreds, then dozens of farms, there are now only two, with the Sayre Baldwin's Carwytham Farm in Bridgehampton the most significant in terms of production. Slightly more than 200 cows are milked there twice daily, with the milk shipped off every other day to East Northport and the Oak Tree

Dairy. Manager Claes Cassel, who has been in the dairy business since he was eight, now uses the most modern techniques of artificial insemination to produce cows for his own farm and others upstate. There is one beef feed lot in the Town of Yaphank.

"Dairying existed here because we were so close to New York City," says Dale Bennett, curator at Old Bethpage Village Restoration. "We have little area to turn the cows onto, we don't have enough to provide the full pasture. But when I say we weren't an important dairy district, that doesn't mean that most farms didn't have cows. They did."

In the 1800s Bennett says that farms closest to the city grew vegetables primarily for the city market, while farther east there were more general farms, with a few cows, beef cattle, some chickens, and a range of crops such as corn, wheat, oats, rye, hay, and probably some potatoes. As the city grew and pushed eastward, farmers retreated and changed from a mix of crops to specialized truck farming and an emphasis on high profit crops like potatoes. "I would like to see a move to more intensive vegetable farming," says Bennett. "That's my personal desire because more people could make a living farming and would be producing more food closer to where it's consumed."

Richard Hendrickson remembers those days when all farmers raised a few chickens, a pig or two, and when farms were self sufficient. "You made smoked sausage because that was the way it was kept," says Hendrickson, who has a farm in Bridgehampton. "Beef was used up right away because all you had to keep it was a chunk of pond ice. Seafood—you would go to the bay and get clams or oysters with half a load of seaweed. Layered under seaweed they would keep a week, week and a half. The vegetables in the garden were the turnips, cabbage, the potatoes, and those things were put down in the cellar."

"But now," says Hendrickson, "we import a lot of our lobsters from Maine. We get a lot of our fish from other states, Nova Scotia. We bring a lot of our fruits and vegetables from New Jersey and Delaware, Maryland, Virginia. The same with our chickens, the same with our eggs. There are only two dairies left here, two small poultry farms left...I don't have the answer, I love farming, I really do. I don't mind the hard work."

Even with the changes and the move to develop the land for real estate, the farmers want to stay put. "It is a basic love for the soil, it's tremendous," says Tiska. "It's a nice way to live if you make the living. There are a lot of heartaches and frustrations that come along, but a lot of time you get years where it goes nice, too, beautiful crops and the price is pretty good. I have a 250-acre backyard and I watch the seasons go by. Besides, what is money worth? Is money the answer to everything? How much money do you want?" Adds Corwith, "It's a way of life. It's not like going to a job and working for someone else. You grow up in this way of life."

At Sea

In the beginning Long Island had whaling and oystering. Now it has aquaculture and joint ventures with factory ships capable of freezing as much as 80,000 pounds in a day.

Baymen and fishermen have always made a living off this 120-mile-long island, with plenty of sheltered ports and the Great South Bay teaming with oysters and clams. But the industry is, and has always been, changing.

Quality, however, isn't. The literally centuries-old belief in the superiority of Long Island clams and oysters is still espoused today. "You can talk to any Long Islander and he will say you cannot beat a Long Island product," says Kevin DeVries, co-owner of Fire Island Fisheries in Bay Shore. "You cannot beat a Peconic Bay scallop, a Long Island clam."

"Mother Nature gives us a better product," says John Mulhall of Long Island Oyster Farms, Inc., in Greenport. "The quality of oysters," says Dave Relyea of Frank M. Flower & Sons in Oyster Bay, "tends to be judged by the saltiness. Ours are fairly salty, in New Orleans they are very mild. If you are used to salty, the others tend to be rather bland." The Peconic Bay scallop is, according to fishing expert A.J. McClane, the finest in the world, with the only competition coming from Peru.

But don't take the word of confirmed chauvinists. Consider money. "Our quality is best and I would document that from a business point of view," says Mulhall. "Long Island commands the highest price so that takes it out of the realm of opinion and subjectivity." The Long Island clam also commands the highest price, even as Rhode Island, the Carolinas, and Florida flood the market with their versions. "The Long Island clam goes to the fussiest restaurants and clients," says Bill Zeller of Captree Clam in West Islip. "The Florida clam doesn't have as much meat, because it is faster growing. The deep-growing clams from Rhode Island have a thin shell and a lot of breakage. The Long Island clam…it just seems it's always been the best."

Vincent Daley clamming the Great South Bay

Bill Pell, who owns docks in Greenport and Shinnecock, says the Long Island fisherman gets top dollar; "We have the best quality, this is what we are known for." Adds Paul Flagg, owner of Great Circle Fisheries in East Hampton, "Montauk has to be one of the richest areas around, it's got some of everything. That's what's great about it. And Montauk fish is about the most expensive fish you can find. Fishermen get top dollar, obviously because of the quality."

Yet while quality stands generally unassailed, both industries—shellfish and finfish—find themselves in flux.

For the fisherman, there is guarded optimism. The 200-mile limit, set in 1977, gave them hope to buy bigger boats and get organized for marketing and sales strength. Not that the future is assured, but more are getting into the business, an estimated twenty-five percent increase in the last five years, and a fledgling processing industry may be able to offer support.

For the baymen who have worked the Great South Bay a lifetime, and their fathers a lifetime before them, the clam is no longer down on that bottom in numbers like before. Hard-shell clam landings still lead the industry, contributing $6.8 million to the total $10.9 million estimated value of Long Island shellfish.

The abundance of shellfish is cyclical and clams may be at the low end of their natural ebb and flow; in 1954, the harvest was only 85,090 bushels, while in 1947 it was more than five times that. "Usually there's a seven-year cycle for clams," says DeVries. "Some of the diggers I know are seeing more small clams." Seed clams mean a recent set and an upbeat future. "I'm definitely more optimistic, looks like production is coming in," he says.

Ken Feustel, waterways manager for the Town of Babylon, doesn't believe there is any predictable cycle, or much of anything predictable about the hard clam. "We don't know all the interactions, there are a number of different variables at any one time. We do know the density of clams is continuing to decrease," says Feustel.

Each clam harvest, says Jeff Kassner, bay management specialist for the Town of Brookhaven, is the result of four factors: the conditions of the bay itself (salinity, water quality), the shellfish, the baymen, and the management techniques of the supervising towns. "One year the bay may determine the size of the set, another year the baymen may be the most important factor," says Kassner. The reason the harvest was so high in the late 1960s, Kassner hypothesizes, may not be due exclusively to a larger number of clams out there, but also to more baymen working more efficiently.

Overharvesting, poor management of the bay, inadequate regulation, pollution, predators—nowadays there are fewer clams being harvested and there are fewer people digging for them. For a while, fewer people wanted to buy them after reports of gastroenteritis from the consumption of fresh clams. "The Great South Bay probably has been lumped together with other areas that more likely were the culprits," says Feustel. "But the way the system is set up, it makes it impossible to trace the problem to a source, much less an individual. That's a problem and it continues." Baymen have banded together under the Green Seal Program, designed to identify where each bushel came from; an unbreakable seal is affixed to prevent clams from uncertified areas becoming mixed up with those from certified waters. Of course, it depends upon the honesty of the bayman, and a poacher or dishonest buyer is not likely to record that his clams came from uncertified waters.

The towns are trying to come up with ways to reverse the decline and help ease the impact on baymen. They can give a break to baymen in the winter; when there is less than one-quarter inch of rainfall over twenty-four hours for seven consecutive days, certain areas of the uncertified waters in the Great South Bay can be opened to clamming. It's generally the storm water runoff that causes the problems, although the bay's rivers and creeks have been closed to clamming since the turn of the century. "Standard practice has been to run road drainage into canals," says Feustel. "When it rains, the water takes road debris and animal waste along with it, causing an increase in the coliform count. In the absence of rainfall, the count is generally low."

Feustel says Babylon is putting out about one million clams a year into the bay, raising seed clams purchased from a commercial hatchery in a protected nursery to a size where they are less vulnerable to predators. These clams have a unique genetic character, a color pattern that makes them stand out from the clams indigenous to the bay, letting the town keep track of its success. "The baymen have nicknames for them—Indian clams, bulleyes—they have shell markings, blobs of red or red zigzags," says Feustel.

The Town of Islip is putting gravel down on an acre of bay bottom for a couple million seed clams; predators, it seems, don't like craggy bottoms while clams do just fine. In Brookhaven, the town raises clams in tanks on land, fed by flowing seawater pumped from Long Island Sound. "Our goal is to put out one million per year," says Kassner.

A vast oyster industry once thrived in the Great South Bay—think of Bluepoint oysters—and along the North Shore—consider Oyster Bay. "This used to be a real big industry, thousands of people in hundreds of boats. This is what is left," says David Relyea of Frank M. Flower & Sons. "When I first came into the business," adds George White, marketing manager for Flower, "oysters reproduced so much, we thought there wasn't any way everyone in the world would eat them all, much less America."

In 1895, about five hundred boats and about eleven hundred men worked the oyster industry in the Great South Bay, according to an article then in the *Brooklyn Times*. But even by the 1840s, the natural oyster there was disappearing. A schooner loaded with oysters from Virginia is said to have saved the day, according to the newspaper account. "Unable to find a market in which to dispose of her cargo and the weather becoming warm, she was compelled to hoist her sails and seek a suitable spot in which to dump her precious load," the article states. The ship spread oysters through the bay. "From that time on the oysters continued to increase in a wonderful manner."

Seed oysters did thrive in the bay until 1931 when the opening of the Moriches Inlet increased the salinity of the bay, causing an explosion of oyster predators; while older oysters can do quite well in saltier water, young oysters don't thrive. Then the hurricane of 1938 wiped out the oyster. Buried under the churned up bottom, the oysters were unable to climb out. A particularly vicious parasite, MSX, also contributed to the demise.

The heyday of oyster landings was probably 1904 when 9,108 metric tons were landed. There is little natural production now, and H. Butler Flower in Oyster Bay and the Long Island Oyster Farms in

Greenport carry the standard today, with hatchery and planting operations together producing millions of juvenile oysters per year.

The Long Island lobster hasn't gotten much press, overshadowed by its northern brother in Maine. But according to Neil Tully, owner of Tully's Lobster Company in Hampton Bays, "New York is a good lobster producer, very good. Long Island Sound has a lot of lobsters. The lobstermen do well from Port Jefferson east." There are lobsters west of there, all the way to the Throgs Neck Bridge, Tully says, but it's impractical to set out pots. "There's too much theft, you can't sleep on the lobster gear."

Hauling up the lobster pots—some lobstermen set out as many as 800 to 1,000—is a young man's job, says Tully. "You lift about 500 traps per day, and the average weight is about 150 pounds a trap. Sure, there's a motor to pull the traps up from the bottom, but you still have to heave them over the side and to the back of the boat. Harvesting a pound a pot is a good take," says Tully. But of course it never works out that way. "You may get five empty pots, then six pounds in one trap." The lobsterman is obligated to toss back any lobster smaller than 3³/₁₆th inches measured from the rear end of the eye socket to the rear end of the body shell, or a female lobster with eggs still attached to her. Generally, while one person sorts the pot, another bands the feisty lobsters while a third carries the pots to the back of the boat. When all of the traps on one line have been emptied, the boat turns around, and the traps are dropped off the stern, back to the bottom to entice more lobster with a bait of fish.

"Offshore lobstermen fishing the continental shelf might do 3,000 to 5,000 pounds a trip," says Tully, "but their investment is very heavy. You couldn't go offshore with less than a $200,000 fishing boat. You'd need almost $200,000 worth of traps. Your crew is large; you're out for thirty-six hours. It's a massive operation."

Scalloping on Long Island is anything but a massive operation. There aren't that many out there in Peconic Bay, their primary home; 1982 was a fairly good year, with a harvest of slightly more than 500,000 pounds. Meanwhile 584,980 pounds of sea scallops were harvested, some within twelve miles of Long Island, qualifying it as a local product if you stretch a bit. "More and more Long Island boats are starting to harvest sea scallops," says John Scotti, with New York Sea Grant Extension Program.

That year, 1982, however, was the year of the southern or calico scallop. From a harvest of zero the year before, the landings went to seven million pounds; it can undercut the price of both the bay scallop and sea scallop because it is harvested by large dredge boats and opened by machine rather than by hand. The competitor from southern waters is a different species, significantly smaller than the bay scallop known as *argopecten gibbus* compared to *aequipecten irradians* (bay scallop). The calicos are white because they are shucked using steam or hot water. "I think what happens," says Scotti, "is that they get semicooked. I don't know what their flavor would be if they were handled naturally, but it is economically unfeasible to open them by hand."

And therein lies the primary difference: flavor. Bay scallops are sweet and luscious, good raw or cooked briefly. Calicos don't have the intensity of flavor. "You're talking about a warm water species versus a cold water one," says Scotti. "Generally, most shellfish from cooler water has a better taste and shelf life."

Calicos will be cheaper and are sometimes mismarked as Long Island bay scallops. Rest assured, unless it's between the third Monday in September and March 31st, you aren't buying true Peconic Bay scallops or else you're buying frozen ones. "The main reason for a season," says Steve Hendrickson, marine resources specialist with the New York State Department of Environmental Conservation, "is that they are a fairly limited resource. When harvest is begun, it doesn't take long to harvest most of the resource."

Long Island's commercial fishery has been small relative to Massachusetts, which landed about nine times as much fish and shellfish, or Rhode Island with three times as many landings in 1983. "The reason is not that we don't have the resources; we do have access to fishing grounds, we have a tremendous coastal area," says Scotti. "Those states haven't enjoyed the diverse economies that New York has. Here there never has been a big interest in government to support the industry. Massachusetts and Rhode Island have supported the development because they don't have the other economies that New York has."

"But," adds Scotti, "it looks like there's a turnaround coming. Five years ago 40- to 50-foot boats were the norm, now it's pretty common to see 60- and 75-foot boats. There is more direct marketing by

fishermen and better marketing efforts for underutilized species." And New York government is giving some support to the industry in the form of $2 million to build new docks in Greenport and Shinnecock.

"The fishermen who have been in business for a number of years are changing to more modern equipment, more economical equipment," says Pell. "We're in a flux of change, the 200-mile limit really started it out." Long Island is one of the ideal spots for fishing boats, Pell maintains. "Look at the history. In the summertime you see the southern fleet come up and work out of Long Island. Your Gloucester, your Maine fleet comes down when the winter fleet is bad. We are right in the middle."

John Rempe, a fisherman out of Greenport, takes advantage of the migrating fish. "A lot of the fish we catch come here for the summer, then they leave because it gets too cold for them. They can't stand the cold temperature," he says. "We have others that move out in the summertime because they can't stand the warm water. Herring move out in June and won't come back until late fall. Your summer flounder is a fluke which stays in the ocean in wintertime and comes in here in the summer. And the winter flounder, the blackback, is just the opposite. They come in in the fall and bed down in the mud. As the water starts to get warmer they move out into the ocean."

International trade is where Long Island fishermen can make the most gains, according to Flagg. "There are so many products here that are very good to eat that are wasted and not used, specifically skate, dogfish, squid, butterfish, even mackerel. We're probably the greatest fish market in the world but we have such limited tastes." Flagg is going for the upscale international market by selling fresh tuna to Japan, convincing local fishermen to go for the 400- to 500-pound tuna that the Japanese like the best and to handle it so the quality is maintained. "There are certain methods where you bleed and chill the fish, special ways to produce a superior product. What you do for those first 20 minutes it is

OPPOSITE ABOVE *Digging for steamer clams in Mt. Sinai harbor*

OPPOSITE BELOW *Scallopers returning home at the end of the day, East Hampton*

ABOVE *While her granddaughter watches, Isabella Lore cleans her catch of mussels*

out of the water is very important," says Flagg, who studied Japanese techniques. And it's so crucial because one fish could cost him $3,000 or $4,000.

Phil McSweeney organized the Montauk fishermen to go for squid in a joint venture. They supply the fish to a huge Japanese vessel that stays offshore three miles and processes the catch as well as to onshore dealers—all told that totals more than three million pounds. Only recently have U.S. consumers started enjoying squid, and there's plenty out there to harvest.

Squid was not one of the biggest items caught in New York waters in 1983; whiting led the list with 4,545,337 pounds, followed by the ever popular flounder, bluefish, butterfish, fluke, porgies, and tilefish.

But this does not reflect the fish caught by sportsfishermen. There is some friction between the two groups, with commercial fishermen protesting that when the sportsman sells his fish cheaply because of his low overhead, he undercuts the commercial price and makes it tough for the guy who goes out year-round to earn a living. The sportsman fears overfishing by the commercial fleet will threaten stocks of fish that he enjoys catching.

This natural antagonism came to a head over the question of striped bass, the beloved sports fish and profitable catch for any fishermen. Once prolific, the bass is disappearing from local waters due to many factors: pollution in spawning grounds and possibly overfishing. New York State passed a law setting the minimum legal size at 24 inches, a size believed to ensure that the fish has already spawned and contributed to the next generation. While commercial fishermen file protests, this law has had the effect of virtually wiping out the haul seiner. Only four or five crews remain on the East End, working off the beaches around Amagansett, setting out nets from shore in what has been called the oldest method of fishing.

Most fishermen run trawlers or draggers, pulling their nets behind them. Others, like Rempe, set up pound nets to catch the fish swimming by. "More fish are caught dragging than any other way that I know," says Rempe. "A dragger can work all year long, especially the offshore boats. They go out into deeper water; that's where the fish are. The smaller boats work most of the year, but when the weather's bad and there's really nothing to fish for in the bay…"

Rempe pulls up his nets in late fall to repair for the next season starting early spring. "All your fish generally travel parallel with the beach," he says. "When they run into any obstacle their instinct is to go into deeper water." The net guides the fish into an inner pound, connected to a funnel which leads into a box that is then hauled up, releasing the fish on board. The smart fish find their way back out the funnel; "We only catch the dumb ones," he says. "Now the striped bass is one of the smartest fish in the water. I've gone out in the evening and seen them in the trap and in the morning they're gone."

The cost of bringing in the catch is not cheap; a single trap may cost $5,000. Pulling a trawler out for an annual overhaul can run as much as $10,000, tow wire alone is $650, not to mention fuel, the crew, and the cost of the boat itself. And the ocean has claimed fishermen during fierce storms. "People have this idea that we just go out and fish," says McSweeney, "that we just jump in the boat and it doesn't cost us anything to operate." Yet when the fish are running and the market is favorable, there is much money to be made. And there is a satisfaction that can't be translated into dollars.

"It's great when you go all the way out for these tuna," says Flagg, "and you pass different zones. When you enter into that last zone along the continental slope where you come into some very clear water, the whole ocean can come alive. Bait fish on top, whales, birds. It leaps alive."

"Once you start fishing, it gets in your blood and it never gets out," says Rempe. "You don't want to do anything else. Besides being your own boss there's nothing more beautiful than seeing the sun come up in the morning. There have been times when I've been out in bad weather that I've wished I was back home, but there's really no place else in the world that I'd prefer to be."

Long Island Vineyards

For the first three or four years, all Alex and Louisa Hargrave had was a good theory and no vinifera grapes to vindicate their faith. After all, the climate should be right and the soil acceptable, but no one had turned potato fields into vineyards before.

"Those first five years, there were just too many unknowns involved, and the financial risk was too high," says Hargrave. "The first few years we started producing, we had a hurricane. We got absolutely wiped out by birds one year and a third year it was very rainy. We thought maybe this was the wrong idea.

"We weren't smart enough to change our plans at that point and so we kept doing it. We've run into four truly magnificent seasons and it's all that we had hoped, all that we researched," he says.

"When we first started everyone thought how could it be any good because it's part of New York. They thought it was going to be more grape jelly wine and so nothing I could say could change anybody's attitude. They had to see the wines over a number of vintages, see that they lived and developed in the bottle. See that they fit very nicely on a Thanksgiving table. And voilà."

Not quite instantly, but slowly others are following the pioneering efforts of the Hargraves on the East End. David Mudd, a former Eastern Airline pilot, became a believer in Hargrave's theories even before they came to fruition, and planted his first acre. Now Mudd oversees more than 300 acres for other investors in Mudd's Vineyard, his company that installs and maintains vineyards. Dr. Herodotus Damianos, a physician specializing in internal medicine, became convinced by both the resiliency of the vines in his own backyard and the studies of Cornell University with farmer John Wickham that the North Fork was the place to make wine. In 1979 he began planting on 120 acres at his vineyard and winery Pindar in Peconic and by 1983 he harvested his first Winter White, developing the largest vineyard and winery on the Island. Pat and Peter Lenz, formerly owners of a restaurant, A Moveable Feast, decided against California's Napa Valley when the winery bug hit them and settled instead in Peconic.

Lyle Greenfield, an advertising executive, caught Hargrave's enthusiasm and planted in Bridgehampton.

And there has been growing recognition for these first efforts. Hargrave's wines have captured five gold medals at the New York State Fair for Chardonnay, Sauvignon Blanc, and Riesling, and best in show in the 1984 fair for his 1982 Riesling. Bridgehampton's 1983 Chardonnay received a silver, while Hargrave's 1983 Collector Series Chardonnay won a bronze. The Lenz 1983 Gewürztraminer, their first wine, earned a bronze, the only medal awarded in that classification. Hargrave has also earned international acclaim; his 1982 Collector's Series Chardonnay, with a label by Elaine de Kooning, the East Hampton artist, was given the Prix d'Honneur, in an international food show, competing against 100 wines from five continents.

How much more growth and certainly how fast Long Island's wine industry will develop are under some debate. As of this writing, slightly more than 1,000 acres have been planted, with five wineries in production as of 1984.

The highly optimistic Mudd believes 6,000 to 8,000 acres are required to develop a good healthy region. Others, concerned that overproduction without careful, personalized winemaking to realize all the potential, shy away from grandiose claims. Certainly, though, the question whether Long Island is well suited to vinifera grapes—the European grape stock producing some of the world's finest wines—and not just the native labrusca grapes long associated with foxy, sweet wines has been answered with a firm *yes*.

"Because of the climate we can grow many different types of vinifera," says Pat Lenz, "particularly red varieties which is unique in New York. We have a long enough growing season for it and the winters are mild enough so that the vines winter over and there's not that much winterkill. Providing we have a decent October we can ripen cabernet sauvignon fairly successfully a fair number of years out of ten, as good as in France I think."

But she doesn't foresee a Long Island wine industry developing as fast as you can set down root-

Sheep, shown here at Hargrave Vineyard, help do summer hedging, although the real pruning is done by a vineyard flail

stock. "I still think it's going to be a relatively small area compared to a lot of other grape-growing regions," she says. "It is possible to double and it is possible to triple our size, and I just think it depends on the success of the wines and if the people are willing to do it."

For the wine industry to prosper, it must be done in a "tremendous style and effort from everyone concerned," says Judith Betts, the marketing and sales manager for Pindar. "There is no room for those people looking for the easy buck."

Hargrave is concerned by excessive hype promising that Long Island is a gold mine for grapes. "It is good earth, and it is a lot of work. Wine is a personal statement," he says. Long Island, furthermore, will not ever get the incredible production that a San Joaquin Valley vineyard might expect, upwards of

ten to twelve tons per acre. "We are limited by our winter, they have no winter," he says. "I think the strength of Long Island will be many small producers making personal statements in their wine much the way Bordeaux or Burgundy has achieved it."

Vinifera grapes had never been tried on Long Island, Hargrave discovered, because one William Prince, the foremost small fruit expert in the early 1800s, tried an experiment at his nursery in Flushing and failed. Hargrave, who has researched the subject, found that Prince had two problems—sunburn and powdered mildew. "Prince felt that grapes weren't indicated on Long Island because of his experience in Flushing. The first man who planted a vineyard on the Hudson was Andrew Caywood. He went to Prince and said 'What should I plant and where'," says Hargrave. Prince convinced Caywood

Four Long Island wines, photographed at Pindar Vineyard in Peconic

to head to the "highlands" of the Hudson River. "People followed the Hudson thence to the Finger Lakes. They thought they were so far out west that they called their wineries things like Great Western. The industry went along Lake Erie to Michigan and separately was building up with Michigan grapes in California."

"So Long Island was left out." A mixture to control the mildew that stymied Prince in Flushing was developed in 1853, the year after Prince died. Had the mixture been available, had Prince been willing to try the less humid North Fork, history might have been different, Hargrave speculates.

Another plant specialist further conspired in 1911 to keep vinifera from being tried on Long Island. "U.P. Hedrick was in charge of testing better grape varieties and they used Geneva, New York, as the place they would test all fruit," says Hargrave. If it succeeded in Geneva, they would recommend it generally to everybody else. "Vinifera was killed back by minus 40 degree winters and so they said it's impossible to grow vinifera in New York. And so this was gospel. And it certainly was true you couldn't grow vinifera in Geneva."

Then, in the early 1950s, Dr. Konstantin Frank experimented on a small plot of land at Gold Seal Vineyards in the Finger Lakes region, using his considerable grape-growing talents honed in the Ukraine to raise vinifera. "It took a plant genius to do it and that gave me the confidence," says Hargrave. "Without his experience up there, I would never have considered it, despite all the theories of the Sound and the Bay and the sandy soil and the drain-off and all that."

Those theories now having been substantiated, Mudd uses them to convince potential investors. "We have lousy springs here, we go from winter underwear to short sleeves in one day, usually towards the end of May," he says. "For us natives, it's a terrible thing because we just don't have the springtimes that other areas do. This is due to the fact that the Sound is just across the treetops there and the Peconic Bay is just the other side, less than a half mile away. Both of those bodies are so cold that when we get a warm day west of here or in Connecticut, the land has a chance to warm up. But we don't get that condition because the lands don't warm up as quickly here."

The advantage to all that is the buds will rarely break until the danger of frost is past. "We have one of the longest frost-free growing regions in the temperate northeast," says Hargrave. And Long Island also doesn't face the extremely high temperatures of California. Once the bud breaks out, every day over 90 degrees takes more out of the plant than it puts in; in that very high heat, the grape simply shuts down and doesn't continue to mature in a balanced way. On Long Island, there are few days over 90 degrees, and certainly far fewer than in California.

And because the vinifera grapevine is a deep-rooted plant, it's scarcely bothered by what the vintners hope will be lack of rainfall at the end of the growing season. "The vine has the ability to cope with moisture deprivation, its leaves close up if it's too dry so it doesn't expend its own energy," says Hargrave. "The vines know how to cope with moisture deprivation, they love it. This accelerates their one function, which is to provide for their reproduction." Then, once the seeds are ripe, the plants start putting their energy into creating extra sugar, says Hargrave, which stores up for the plant's immediate survival the next winter and just happens to make ripe fruit. "The old Romans knew exactly how to tell when their vineyards were ripe," says Hargrave, "because they could see when the grape becomes dusky. Another thing in white grapes is that the grape gets totally translucent so the two seeds in the center are like jewels hanging. It's really a lovely sight."

Of course, like every other agricultural generalization, there will be the exception, the thoroughly rainy season. Even so, that's not all bad. "We've had so much rain this year [1984] but we've never had the grapes standing in water," says Pat Lenz. "The soil drains and it's not pure sand, but a sandy loam. If you prepare the soil well before you plant, the grapevine roots can go down deeply enough which really makes for a better vine. Somehow the minerals way down deep make for a more interesting grape."

Generally, fall is also kind to the vine, with a killing frost holding off until as late as Thanksgiving, allowing the plant to recover from the stress of producing grapes before winter sets in.

The South Fork has a slightly different microclimate than the North Fork, which is somewhat less conducive to the grape although certainly a warmer home than upstate. "We have a much cooler temperature in the spring," says Rich Harbich, winemaker and vineyard manager at the Bridgehampton Winery. "This will delay the growth of the vine. We will always be behind the North Fork during the growth season, at bloom, berry set, and ripening, a few days to two weeks behind." The South Fork has fewer growing degree days, a way of measuring the amount of heat that a given growing season will produce. And frost can hit the South Fork earlier, as well. "But this is still the place to grow vinifera," says Harbich. "Our main advantage is that we have cooler weather, so there is slower ripening. That leaves more acidity and a greater production of aromatic compounds and flavors that make the grape variety unique. The slower the change of temperature takes place, the more delicate the flavor and aroma will be."

"In many ways," says Hargrave, "the most creative thing a winemaker ever does is decide where he plants his vineyard, because you're really harvesting wine, you're not making it. You can't manipulate the grapes that much; once they come to you, they've got their potential. You've either succeeded in the field in ripening them, or you've not. There are many things you can do in the cellar which diminish what you've done in the field but there are none that can make it better."

From the start of harvest, usually the second week of September with Pinot Noir, Hargrave says he uses the tools of the winemaking trade to "make a delicious wine. I've gotten very uncomplicated about it, I want it to be delicious." And for Long Island grapes, he predicts very characteristic wines with the ultimate flavor of the fruit. "We don't have a heavy soil, so we don't have wines that make your teeth rattle. We don't have any odd seabed mineralization here and so you don't expect any sort of mysterious affinity with lobster to emerge," he says. "We have a very neutral soil. I feel a classic quality for Long Island will be something that rings ripe fruit like a clear bell."

It's still too early to see which grape is going to do the best, according to Pat Lenz. But she's excited about Pinot Noir, the troublesome grape that can produce a great Burgundy occasionally, and is generally an unsuccessful wine in California. "We planted Pinot Noir predominantly to do a champagne with, but we didn't want to get involved with that our first year." When their winemaker saw that the Pinot was ripening well, the Lenz's decided to let him try his hand. "It's a Beaune style, it's light but it's not thin, it's damn good and Beaune better watch out," she says, teasing. The Lenz's have also released a spicy, light Gewürztraminer and a Chardonnay for the first season of their 30-acre winery.

At Pindar (named for Damianos's son who in turn is named for an ancient Greek poet whose words so moved Alexander the Great that he spared Pindar's home town from destruction) Winter White is one of their early hits. It is a blend of a French hybrid, Cayuga White, and young Chardonnay; on Long Island's soil, the hybrid reveals its heritage of Chardonnay. Seventy percent of the vines are white —Riesling and Gewürztraminer in addition to the Cayuga white and Chardonnay. And Damianos plans to increase his plantings of red grapes, Pinot Noir, Merlot, Cabernet Sauvignon, and a blending grape, Petit Verdot. Damianos decided on Riesling and Gewürztraminer because he wanted varieties that would enhance the aquaculture of Long Island,

says Betts. "We have such marvelous fresh fish, Peconic bay scallops, clams and oysters, he wanted white varieties to complement them," she says.

Hargrave has a full line—from a fresh young Sauvignon Blanc to a Cabernet Sauvignon aged three years in oak—including a special release Chardonnay with a label designed each year by a different local artist in the style of Chateau Mouton Rothschild.

Marketing, that's what they call it. And that's what Harbich believes will be his biggest challenge. "There's no question we can produce good, even great wines," says Harbich, who is aiming for the kind of wine to complement the food. A big oakey, old-style California Chardonnay, for instance, would overwhelm the local flounder, delicately fried.

"The greatest affinity we've seen is between Sauvignon Blanc and bay scallops," says Hargrave. "It's heaven. There was another time when a wonderful guy who was working for us got a pheasant locally and made pheasant pâté and we had it with a blanc noir. It was possibly the finest taste combination I've ever had in my entire life.

"Generally I think that very well-made wine has an extra reason to fit into fresh produce and complements it by its own nature. We have the advantage that the wine doesn't have to travel or be transported. The wines can be fresher, cleaner because we don't have to sterile-filter them, we don't have to clobber them with chemicals to make sure they make a 2,000 mile overland trip with 3,000 shocks per mile. The wine can be what it's supposed to be."

APPETIZERS

Garlic and Caper Vegetable Dip

2 tablespoons capers, drained
3 large cloves garlic, chopped coarsely
12 sprigs parsley
½ cup coarsely chopped fresh chives
1 egg
Heaping ½ teaspoon Dijon mustard
1½ tablespoons lemon juice
¼ teaspoon salt
½ teaspoon pepper
¾ cup olive oil
¼ cup vegetable oil
1 cup sour cream

1. In a blender or food processor, combine the capers, garlic, parsley, and chives. Process until chopped very fine. Transfer to a mixing bowl.

2. In the same container, add the egg, mustard, lemon juice, and salt and pepper. Process until well blended, 2 to 3 seconds.

3. With machine on, slowly add the olive and vegetable oils in a thin stream. You should have a thick mayonnaise. Add the chopped ingredients to the mayonnaise and process a few more seconds.

4. Pour into a bowl, stir in the sour cream, taste, and add more salt and lemon juice if desired. Chill well before serving, preferably for at least 8 hours to blend flavors. Serve as a dip for fresh vegetables.

Makes about 2¹/₄ cups.

Eggplant Relish

Simple to do, yet a bit different than most relishes. A good appetizer to serve at dinner parties.

1 medium eggplant, a little less than 1 pound
1 large green or red pepper
1 medium onion, diced
2 tablespoons vegetable oil
Salt and freshly ground black pepper to taste

1. Wash eggplant and pepper but leave whole. Place eggplant and pepper on rack in a preheated 375 degree oven. Place onion in an ovenproof dish with the vegetable oil and cover with foil. Bake about 1 hour, or until eggplant is soft. Turn vegetables after 30 minutes. Vegetables will get a little charred on the outside.

2. Remove vegetables from oven. Wrap pepper in foil or plastic wrap while it is still hot. When cool, peel and seed pepper. When eggplant cools, peel skin; scrape any remaining eggplant off skin. If eggplant is watery, drain off some liquid. Chop eggplant coarsely and place with pepper and onion in its cooking liquid in a food processor. Blend briefly using on/off motion about 5 times. Season with salt and pepper. Serve with crackers or toasted pita squares.

Makes 4 servings.

NOTE: The cooked, peeled, and chopped vegetable mixture may be frozen.

Homemade Mayonnaise

2 egg yolks
1/2 teaspoon Dijon mustard
1/4 teaspoon salt
Pinch cayenne pepper or a few drops Tabasco
1 tablespoon white wine vinegar
1 1/2 cups oil, a mixture of olive and vegetable

1. Place egg yolks, mustard, salt, and pepper or Tabasco in a blender or food processor. Blend briefly, then add vinegar and blend again. While machine is running, slowly add the oil in a very thin stream. As the emulsion starts to form, you can add the oil more quickly. You may not need all of the oil. Taste and adjust seasonings. May be refrigerated for up to 10 days.

2. If preparing by hand, beat yolks, mustard, salt, pepper or Tabasco, and vinegar in a bowl with a wire whisk. Slowly add oil.

Makes about 1 1/4 cups.

Zucchini and Roquefort Canapés

It's tough to keep up with a zucchini plant in full production; here's yet another idea for the overflow from Yvonne Gill, author of the Food Enthusiast Newsletter.

3 zucchini, each 5 to 6 inches long, about 1 pound
8 ounces Roquefort cheese, at room temperature
1/4 pound unsalted butter (1 stick), at room temperature
2 tablespoons dry sherry or any fruit vinegar
24 pecan halves, toasted

1. Wash zucchini and remove ends. Cut on a diagonal into slices about 1/4 inch thick, holding the knife at an angle to get long, attractive slices.

2. Cream the cheese and butter together with the sherry or vinegar until smooth.

3. Fit a large pastry bag with a star tip and load the cheese-butter mixture into the bag. Pipe a rosette onto each zucchini slice. Place a toasted pecan half on the rosette, tipping the nut on an angle.

4. Chill, uncovered, to firm the rosette. The canapés will hold for about 6 hours if placed in a recessed dish (so that the covering won't squash the rosettes) and covered with foil or plastic wrap.

Makes about 24 canapés.

Duck and Chicken Liver Spread

The more duck livers you have, the better, for this incredibly rich spread I created while working on duck recipes. Whenever you make duck freeze the duck livers until you have a good supply on hand. Be sure to use a bland cracker or toast so as not to detract from the delicate flavor.

1 pound duck and chicken livers (at least half should be duck livers if possible)
2 cloves garlic, smashed
Orange juice, about 2 cups
1 tablespoon butter
1 small onion, chopped
1 clove garlic, chopped
Pinch thyme
1 bay leaf
Pinch cayenne pepper
1/4 teaspoon quatre épice or large pinch allspice and large pinch cinnamon, combined
Salt and pepper to taste
1 tablespoon Cognac or port
8 to 12 tablespoons unsalted butter, at room temperature

1. Clean livers of any membrane or connective tissue. Marinate livers with 2 cloves garlic in orange juice to cover at least 4 hours or overnight.

2. Remove livers from marinade and discard. Pat livers dry. Melt the 1 tablespoon butter in a small sauté pan and cook onion and garlic briefly. Add livers, thyme, bay leaf, cayenne, quatre épice, salt and pepper, and cook, stirring, about 10 minutes. Add Cognac, set cover ajar, and cook another 10 minutes.

3. Remove bay leaf and place contents of pan in a food processor. Add 8 tablespoons of the butter and purée until very smooth. Pour into a serving crock.

Refrigerate overnight and serve the next day. Be sure to let spread come to room temperature before serving.

Makes 8 servings.

NOTE: If you want to save the spread for a few days, melt remaining 4 tablespoons butter and clarify. Pour enough clarified butter over the top to seal. You may also freeze this for 2 to 3 months.

Libby's Duck Pâté

One of the delicious ways to serve Long Island duck is as a pâté—rich, intense flavors in each thin slice, garnished with cornichons, if desired. This version comes from Libby Hillman, cooking school teacher, cookbook author, and contributor to *Newsday*.

1 5- to 6-pound duck
¼ cup tawny port wine
½ pound mushrooms, cut in quarters
½ teaspoon thyme
1 pound bacon, sliced
½ pound veal
½ pound lean pork
½ pound fresh pork fat
3 shallots, peeled
4 to 6 cloves garlic, peeled
2 slices white bread soaked in ½ cup cream
1 duck liver
½ pound chicken livers or additional duck
   livers if you have them
3 eggs
¼ cup brandy
¼ teaspoon ground cloves, ¼ teaspoon
   cinnamon, ¼ teaspoon freshly grated
   nutmeg
2 teaspoons salt
2 teaspoons pepper
½ pound ham, cubed
¼ cup green peppercorns
12 water chestnuts, cut in quarters
Fresh parsley or watercress, finely chopped,
   and cornichons for garnish

1. To bone the duck: Place the duck on its breast. Cut through the skin down along the back-bone from neck to tail. Carefully separate the skin from the flesh, keeping the skin intact if possible. Do not fret if the skin tears; it will be used to cover the pâté as it cooks. Set aside skin.

2. Proceed to cut away the duck flesh close to the bone; remove the duck to a bowl. Reserve the breasts in 2 large sections. Cut the wings and legs off. Remove the skin and scrape off the flesh from the bones.

3. Cut the breast halves into thin slices. Marinate them for a few hours or overnight in the port wine with the mushrooms and thyme. These will be used later when layering the pâté.

4. Line 2 8-by-3-inch bread loaf pans with slices of bacon. Preheat oven to 400 degrees. Set aside a shallow pan large enough to hold both loaf pans. If you don't have a pan that is large enough, use 2 smaller for each.

5. Use a food processor or meat grinder to grind duck flesh, veal, pork, and pork fat together. Transfer ground mixture to a large bowl. In the same machine, process the shallots, garlic, cream-soaked bread, livers, eggs, brandy, cloves, cinnamon, nutmeg, salt and pepper. Combine with meat mixture.

6. Add the ham, green peppercorns, and water chestnuts to mixture. Stir well to combine ingredients thoroughly. Test a small ball for seasoning by simmering it in water for a few minutes. Taste and adjust seasoning as needed.

7. Spread a thin layer of the duck mixture in each loaf pan. Arrange slices of marinated duck breast and mushrooms. Continue to alternate layers until mixture is divided evenly between pans. Place duck skin directly on top to seal and cover with aluminum foil. Place pans in larger pan. Add boiling water to come halfway up sides of bread pans. Bake for 1½ to 2 hours, or until juices run clear when tester is inserted.

8. Remove pâté from oven and set on cooling racks. Loosen foil around edges but leave it in place. Set a brick or heavy objects such as cans on the foil to weight down the pâté for easier slicing. Cool. Remove weight and refrigerate for 1 or 2 days before serving, to allow flavors to blend.

9. To unmold, run a knife around the sides. Remove the duck skin and discard. Set the pan in warm water to release the bottom fat. Turn upside down on a board. Trim if necessary, slice thinly, and arrange on serving platter. Garnish with finely chopped parsley or watercress and cornichons.

Makes 20 to 30 slices, or enough to serve a large crowd.

ABOVE *Spinach Dip is served at an outing on Fire Island (recipe, page 32)*

LEFT *A sunset buffet on the deck, Dunewood, Fire Island*

BELOW *Dockside cocktail hour, Westhampton Beach*

OPPOSITE *Oysters on the half shell, Greenport*

Spinach Dip

1 pound fresh spinach or 1 10-ounce
    package frozen
1 8-ounce can water chestnuts, chopped
1 carrot, peeled and shredded
1 pimiento, chopped
1 shallot, minced
1 clove garlic, very finely minced
1 1/2 to 2 cups sour cream
1/2 cup mayonnaise
Salt and pepper to taste
Dash Tabasco sauce
Juice of 1/4 lemon

1. If using fresh spinach, wash thoroughly, then cook, with just the water clinging to the leaves, in a covered pan until tender. Drain thoroughly, chop, and squeeze out any moisture.

2. If using frozen spinach, thaw, chop, and squeeze out any moisture.

3. Combine spinach, water chestnuts, carrot, pimiento, shallot, and garlic. Stir together sour cream and mayonnaise, then add to vegetables. Season with salt, pepper, Tabasco, and lemon juice. It should be highly seasoned. Serve with sliced fresh vegetables or crackers.

Makes 6 to 8 servings.

Asparagus Vinaigrette

1 pound asparagus
2 tablespoons Dijon mustard
2 tablespoons red wine vinegar
About 1/2 cup vegetable oil (substitute olive oil
    for part or all of the vegetable oil if desired)
Salt and pepper
2 tablespoons minced fresh chives
1/2 red pepper, chopped

1. Break off woody ends of asparagus and peel stems if desired. Cook until tender, about 5 to 7 minutes; the asparagus should bend just slightly when done. Rinse under cold running water to stop the cooking.

2. Place mustard in a small bowl and stir with a wire whisk. Add vinegar and continue whisking. Slowly add oil in a thin stream, whisking constantly. If desired, place a towel under the bowl to anchor it. Season with salt and lots of pepper.

3. To serve, arrange asparagus on plates and nap the center with the vinaigrette. Sprinkle with chives and red pepper.

Makes 4 to 6 servings.

Hewlett Fish Market's Seafood Salad

The Hewlett Fish Market on the South Shore prepares a full line of appetizers and main dishes to go; this is one of my favorites.

2 to 2 1/2 pounds squid, cleaned and cut into
    1/4-inch pieces (see page 110)
2 29-ounce cans cooked conch
4 ribs celery, cut into 1/4-inch pieces
12 to 15 black olives, halved
2 or 3 slices red peppers packed in vinegar, cut
    into 1/4-inch dice
3/4 cup good-quality virgin olive oil
1/4 to 1/2 cup freshly squeezed lemon juice
2 tablespoons freshly chopped parsley
1/2 teaspoon oregano
Salt and pepper to taste
Pinch ground red pepper flakes
3 to 4 cloves garlic, finely minced

1. In a large pot, bring 4 quarts of water and 1 tablespoon salt to a rolling boil. Add squid. When the water returns to a boil, cook squid for 15 minutes in a rolling boil.

2. Turn off burner and let squid remain in pot for 15 minutes. Drain, and set aside. Allow to cool.

3. In a large bowl, mix squid with conch, celery, olives, red peppers, oil, lemon juice, parsley, oregano, salt and pepper, red pepper flakes, and garlic. Toss well. Chill overnight.

Makes 6 to 8 servings.

Cucumbers filled with Fish Mousseline

Robert Schoolsky, *Newsday*'s wine writer, not only knows his way around a cellar but is a master in the kitchen as well. His elegant appetizer is a tribute to the best principles of the new-style cooking: beautiful as well as delicious.

> 1/2 pound any firm-textured fish such as whiting, scrod, or scallops, cut into small pieces
> 1 egg
> 2 tablespoons heavy cream
> Salt and pepper to taste
> 3 large cucumbers
> Fish stock or bottled clam juice
> 5 to 6 large ripe tomatoes, peeled and seeds removed
> Lemon juice to taste
> 8 green beans, trimmed
> 3 carrots, peeled

1. In a food processor combine the fish, egg, cream, salt, and pepper. Process until mixture is smooth, about 20 seconds.

2. Peel cucumbers and cut off ends. With a corer, remove all seeds. Stuff the fish mixture into the hollow cucumbers.

3. Place cucumbers in a shallow baking dish. Cover with fish stock or clam juice and poach on top of the stove for 15 minutes. Remove from stock and refrigerate. Fish mixture may extend beyond ends of cucumbers while poaching or during refrigeration. Trim excess.

4. Purée the tomatoes. Let drain in a fine sieve. Add lemon juice to taste. Cut the beans and carrots into 1 1/2-inch lengths and blanch quickly, about 1 minute, in boiling water. Rinse under cold water, and pat dry. Chill.

5. To serve, ladle equal amounts of tomato purée on each of 4 plates. Slice each cucumber into rounds about 1/4 inch thick. Arrange cucumber rounds on the tomato purée in an attractive design, alternating with the beans and carrots.

Makes 4 servings.

Bluefish Seviche

Chopped green pepper may be added to this seviche. Or, you might consider a few dashes Tabasco for spicy heat.

> 1 pound bluefish fillets
> White vinegar
> 1 tablespoon minced fresh parsley
> 1 1/2 tablespoons grated onion
> 1 large tomato, peeled, seeded, and diced
> Salt and pepper to taste
> 2 tablespoons dry white wine
> 1 teaspoon Dijon mustard
> 2 tablespoons prepared chili sauce
> 1 teaspoon prepared horseradish

1. Cut raw fish fillets in cubes or strips, place in a porcelain or glass dish and cover with vinegar. Marinate for 2 hours—the vinegar will "cook" the fish.

2. Drain fish, mix with parsley, onion, tomato, salt, and pepper. Blend wine with 1 tablespoon of the vinegar, mustard, chili sauce, and horseradish. Add to fish, mix well and chill an hour or so.

Makes 6 to 8 servings.

Chili-Horseradish Dip for Clams

Use only the freshest clams you can find from a reliable fish store. Then serve them simply with lemon wedges and this spicy dip.

> 3/4 cup ketchup
> 2 tablespoons grated horseradish
> 2 teaspoons Worcestershire sauce
> 1/2 teaspoon Dijon mustard
> 1 tablespoon lemon juice
> 1 scallion, minced, including part of the green
> Tabasco sauce to taste

Combine all ingredients.

Makes about 1 1/4 cups.

Robert Lipinski's Steamers

Robert A. Lipinski, free lance wine and food writer and consultant, says he would be content to sit and eat steamers all afternoon on a hot sunny day. This is his approach, devised because he enjoys drinking the broth as well. Be sure to watch the amount of black pepper; even a devotee can get carried away.

6 dozen steamers
3 carrots, peeled and coarsely chopped
4 onions, sliced
4 ribs celery, chopped
4 cups very dry white wine
1 quart water
1 teaspoon freshly ground black pepper
3/4 teaspoon thyme
3 cloves garlic, minced
Dash red pepper flakes, optional

1. Clean steamers by packing them tightly in a large tub with plenty of ice and seltzer. Let them soak for a good four hours.
2. Then, put them in a salad spinner, again packed tightly, and run. If they are not tight enough, the shells will crack. Place steamers in the top of a steamer rack.
3. In bottom of steamer pot, put the carrots, onions, celery, wine, water, pepper, thyme, and garlic, adding red pepper if desired. Taste and adjust seasonings.
4. Cover steamers and cook until clams open, about 15 to 20 minutes. Serve steamers with the broth on the side. Or strain the broth and save it for soup.

Makes 4 to 6 servings.

Clams with Parsley and Garlic Sauce

Hazelnuts add unexpected flavor here. To remove the skins from the hazelnuts, heat them briefly in a 350 degree oven; you can then slip the skins off easily.

32 cherrystone or littleneck clams
Coarse salt
1 bunch fresh parsley
4 cloves garlic
1/4 cup coarsely chopped fresh chives
1/3 cup hazelnuts or filberts
1/4 pound (1 stick) unsalted butter
Salt and pepper to taste

1. Scrub the clams. Just before serving, open clams, reserving liquid. Discard top shell. Or have fish store open clams, reserving the liquid.
2. Place salt in one large ovenproof dish to cover, or in four small ones, and nestle clams on top, 8 to a dish. Set aside.
3. In a food processor or blender, combine the parsley, garlic, chives, and hazelnuts until finely chopped.
4. Heat the butter in a small saucepan, add parsley mixture and heat briefly, about 30 seconds. Season with salt and pepper, if desired, then spoon onto the clams.
5. Preheat oven to broil. Broil until the clams are cooked, about 5 minutes; do not overcook. Serve with crusty French bread.

Makes 4 to 6 appetizer servings.

Stuffed Clams

40 cherrystone clams, with their shells
2 tablespoons butter
2 slices bacon, minced
3 cloves garlic, minced
2 fresh plum tomatoes, peeled, seeded, and diced
1/2 green pepper, minced
3/4 cup dry, unseasoned bread crumbs
Coarse salt

1. Scrub the clams well before opening them. Remove the clam meat and chop coarsely. If you buy them already shucked, be sure to ask for the shells.
2. In a small skillet, heat the butter, add the bacon and cook briefly; add the garlic, tomatoes, and green pepper. Cook until the green pepper is soft, 5 to 8 minutes.
3. Off the heat, stir in the bread crumbs and then the chopped clams. Scoop generous portions of the clam mixture into 32 shells—that way you get more clams per bite.
4. Preheat oven to broil. Pour salt into a large oven-proof dish to cover bottom. Nestle clams in the salt.
5. Broil about 8 to 10 minutes, or until top is crispy.

Makes 4 to 6 servings.

Clam Fritters

In response to a reader request to her popular Feedback column in *Newsday,* Marie Bianco developed this recipe.

2 cups finely minced clams, drained
2 egg yolks, well beaten
1 cup cracker or dry bread crumbs
2 tablespoons minced fresh parsley
Salt and pepper to taste
Clam juice
3 egg whites

1. In a large mixing bowl, combine clams, egg yolks, crumbs, parsley, salt and pepper, and enough clam juice to make a heavy batter. Mix well.
2. Beat egg whites until stiff and fold into clam mixture.

3. In a deep fryer heat vegetable shortening to 375 degrees. Add batter to hot fat by tablespoonfuls and fry, turning once, until brown on all sides.

Makes 3 to 4 dozen.

Green Beans with Lobster Salad

1 1/2 pounds fresh green beans
3 tablespoons vinegar
10 tablespoons oil, half olive, half vegetable
1 tablespoon fresh tarragon, chopped, or
    1 teaspoon dried
Salt and pepper to taste
1 clove garlic, minced
2 1 1/2-pound lobsters, cooked (see page 119)

1. Clean beans and cook in a large pot of boiling, salted water until just tender, about 5 minutes. Refresh under cold running water.
2. Stir to combine the vinegar, oils, tarragon, salt, pepper, and garlic. Remove lobster from its shell and cut into bite-size pieces.
3. Marinate beans in half of the vinaigrette. Marinate lobster in remaining vinaigrette. Let stand at least 1 hour before serving. To serve, mound the lobster salad with the green beans.

Makes 4 servings.

Mussels in White Wine Butter Sauce (recipe, page 36)

Cold Lobster Rémoulade

5 cooked lobsters (each about 1¹/₂ pounds),
     chilled (see page 119)
³/₄ cup mayonnaise, preferably homemade
     (see page 28)
1 teaspoon anchovy paste
1¹/₂ teaspoons Dijon mustard
1¹/₂ tablespoons chopped sour gherkins,
     French cornichons preferred
2 teaspoons capers, drained and smashed
1 tablespoon chopped fresh tarragon or
     1 teaspoon dried
2 tablespoons finely minced fresh parsley
Freshly ground pepper

1. Remove the cooked, chilled meat from the shells and cut into bite-size pieces.

2. For the rémoulade, combine the mayonnaise, anchovy paste, mustard, relish, capers, tarragon, parsley, and pepper. Taste and adjust seasonings as needed. Serve the lobster with the sauce on the side or combine with just enough sauce to coat lightly.

Makes 6 to 8 servings.

Mackerel in White Wine

2 tablespoons olive oil
2 small onions, thinly sliced
2 carrots, pared, sliced into thin rounds
6 small mackerel, cleaned
¹/₂ lemon, sliced
1 cup water or clam juice
2 cups dry white wine
1¹/₂ tablespoons lemon juice
Salt and pepper to taste
1 teaspoon tarragon
Pinch of thyme
3 sprigs parsley
6 black peppercorns
2 cloves
1 bay leaf

1. Line the bottom of a lightly oiled baking dish with half of the onion and carrot slices. Place fish on top in one layer, cover with remaining onion and carrot and the thinly sliced lemon. Blend water or clam juice, wine, lemon juice, and remaining tablespoon of oil. Pour over fish. Season with salt and pepper, add tarragon, thyme, parsley, peppercorns, and cloves; put bay leaf on top.

2. Cover dish with a tight-fitting lid or aluminum foil. Bring to a boil, reduce heat, and simmer for about 10 minutes until fish flakes easily. Remove from heat, place fish carefully in a serving dish, strain cooking liquid over them, garnish with some of the carrot rounds and lemon slices. Chill before serving.

Makes 6 servings.

TO CLEAN MUSSELS

Mussels are delicious but time-consuming to clean. It is, however, crucial that they be scrubbed and free from sand, particularly if you intend to consume the liquid they have been cooked in. If there is time, you can soak the mussels in cold water that has a tablespoon of vinegar, flour, or cornmeal in it. This encourages them to disgorge the sand.

Discard any cracked or open mussels. Grab the mussels with your thumb and forefinger and slide your thumb sideways. A live, healthy mussel will not slide apart. Use a pair of rubber gloves to protect your hands. Scrub mussels with a stiff brush and scrape off barnacles with a knife. Pull or scrub off the "beard," officially called the byssus, which a mussel uses to attach itself to rocks and pilings. Rinse again thoroughly.

Mussels in White Wine Butter Sauce

This is one of Joe Dombroski's specialties.

5 pounds mussels
1 onion, sliced
¹/₂ cup white wine

2 cloves garlic, minced
2 lemons, sliced
2 teaspoons oregano

Butter sauce:
1/4 pound (1 stick) unsalted butter
3 cloves garlic, minced
1 teaspoon oregano

1. Clean mussels and remove beard (see page 36). Mince a couple slices of the onion. Combine minced onion with wine and garlic in bottom of large roasting pan or stockpot. Cook over high heat briefly, just to combine flavors. Add a few slices of lemon, then some of the mussels, and a few slices of onion and lemon. Repeat pattern, using all of the mussels, onion, and lemon slices. Sprinkle 2 teaspoons of the oregano on top.

2. Cover and steam mussels, shaking pan occasionally.

3. Meanwhile, prepare the sauce. Heat butter in a saucepan, add the garlic and oregano and cook briefly, a minute or two.

4. When all mussels have opened, remove from heat. Discard any that have not opened. Remove mussels to a serving bowl. Pour off cooking liquid, leaving about a depth of 1/2 to 1 inch in pan. Add butter sauce and heat, stirring to combine. Taste and adjust seasoning as needed.

5. Divide mussels among 6 to 8 serving bowls and pour the sauce over them. Serve with crusty bread.

Makes 6 to 8 servings.

Mussels in Green Sauce

Mussels may be used a variety of ways; here they are adapted to Spanish cuisine, napped in a piquant green sauce.

To steam mussels:
1 onion, peeled and quartered
2 sprigs parsley
1 bay leaf, cut in half
1 sprig fresh thyme or 1/2 teaspoon dried
1 clove garlic, unpeeled and smashed
8 black peppercorns

1/2 teaspoon red pepper flakes
1 cup dry white wine
2 pounds mussels, 30 to 40, depending on size, trimmed and cleaned (see page 36)

For Green Sauce:
1 cup reserved mussel broth
1 clove garlic
2 shallots
1 egg
1 teaspoon Dijon mustard
1 tablespoon lemon juice
1 teaspoon coarse salt
1 teaspoon freshly ground pepper
2 cups mixed greens (such as spinach, watercress, lettuce, parsley, scallions)
1 1/2 cups olive oil or combination of olive and vegetable oil
1/4 cup capers, rinsed and drained
Italian parsley sprigs

1. Put the onion, parsley, bay leaf, thyme, garlic, peppercorns, red pepper flakes, and wine in a large soup pot, and stir to combine; add mussels. Cover and bring to a boil. Shake the pot after a few minutes to redistribute the mussels. They should open in 5 to 7 minutes. Give them 10 minutes if necessary and then discard the unopened ones.

2. Remove mussels to a platter, cool slightly. Allow broth to cool in the pot. Open mussels, remove and discard the rubberlike band around each mussel. Leave mussel in the half shell, and discard top half. Set mussels on a clean tray.

3. To make the sauce, strain mussel broth without disturbing any sand that may have settled to the bottom of the pot. Reserve 1 cup. Boil reserved mussel broth with the garlic and shallots until reduced to a few tablespoons.

4. In a food processor or blender, combine the egg, mustard, lemon juice, salt, pepper, 1 tablespoon of the reduced mussel broth and the greens. Process for 30 seconds or until mixture is light green. Slowly dribble in the oil while machine is running. Mixture will become very thick. Add 1 or 2 tablespoons reduced broth. Taste and adjust seasoning.

5. Nap each mussel with a small amount of sauce. Garnish the top with a few capers and 1 flat leaf of Italian parsley.

Makes 8 to 12 servings.

On Oysters

The people who make up the various Long Island oyster companies aren't fishermen really, they're underwater farmers. They control the land and the crops on them, grooming the bay bottom and "planting" the seedlings just as any farmer tills his soil and puts down seeds.

"We're very close to land farmers except we cannot sell the crop unless we send a diver down," said John Mulhall, president of the Long Island Oyster Farms, Inc., in Greenport. Actually, his company dredges 6,000 acres in Gardiners Bay, cleaning the bottom much like a vacuum cleaner.

If Mulhall's company didn't put the seed oysters there in the first place, there wouldn't be any to

H. Butler Flower

harvest commercially, the "natural" set having disappeared decades ago. Actually, the company sends boats every summer to New Haven, Connecticut, where oysters do breed naturally and brings back two-year-old bivalves to grow one more year to maturity in Long Island waters.

"Why isn't this area good for spawning? The water currents, temperature, salinity, the amount of algae available for growth are all factors, variables that don't come together to make the right combination." Then he shrugs, implying that the exact reason eludes experts. So, why Connecticut? Probably the abundance of rivers feeding into the Sound. But the odds are against the oyster; one female may put out fifteen million eggs and an infinitesimal percentage make it to maturity.

H. Butler Flower, whose grandfather began the company Frank M. Flower & Sons, Inc. in 1887, also once brought back oysters from Connecticut. Now he circumvents that problem by hatching his own. Since the early 1970s, he has been planting seed oysters on twenty-five hundred acres of bay bottom leased from the Town of Oyster Bay.

From February through July, biologist David Relyea convinces breeder oysters that it's summer and gets them to spawn. "We need 12 oysters per week to keep the hatchery going," says Relyea. After spending two weeks in 75-degree salt water getting their fill of algae and other nutrients, the breeder oysters spawn, each dozen producing anywhere from one hundred million to two hundred million larvae.

"Within 24 hours, we have swimming larvae, each has two shells, microscopic, of course," says Relyea. However, only the fastest-growing are kept, as the developing oysters are frequently filtered for size. In three weeks, the oysters are ready to metamorphose, that is, lose their swimming apparatus (velum) and attach themselves to the material that will become home base.

"We cover the bottom of the tank with ground-up hard clam shells, the larvae attach to this and that's where they will stay for the rest of their lives," Relyea says. When they reach 1½ inches in length, they are ready to plant on seed beds in the harbor with hard bottoms where the oysters are unlikely to

Crewmen aboard the Frank M. Flower & Sons boat sort oysters

be covered with silt, and that are relatively free from the natural predators—oyster drills, starfish, and crabs. Since they no longer are able to swim, they can't climb out from under mud, unlike a clam that is able to work its way free.

"After one year, we transplant from seed beds to areas where small oysters can't make it, but a larger one does," says Relyea. The bigger they are, the better they are able to resist the probing of the oyster drill that bores through the shells or the starfish that surrounds the oyster and digests it in its shell. "When they're two or three years old, they're ready for harvest." Growth occurs twice a year, explains Butler, every spring and fall. "They don't grow when it's very cold or when they spawn."

Harvesting is a bit more romantic here; instead of a huge factory ship, smaller oyster boats drag dredges over the side. The teeth in the dredges flip the oysters up into a cage; when the dredges are emptied onto the boat, the oysters are culled and sized.

Mulhall's oyster company markets about twenty-five million oysters, though if Mother Nature would cooperate, he would gladly sell more to buyers throughout the country. Flower, too, faces more demand than supply. Ironically, his company sends coals to Newcastle with shipments of oysters to the prime producing areas of Maryland and Virginia. "And they just want more, even though we sell for about $50 to $55 a bushel and they could buy local oysters for $10 to $15," he says.

Flower is partial to his own product, too. "I like them in butter, pepper and salt, a little cream or half and half. I cook the oysters by themselves, you can watch them better. As soon as the gills curl up, they are done. You can overcook them and they get tough." Mulhall prefers his oysters raw. "Just eat them on the half shell. Plain. If you have a cocktail sauce, I like it hot, with fresh horseradish, a new bottle every time," he says. "But I love the product I work with, so I'm very biased."

Peppers Stuffed with Mussels and Lobster

Marvin Krosinsky and Debbie Coccaro, old friends and good cooks, made up this appetizer that is not only delicious but also great for using up any leftover cooked mussels. When selecting mussels, Krosinsky looks for closed, fresh-smelling mussels.

> 2 pounds mussels
> 2 tablespoons butter
> 2 cloves garlic, chopped
> 3 shallots, peeled and chopped, or 1/2 cup
>   chopped onions
> 1 cup chopped mushrooms
> 1/4 cup diced celery
> 2 tablespoons chopped fresh Italian parsley
> 2 tablespoons chopped fresh dill
> 1/8 teaspoon oregano
> 1/8 teaspoon rosemary
> 1/2 pound cooked lobster meat
> 12 ounces farmer cheese or cream cheese
> 12 medium frying peppers
> Olive oil

1. Clean the mussels, according to instructions, page 36.

2. Place mussels in a deep pot. Add water to cover, bring to a boil, and cook until shells open; check after 3 minutes. Do not overcook. Remove mussels and cool. Discard any mussels that have not opened. Remove mussels from shells and set aside.

3. Melt the butter and in it lightly sauté the garlic, shallots, mushrooms, and celery. Add parsley, dill, oregano, and rosemary. Chop mussels and lobster and combine with garlic-onion mixture. Pour into a blender or food processor and run machine briefly. Do not purée; you want some texture. Place in a bowl and stir in the cheese.

4. Cut off top of peppers and remove seeds and white membrane. Working gently, stuff with mussel mixture; try to get down into the bottom of the pepper without breaking the skin. Press down the mixture. Arrange in a large baking pan and drizzle each pepper with a little olive oil. Bake in a preheated 350 degree oven for 20 to 25 minutes, until peppers are browned but not burned.

Makes 12 stuffed peppers.

HOW TO OPEN AN OYSTER

There is the easy way to shuck an oyster that leaves the shell slightly damaged. Then, there's the hard way to obtain a perfect shell. Take your pick.

1. Break off a small piece of the shell with a pliers; insert the oyster knife and run it around the oyster to pry off the shell.

2. Work the oyster knife into the hinge with a gentle twisting motion. The oyster shell will "give" or open slightly. Then run the knife around the oyster to open completely.

Sauce Mignonette for Oysters

Serious oyster lovers go for just a squeeze of lemon juice, but a simple mignonette sauce is also appropriate.

> 1/4 cup finely minced shallots
> 2 tablespoons crushed or coarsely ground
>   black pepper
> 1/2 cup white wine vinegar
> 1/2 teaspoon salt
> 1/2 teaspoon chervil
> 1 teaspoon minced fresh parsley

Blend all ingredients and serve with oysters.

Makes about 1 cup.

Scalloped Oysters

> 1 1/2 cups bread crumbs
> 3 cups cracker crumbs
> 1 1/2 cups melted butter
> 3 pints shucked oysters, liquid reserved

Salt and pepper to taste
Grated nutmeg to taste
6 tablespoons cream
1 cup plus 2 tablespoons oyster liquid

1. Mix the crumbs and butter together. Spread a thin layer of crumbs in a shallow, buttered baking dish. Cover with half of the oysters. Sprinkle with salt, pepper, and a grating of nutmeg. Add half of the cream and half of the oyster liquid. Repeat layering. Cover top with crumbs.

2. Bake in a preheated 450 degree oven for 20 minutes.

Makes 10 servings.

Oysters with Curry Flavor

This hot appetizer may be served on a platter with toothpicks for dipping the oysters in the cucumber sauce—it is particularly suited to a buffet-style party.

For sauce:
1 cup plain low-fat yogurt
1 cucumber, peeled, cut in half lengthwise with
  seeds scooped out
2 cloves garlic, minced
Salt and pepper

3 dozen oysters, shucked
3 tablespoons oil
1 tablespoon curry powder
2 teaspoons minced ginger
2 cloves garlic, minced
2 scallions, minced, including some of
  the green
1/8 teaspoon powdered cardamom
1/8 teaspoon cayenne pepper
1/2 teaspoon turmeric
2 tablespoons raisins, soaked in hot water for
  20 minutes, drained, and minced

1. In a food processor or blender, combine yogurt, cucumber, garlic, and salt and pepper to taste. Blend briefly, but do not overprocess.

2. Pat oysters dry with a paper towel. In a large sauté pan, heat oil and add the curry powder, ginger,

garlic, scallions, cardamom, cayenne, and turmeric. Heat briefly, stirring constantly. Add oysters and raisins and toss to coat with spices. Cook briefly over medium heat, just until oysters start to curl. Remove from heat. Serve with the yogurt-cucumber sauce.

Makes 6 to 8 servings.

Baked Oysters with Garlic and Pernod

John C. Ross, owner of Ross' Restaurant in Southold, prides himself in serving the best of Long Island foods. This appetizer is an example of the combination of a great idea with a terrific product.

24 oysters, on the half shell
Coarse salt
2 strips bacon
2 1/2 tablespoons finely minced garlic
4 tablespoons bread crumbs
3/4 pound unsalted butter (3 sticks)
Chopped fresh parsley, about 4 sprigs
Paprika
Pernod
Lemon wedges

1. Nestle oysters in a bed of coarse salt on one large ovenproof tray or on 4 individual ovenproof plates. Cook bacon until nearly done, drain, and cut into 1/2-inch slices. Set aside. Combine the garlic and bread crumbs. Melt the butter and spoon about 1 tablespoon on each oyster. Top each with the garlic and bread crumb mixture. Sprinkle parsley and paprika on top as desired. Sprinkle each oyster with a very small amount of pernod, as the anise flavor is quite pronounced. Top each oyster with a 1/2-inch piece of bacon.

2. Place the oysters on the middle shelf of a preheated 425 degree oven and cook until bacon is crisp, about 5 minutes. Serve with lemon wedges.

Makes 4 servings.

FROM THE TOP, CLOCKWISE *Scallop baymen at dawn, East Hampton; Oysters; A solo clammer, Great South Bay*

OPPOSITE *Going out to seed oyster beds, Oyster Bay harbor*

Oysters with Ham and Minted Cream

This smooth oyster appetizer is served at the American Bounty Restaurant at the Culinary Institute of America in Hyde Park, New York.

    4 tablespoons unsalted butter
    4 tablespoons white wine
    24 oysters, shucked
    1/3 cup Virginia ham, thinly sliced, then
        roughly chopped
    1 1/4 cups heavy cream
    1 generous tablespoon chopped fresh mint
    Toast points

1. Bring the butter and wine to a simmer; add oysters and poach gently, 2 to 3 minutes. Add the ham and toss to combine.

2. Add cream and mint and bring to a simmer. When slightly reduced, pour gently into a serving casserole. Serve with toast.

Makes 4 servings.

Heavenly Fried Oysters with Chili Sauce

These batter-fried oysters are the perfect answer for those who shy away from eating them raw.

    3 dozen oysters, shucked and drained
        (see page 40)
    5 cups ice water
    1 1/2 tablespoons salt
    4 egg whites
    1/4 cup cornstarch
    1 teaspoon salt

Chili Sauce:
    1 tablespoon vegetable oil
    2 teaspoons chili powder
    1/2 teaspoon cumin
    1/4 teaspoon oregano

    1/2 green pepper, minced
    1 small onion, minced
    1 8-ounce can tomato sauce
    Pinch sugar
    Salt and pepper to taste
    1 lemon

    2 cups vegetable oil

1. Soak oysters in ice water with 1 1/2 tablespoons salt for 30 minutes. Drain oysters, rinse under cold water and pat dry with paper towels.

2. In a bowl big enough to hold the oysters, combine the egg whites, cornstarch, and salt just until blended. Add the oysters and coat well with the mixture. Let stand in refrigerator, covered, for 12 to 24 hours.

3. Meanwhile, make the sauce. Heat the oil in a skillet, add the chili powder, cumin, oregano, green pepper, and onion and sauté until onion is golden. Add tomato sauce and a pinch of sugar. Cook over high heat about 10 minutes or until thickened. Add salt, pepper, and lemon juice to taste. Set aside.

4. Heat the 2 cups vegetable oil in a large skillet until very hot but not smoking. Add oysters to oil, 1 at a time, loosening gently with a slotted spoon if they stick to the bottom. Cook 2 minutes, then turn and cook for 2 to 3 minutes more or until edges curl. Remove with slotted spoon and drain on paper towels. Serve while hot with chili sauce.

Makes 6 servings.

Peconic Bay Scallops with Japanese Dipping Sauce

The fresh, sweet flavor of Peconic Bay's scallops is even more intense when you serve them raw.

    1 pound Peconic Bay scallops
    6 tablespoons soy sauce
    2 tablespoons rice wine vinegar
    6 tablespoons dry sherry
    2 teaspoons minced fresh ginger
    Pinch cayenne pepper
    4 tablespoons sugar

Wash the scallops and pat dry. Place them in a serving bowl nestled in a larger one filled with crushed ice. For the dipping sauce, combine the soy sauce, vinegar, sherry, ginger, pepper, and sugar, stirring well. Dip sparingly.

Makes 4 to 6 servings.

Scallops in Mustard Cream

The secret here is to use enough mustard to provide tang but not so much that it overwhelms the scallops' delicate taste. When Peconic bay scallops are not in season, I've substituted sea scallops, cut in half if they are large. The result is still pleasing.

1 1/2 pounds bay scallops
Finely ground cornmeal
2 tablespoons butter
2 tablespoons oil
1/2 cup white wine
1 cup heavy cream
1 to 1 1/2 tablespoons grainy mustard
Freshly ground black pepper
Juice of 1/2 lemon

1. Toss scallops in cornmeal and shake loose excess. Refrigerate for at least 1 hour before cooking.

2. Heat butter and oil in a sauté pan and cook scallops, a few at a time, until golden on all sides, just a couple of minutes. Remove and keep warm. Add extra butter as needed.

3. Add wine and stir constantly over high heat. Reduce slightly. Pour in cream and further reduce until slightly thickened. Mixture should coat the back of a spoon. Reduce heat.

4. Stir in mustard; do not boil or mustard will become bitter. Return scallops to pan to reheat. Season with pepper and lemon juice.

Makes 6 servings.

Coquilles St. Jacques Marinière

Karen Frame Pancake perfected this combination of mussels and Peconic Bay scallops for her restaurant, Peche Mignon, in Huntington.

1 1/2 pounds mussels
1 cup dry white wine
2 teaspoons chopped shallots
2 pounds Peconic Bay scallops
1 cup dry white wine

Marinière Sauce:
1/2 cup dry white wine
1/2 cup reserved mussel liquor
1 1/2 tablespoons chopped shallots
2 tablespoons heavy cream
5 tablespoons sweet butter

1. Debeard mussels and rinse well in several changes of fresh water. Place in a pot with 1 cup of white wine and 2 teaspoons shallots. Cover and steam over high heat, shaking the pan vigorously back and forth until the mussels open. Strain the liquid and reserve 1/2 cup for the sauce. Remove mussels from their shells and set aside, covered. Discard any mussels that have not opened.

2. Put the scallops and 1 cup white wine in a nonaluminum pan to soak; later, they will be cooked for about 1 minute when the sauce is almost finished.

3. For the sauce: In a small nonaluminum saucepan put the 1/2 cup wine, reserved mussel liquor, and shallots. Reduce over high heat to about 1/3 cup. Add the heavy cream and bring to a slow boil. Stirring constantly, add the butter one tablespoon at a time until completely absorbed.

4. Meanwhile, cover the scallops and simmer for 1 minute. Remove the scallops to serving plates. Add mussels to the hot scallop liquid to reheat gently. Strain the marinière sauce over the scallops and garnish with the mussels.

Makes 6 servings.

SOUPS & SALADS

Basic Chicken Stock

I prefer to roast the bones slightly before adding; I think it makes a richer, tastier stock.

Neck and bones from 2 3½-pound chickens or
   3 pounds chicken wings
1 large onion
2 carrots, coarsely chopped
1 large slice fresh ginger
2 ribs celery, coarsely chopped
12 peppercorns
2 bay leaves

1. Place neck and bones or wings in a large soup kettle. Cut onion in eighths, but do not peel, and add to kettle. Add the carrots, ginger, celery, peppercorns, and bay leaves. Cover with water.

2. Bring to a boil, reduce to a simmer, and remove froth from top. Cook about 1½ to 2 hours. Strain and skim off fat. This is easily done by first chilling the stock, preferably in a bowl set in ice water. Remove solidified fat.

3. Return to kettle and reduce stock to about 3 to 4 cups. Can be refrigerated for a day or two. Otherwise freeze for up to 3 months.

Makes 3 to 4 cups.

Basic Beef Stock

Beef bones with meat, about 2½ pounds
Beef marrow bones, about 2½ pounds
1 quart boiling water
2 large onions, peeled and coarsely chopped
2 leeks, washed, trimmed of green, and
   coarsely chopped
3 carrots, lightly scraped, coarsely chopped
2 ribs celery, coarsely chopped
5 quarts cold water
3 sprigs parsley
6 peppercorns or ⅛ teaspoon freshly
   ground pepper
2 bay leaves

1. Heat oven to 425 degrees. Place bones in a roasting pan and allow to brown in oven for about 40 minutes, turning every 10 minutes. Do not let burn.

2. After beef has browned, place roasting pan on top of the stove; carefully pour in boiling water, scraping up drippings. When all scrapings have been incorporated, place the bones and the liquid in a sturdy soup kettle.

3. Add the onions, leeks, carrots, celery, cold water, parsley, peppercorns, and bay leaves. Bring to a boil, then reduce heat to a simmer; skim off the froth and discard. Partially cover and simmer for 4 to 5 hours. Check pot occasionally, and add water if too much has cooked away. You will end up with 4½ quarts.

4. Strain stock, then skim off fat. Preferably let stock cool by placing the bowl of strained stock in ice water. Remove solidified fat. Return stock to pot to simmer, uncovered, until reduced by one-fourth.

Lettuce fields, early summer at Schmitt Farm, Melville

Basil and Broccoli Soup

Successful basil plants have a tendency to go the way of zucchini, with a seemingly endless supply in sight. Faced with just such a happy dilemma, I conjured up this summer soup.

> 4 cups coarsely chopped broccoli stems
> 2 cups chicken stock (see page 47)
> 3 tablespoons butter
> 3 cloves garlic, minced
> 1/4 cup fresh basil, minced
> Salt and pepper
> Lemon juice
> Grated Parmesan cheese, optional

1. In a saucepan, cook broccoli in stock until very tender, about 25 to 30 minutes. Purée broccoli and stock in batches in a food processor or blender until very smooth.

2. Melt butter in a small saucepan and in it sauté garlic and basil briefly. Add to processor and blend briefly. Stir into soup and season with salt, pepper, and a squeeze of lemon. If too thick, add more chicken stock or heavy cream. To serve, sprinkle with Parmesan cheese if desired.

Makes 4 servings.

Curried Broccoli Soup

Here is a flavorful soup that successfully combines curry, pears, and yogurt with fresh broccoli.

> 2 to 3 tablespoons butter
> 1 tablespoon minced ginger
> 4 cloves garlic, minced
> 1 tablespoon curry powder, or more to taste
> 1 large onion, sliced
> 1 1/2 pounds broccoli, trimmed and
>   cut in chunks
> 1 large or 2 small pears, peeled and chopped
> 4 cups chicken stock (see page 47)
> Salt and pepper to taste

> 1/2 lemon
> 1 cup plain yogurt
> Hot pepper sauce

1. In a large saucepan, briefly sauté in butter the ginger, garlic, curry powder, and onion.

2. Add the broccoli and pears, stir well, then add the stock. Simmer, partially covered, until broccoli is tender, about 20 to 30 minutes.

3. Purée in a food processor or blender and return to pan. Season with salt, pepper and lemon juice to taste.

4. Let cool, then stir in yogurt. Serve with hot pepper sauce that can be drizzled on the soup to taste.

Makes 4 to 6 servings.

Cold Carrot Soup

> 1 pound carrots, peeled and sliced
> 3 cups chicken stock, preferably homemade
>   (see page 47)
> 1 1/2 teaspoons tarragon
> 1 small onion, sliced
> 2 tablespoons orange juice
> 1/2 cup plain, low-fat yogurt
> Freshly ground black pepper to taste
> 3 tablespoons chopped fresh parsley or
>   cilantro for garnish

1. Cook carrots in stock, partially covered, with the tarragon, onion, and orange juice until carrots are tender. Purée carrots in blender or food processor, adding enough broth to get the proper consistency. Chill.

2. To serve, stir in yogurt and season with black pepper. Garnish with parsley.

Makes 4 servings.

Sylvia's and Linda's Corn Chowder

Perfected one bright summer weekend, this is the result of Sylvia Carter's search for the ultimate corn chowder.

8 ears fresh corn, or about 4 cups kernels
¼ pound slab bacon, cut into small chunks
2 small onions, diced
½ cup dry white wine
1½ cups chicken stock, preferably homemade (see page 47)
3 medium potatoes, washed, peeled, and cut into ½-inch pieces
2 teaspoons salt, or to taste
1 teaspoon freshly ground black pepper, or to taste
1 teaspoon chopped fresh thyme, or to taste
2 cups milk
1 cup heavy cream

1. Using a sharp paring knife, scrape corn kernels and milk from the ears of corn. Be sure to scrape close to the ear, releasing as much corn milk as possible. Reserve 1 scraped ear of corn.

2. In a commodious heavy pot, preferably black cast iron, fry the bacon, tossing with a slotted wooden spoon, until crisp. Remove bacon bits to paper towels to drain; reserve. Measure rendered bacon fat and remove all but 3 tablespoons fat. Sauté onions until limp in the bacon fat.

3. Add wine, chicken stock, potatoes, and reserved scraped corn cob. Add some salt and pepper. Simmer until potatoes are tender, about 10 minutes after the liquid comes to a simmer. Remove the corn cob and discard. Using a hand potato masher, coarsely mash the potatoes in the liquid.

4. Add fresh thyme, corn kernels, milk, and cream and mix well. As the mixture heats, taste again for seasoning, adding salt as needed. Once the mixture reaches a gentle simmer, let it simmer, without allowing it to boil, for about 5 minutes. Ladle into bowls and serve immediately, with some crumbled bacon tidbits on top.

Makes 8 servings.

NOTE: Additional fresh thyme might also be sprinkled on top or perhaps chopped scallions. If using dried thyme, use just a pinch, then taste to see if you want more. This is a hearty but delicate soup, and while just enough bacon and thyme taste brings out the flavor of the corn, too much would obscure it.

Conchita's Gazpacho

Alice Ross brought this version of gazpacho back with her from a trip to Spain. It works as well with local vegetables.

2 pounds ripe tomatoes
3 medium cucumbers, peeled
1 large green pepper, seeded
1 small onion, halved
2 to 3 cloves garlic or more to taste, minced
3-inch length of stale Italian bread, soaked in water
1 cup oil (mixed olive and vegetable)
¼ cup vinegar or to taste
Salt to taste

1. Peel tomatoes, if desired. Place in blender or food processor with cucumbers, pepper, onion, and garlic. Squeeze the water from the soaked bread, and add bread to blender. Blend until smooth.

2. Mix in oil and vinegar, adjusting the proportions to your taste. Add salt.

3. Refrigerate several hours or even overnight. Serve chilled, with garnishes of diced cucumbers and green peppers, if desired.

Makes 4 to 6 servings.

NOTE: This gazpacho is often served with toasted croutons flavored with garlic and oil.

Basil and Broccoli Soup (recipe, page 48)

Cold Carrot Soup (recipe, page 48)

Gazpacho

1 cucumber, peeled and diced
1 red onion, minced
2 cloves garlic, minced
2 large, ripe tomatoes, peeled, seeded, and diced
1 green pepper, seeded and diced
2 cups thick tomato juice
1½ cups chicken broth
¼ cup wine vinegar
1 teaspoon oregano
Cayenne pepper or Tabasco sauce to taste
1 teaspoon salt
Freshly ground pepper to taste
Lemon slices for garnish

1. Combine all of the ingredients except lemon slices and chill well for several hours.
2. When ready to serve, put an ice cube into each soup bowl, fill with the gazpacho and garnish with lemon slices.

Makes 4 servings.

Creamy Summer Borscht

For a summertime variation, serve this refreshing, cool borscht.

6 cups beef stock, preferably homemade
   (see page 47)
3 tablespoons sugar
2 bay leaves
2 to 3 tablespoons cider vinegar
1 cup thinly sliced onions
1 pound fresh plum tomatoes, peeled, or
   1 16-ounce can whole tomatoes, drained
2 cups sliced cabbage
2 pounds beets, peeled and cut in julienne
   strips or 1 16-ounce can beets, drained and
   cut in julienne strips
Salt and pepper to taste
1 cup buttermilk
½ cup heavy cream
3 scallions, sliced with some of the green tops

1. In a large saucepan combine stock, sugar, bay leaves, vinegar, onions, tomatoes, cabbage, and beets. Simmer about 30 minutes.
2. Remove bay leaves and season with salt and lots of pepper. When soup has cooled, stir in buttermilk and cream. Refrigerate overnight.
3. To serve, sprinkle bowls with scallions.

Makes about 8 servings.

Cabbage Borscht

To relieve the chill of winter, try this version of a cabbage borscht. The soup is so substantial that perhaps a fresh loaf of pumpernickel and something to drink is all you'll need to serve with it.

2 tablespoons lard or oil
2 pounds beef chuck or shin, cubed
½ cup flour
8 cups beef stock (see page 47)
1 medium head cabbage, quartered, then
   thickly sliced
4 red beets, peeled and cut in strips
4 large tomatoes, peeled and chopped
   (drained, canned tomatoes can be used)
1 large onion, chopped
1 large clove garlic, minced
Juice of 1 medium lemon
1½ tablespoons sugar
½ teaspoon caraway seeds
Salt and pepper to taste

Heat lard in a heavy saucepan or kettle, dredge meat cubes in flour and brown, a few pieces at a time, in hot lard. Add stock, cabbage, beets, tomatoes, onion, garlic, lemon juice, sugar, caraway seeds, salt and pepper to taste. Mix well, cover tightly, and cook over low heat for 2 hours or until meat is tender.

Makes 8 servings.

Dill Vichyssoise

Jules Bond prepares his dill vichyssoise for freezing before adding cream, so he's always at the ready with a smashing soup for dinner parties.

6 tablespoons butter
2 cups leeks, white part only, washed and chopped
1 large onion, sliced thin
1 large clove garlic, minced
2 cups diced, peeled potatoes
1/2 cup chopped fresh dill
4 to 6 cups chicken stock, preferably homemade (see page 47)
Salt and white pepper to taste
1 1/2 cups heavy cream
2 tablespoons minced fresh chives for garnish

1. In a saucepan heat the butter, and add the leeks, onion, and garlic. Cover and cook gently for 5 minutes. Add potatoes, stir and mix, cover again, and cook over gentle heat for 15 minutes. Stir a few times, do not let vegetables brown. Add dill, mix, cover and cook for another 5 minutes. Add chicken stock, season with salt and pepper, cover and simmer for 1 hour until vegetables are very soft.

2. Purée contents of pan in a food processor or rub vegetables through a strainer; return to pan and simmer for 15 more minutes. Blend in cream and bring to a simmer. Remove from heat, correct seasoning. Cool and chill for several hours. Sprinkle with chives when serving.

Makes 6 servings.

Pumpkin-Melon Soup

Loulou Scharf teaches cooking classes in Woodmere, dazzling students with creative combinations as in this soup.

1 large cranshaw melon
4 tablespoons butter
1 1/2 cups peeled, diced pumpkin
4 carrots, peeled and sliced
2 large onions, chopped
4 leeks, white part only, chopped
2 large potatoes, peeled and chopped
2 cups beef consommé
2 cups chicken consommé
Salt and pepper to taste
Butter
1/2 teaspoon cinnamon
Zest of 1 orange and 1 lemon
1/3 cup white roux (a paste of half flour, half butter)
1 pint or more of heavy cream

1. To prepare a tureen from the melon, carefully cut off the top, scoop out melon flesh, and reserve. If melon is not stable, cut a slice off the bottom to level it.

2. Melt butter and in it sauté pumpkin, carrots, onions, leeks, and potatoes until soft. Add melon flesh and the two consommés. Simmer 20 minutes.

3. Purée mixture in a food processor or blender and return to pot. Add salt, pepper, butter, cinnamon, zest, and sufficient white roux to make a thick creamy soup. Refrigerate. Before serving, add heavy cream and pour into melon tureen.

Makes 8 servings.

NOTE: Soup could also be served hot. In this case, add the cream to the soup just after blending in the roux. Heat gently but do not allow to boil.

Curried Squash Soup

The addition of curry, chutney, and yogurt give Indian overtones to this tangy squash soup.

    3 cups chicken stock, preferably homemade
       (see page 47)
    1 2½-pound butternut squash
    2 apples
    2 tablespoons butter
    2 tablespoons chutney or orange marmalade
    1 to 2 tablespoons curry powder
    ¼ cup tomato juice
    ¼ cup red wine
    Dash Tabasco sauce
    1 to 1½ cups plain yogurt
    Salt and pepper to taste
    1 apple, cored and chopped for garnish

1. Bring stock to a simmer in a large saucepan. Meanwhile, peel squash, remove seeds, and cut into chunks. Peel, core, and chop the apples. Cook apples and squash in simmering stock until tender, about 20 minutes. In a separate pan, heat butter and cook chutney and curry powder about 1 minute, stirring. Add tomato juice and wine; cook over high heat until the liquid is reduced by half. Add to the cooked squash and apples.

2. Purée squash and apples in a food processor or blender, adding cooking liquid as needed to get a velvety texture. Return to pan. Stir in some Tabasco, yogurt, and salt and pepper. Heat through but do not boil. Serve with chopped apple.

Makes 6 servings.

Fish Broth, Avgolemono Style

    1 to 1½ pounds head, bones, and skin left from
       charcoal-grilling fish: anything large but not
       too oily, such as weakfish; supplement or
       substitute cod head and collar, blowfish or any
       firm fish
    1 medium onion, halved
    1 rib celery, stem and leaves
    1 bay leaf
    1 parsnip
    1 bunch parsley, stems only (reserve the leaves)
    ½ cup white wine
    Juice of 2 lemons
    2 egg yolks
    4 tablespoons chopped fresh dill for garnish

1. Put fish in a large pot and cover with water. Add the onion, celery, bay leaf, parsnip, and parsley stems. Bring to a boil and simmer over low heat for 1 hour or until broth is strongly flavored. Use the lowest possible heat to prevent boiling, in order to achieve a clear broth.

2. Strain through a towel-lined colander or a fine sieve. Discard vegetables and bones, reserving flaked fish, if desired, to be added to soup at the end.

3. Return broth to pot. Add wine and lemon juice.

4. Beat in egg yolks and simmer gently over low heat, stirring, until slightly thickened, about 3 to 5 minutes. Correct seasonings and garnish with fresh dill and reserved fish, if desired.

Makes 4 servings.

NOTE: Instead of the dill, you could use 2 tablespoons shrimp boil or mixed pickling spices in step 1.

Bisque of Littleneck Clams with Curry and Saffron

Pat Lenz is one of Long Island's finest cooks, first in her restaurant, A Moveable Feast, and now as a retired pro running a winery with her husband Peter. Inspired by Julia Child, she shows a French bent in her cooking.

1 tablespoon curry powder
2 tablespoons diced leek (white part only)
2 tablespoons diced fennel bulb or celery
Fish velouté made with 2 cups fish stock
    (see page 61)
1 cup clam juice
12 to 18 littleneck clams, scrubbed well
½ teaspoon saffron threads
½ teaspoon minced fresh herbs such as thyme,
    oregano, marjoram or Italian parsley
2 egg yolks
½ cup heavy cream
3 tablespoons diced tomato, peeled and seeded
Salt
White pepper
Cayenne pepper

1. Toast curry powder on a square of aluminum foil in a preheated 325 degree oven for 8 to 10 minutes. Set aside.

2. Blanch leek and fennel in boiling water in a small saucepan for 2 minutes. Refresh under cold running water. Pat dry and set aside.

3. Prepare the velouté: melt 2½ tablespoons butter, add 3 tablespoons flour, and stir or whisk to remove lumps. Cook for 2 to 3 minutes, but do not let brown. Remove from heat and beat in the 2 cups fish stock. Return to heat, bring to a boil, reduce heat and cook slowly for at least 5 minutes.

4. Bring the clam juice to a boil in a heavy saucepan. Add clams, cover. Remove from heat and set aside until clams open. With a slotted spoon, remove clams (still in their shells) to a bowl until ready to serve. Reserve clam juice.

5. Add toasted curry powder, saffron threads, herbs, and fish velouté to clam juice remaining in saucepan. Stir over medium heat until simmering. Continue to simmer 10 to 15 minutes.

6. Mix egg yolks and heavy cream together in a bowl. Slowly whisk a few tablespoons of the hot clam juice mixture into the egg yolk-cream mixture. Then slowly whisk egg yolk mixture into soup. Do not boil or soup will curdle.

7. Add tomato and the reserved leek and fennel to soup. Stir over low heat for 2 minutes. Season to taste with salt, white pepper, and cayenne.

8. Place 2 to 3 clams in their shells in each of six warm soup bowls. Ladle soup over clams and serve immediately.

Makes 6 servings.

Cream of Mussel Soup

This creamy soup is as good served hot or cold, either as a first course or with some good bread and a salad for a cozy supper.

2 quarts mussels
1 cup dry white wine
1 cup water
2 tablespoons minced onion
2 tablespoons minced shallots
1 medium carrot, pared and chopped
1 rib celery, diced
4 tablespoons butter
3 tablespoons flour
2 cups heavy cream
White pepper and salt to taste

1. Scrub mussels under running cold water and remove beards. Place mussels, wine, water, onion, shallots, carrot, and celery in a large, deep saucepan. Cover, bring rapidly to a boil, and cook for 5 to 7 minutes until mussels are opened. Remove mussels from pan, and discard any that have not opened. Remove mussels from shells and reserve.

2. Strain liquid through a kitchen towel or triple layer of cheesecloth into a saucepan and bring to a simmer. Combine flour and butter into a smooth paste. Add the mixture in small pieces to the liquid in the pan, stirring until dissolved and the soup starts to thicken. Add the cream, season if needed, and simmer for 5 minutes without letting the soup boil.

3. Rub half of the mussels through a strainer into the soup, add the remaining whole mussels, heat through, and serve.

Makes 4 to 6 servings.

About Clams

The first thing you learn about the clam business is that there is no certainty. There are no definitive answers as to why one year is better than the next. Nor is it clear why clams set in one area more prolifically than in another. Most likely pollution plays a role, as does water temperature and salinity. But fundamentally, there is Mother Nature, unpredictable and mysterious.

"Everything you do in this business is based on Mother Nature," says Vincent J. Daley, an independent bayman, who has spent twenty-five years on the water. When it rains too much, not only does it make life hard for the clam diggers who work the Great South Bay, it puts a crimp in the tourist business. When the resorts are hurting, the demand for clams drops.

The successful bayman outmaneuvers nature, uncovering the patch of littlenecks and successfully bringing them to the surface without alerting the competition that he's onto something. "How much you get depends on who you are and what you're looking for," says Daley. Chowders are generally easier to dig and there may be more of them in certain areas. The drawback is that they're not worth as much, maybe six dollars, up to eight dollars a bushel, varying of course. Littlenecks command top dollar, but you have to work harder and longer to get them. "It drives you crazy when you get only twelve pounds in an hour, that's about seventy or eighty clams," says Daley.

You need 500 clams for the "count," but they're worth a lot more, maybe fifty dollars to sixty dollars, varying, once more, according to supply and demand. Littlenecks, by New York State regulation, are clams, measured across the hinge, that are from 1 inch through 1 7/16ths inches; cherrystones are larger than 1 7/16th through 1 5/8th inches; larger than that, they're called chowders.

To "tong" or dig for clams, Daley opens the handles about a foot and a half and gently rocks them closed, forcing the teeth down into the bottom to roust up the clams and pull them into the basket. "You can feel when you have clams in the basket, but sometimes it's tough when there are a lot of shells," says Daley. He pulls the tongs up and shakes the basket; the clams tumble out the open end and onto the boat and flat deck, no protective railing. A bit unnerving for the beginner.

Daley's son, David M., has joined him on the bay, while his oldest son, Vincent C., has given it up for insurance. His father-in-law, Charles Berberich, has worked the Great South Bay for more than fifty years. "He's 71 and still out there every day; well, he takes Saturdays off now," says Daley. Berberich can make a meal of the clams he's just caught, while Daley prefers them deviled. "I take a half pound of bacon, a few onions, I grind them up, some celery I grind, too," says Daley. "Then I take a half bushel of chowder clams, open them, grind them and clean the shells. You mix that up in iron frying pans, add a little egg, some bread crumbs to firm the texture and put it back into the shells. They're ready to bake. I freeze them on trays, so when I want, I take out a few dozen and cook 'em up. What's good is they have lots of the clam juice in them—just don't grind them too small."

While Daley is partial to littlenecks or cherries, he will harvest mussels or crabs when nature is kind and they are abundant. "A real bayman really works the bay, does a little eeling, scalloping, works the circuit for steamers, mussels," he says.

The last good natural set, everyone seems to agree, was in the early 1970s. As the landings have dropped drastically from 1976 and a height of 700,465 bushels to 178,422 bushels in 1983, the towns of Babylon, Islip, and Brookhaven have started up a variety of programs to plant clams in the bay.

Bluepoints Company, Inc., with more than 13,000 acres of the bay it owns and cultivates, has responded to poor natural sets with an aggressive hatchery program. They are hedging their bets by placing four- to nine-month-old clams in areas that have proven to be good in the past. They also place large numbers of very small clams overboard, letting natural selection take place in the bay.

If the conditions are right, about one-half of one percent of the small clams Bluepoints plants will survive to be harvested five to seven years later, while maybe ninety percent of the older clams make it to maturity. Life is tough for baby clams. "The smaller the clam is when it's put out in the wild, the less chance it has to survive," says Ken Kurkowski, hatchery biologist. "Temperature, food, and predators are the major reasons they don't make it. But if they make it past two years—that's thumbnail size—they start avoiding predators with much greater skill." He adds that any animal that consumes food will consume a clam at one point or another. "That includes ducks, other fish, and people; all have a particular size that they like," Kurkowski says.

A clam can spawn about ten million eggs or sperm in a single season, says Kurkowski, but the odds are only 1 in 29 million that the fertilized egg will grow to market size.

It takes about 750 to 1,000 clams to produce the numbers that the hatchery needs to keep going. "All clams start off as males," he says, "then at a certain size, a percentage will turn female. You can tell which, but only by dissection, and that would defeat the purpose of using them to spawn." When the clams begin to spawn, Kurkowski separates the males from the females, using a cupful of sperm to fertilize the remaining eggs.

From then on, the process resembles the oyster hatchery, with slow-growing clams discarded from the pack in successive filtering of the tanks. After about a week or two, metamorphosis takes place, and the clams that were previously swimmers lose their velum or swimming organ and will settle on the bottom, using a foot to crawl around on. Most of the millions of clams raised each year go out in the bay by November; however, a few are shipped to Northport to winter over in the warm waters of the LILCO power generating station. Hard clams grow more slowly than oysters, taking about five years to reach the size of littlenecks. They only grow in summer; when the water temperature hits 38 to 40 degrees, they lose their stiles or stomachs and go into hibernation.

At Bluepoints, the harvesting is done by dredge boats, with sorting taking place right on board. The company has harvested three times as many clams from an acre that was seeded compared to one that was not, says Kurkowski. "That's our only indication that what we were doing is working."

While Bluepoints harvests about twenty percent of the Great South Bay, that leaves the majority for the independent baymen, men fiercely protective of their independence, in love with the bay.

"I am independent, I don't have anyone to tell me what to do, how to do it, when to do it," says Daley. "How many people do you know who can say that?"

OVERLEAF *Long Island Fishermen's Soup (recipe, page 61)*

Oyster Soup

Don't overcook the oysters; simmer them just until the edges begin to curl.

2 to 3 dozen oysters
4 tablespoons butter
2 tablespoons chopped shallots
2 tablespoons chopped fresh parsley
1/4 cup finely chopped celery
4 cups milk
1/2 cup dry sherry
Dash Worcestershire sauce
Salt to taste
1/4 teaspoon white pepper
Oyster crackers

1. Shuck oysters, reserving any liquid (see page 40).

2. In a medium saucepan, melt the butter and sauté the shallots, parsley, and celery for 5 minutes. Stir in the oyster liquid, milk, and sherry, and slowly bring to just below boiling.

3. Add the oysters and simmer for just a few moments or until the edges curl. Season with Worcestershire, salt, and pepper. Serve with oyster crackers.

Makes 4 servings.

Long Island Fish Chowder

1/2 pound salt pork or bacon, sliced
1 cup sliced carrots
1 cup sliced onions
1 cup broccoli flowerettes
1 cup fresh corn kernels, cut from the cob
1 cup diced, peeled potatoes
4 cups chicken stock, preferably homemade (see page 47)
1 tomato, peeled, seeded, and chopped
1/2 teaspoon basil
1/2 teaspoon oregano
1 teaspoon salt
1/2 teaspoon freshly ground black pepper

1 pound cod or other thick fish fillets, cubed
1/2 pound scallops
1 cup heavy cream

1. In a large stockpot, fry the salt pork until crisp. Remove, drain, and crumble.

2. In the pork fat, sauté the carrots, onions, broccoli, corn, and potatoes for 5 minutes. Add the chicken stock, tomato, basil, oregano, salt, and pepper. Bring to a boil, lower heat, and simmer for 15 minutes.

3. Add the cod and scallops and cook until tender, about 10 minutes. Add cream and heat gently. Garnish with reserved salt pork bits.

Makes 6 servings.

Long Island Clam Chowder

24 cherrystone clams, in the shell
1/4 cup finely chopped salt pork
1 large onion
3 ribs celery
3 large all-purpose potatoes (not baking), peeled
1 28-ounce can tomatoes with their juice
1/2 teaspoon thyme
1/2 teaspoon freshly ground pepper

1. Wash the outside of the clams well and open with a clam knife. If they are difficult to open, place in a freezer for about 15 minutes to relax the muscles. Once opened, put clams through a meat grinder. Do not chop with a knife or meat will be tough.

2. Place clams in a sieve and let clam juice drip into a measuring cup. Measure 1 cup of clam juice and discard the rest. To this, add 2 cups of water. Set aside. Reserve clams.

3. In a skillet large enough to hold the clams and vegetables, fry the salt pork slowly over medium heat.

4. Place onion, celery, and potatoes in grinder and grind on medium blade. Or use food processor, or dice by hand.

5. Add vegetables to the salt pork, and sauté

them, but do not allow to brown. When vegetables begin to soften, add clam juice-water mixture. Bring to a boil, lower heat and simmer, uncovered, for 15 minutes.

6. Chop the tomatoes into small dice, and add, with their juice, to the vegetables. Return chowder to a boil, then simmer for 15 minutes.

7. Add clams, stir to mix, and reduce heat to very low. Simmer until clams are hot. Clams should not boil which makes them tough. Add thyme and pepper, taste and check for seasoning.

Makes 6 to 8 servings.

Long Island Fisherman's Soup

Alice Ross, who has pursued a serious interest in food as a measure of culture, is also a terrific cook as shown in this recipe of hers.

1 dozen *each*: littleneck clams, mussels and
  steamer clams
3 blue claw crabs
2 tablespoons olive oil
2 cloves garlic, minced
1/4 pound chorizo, crumbled, optional
3 to 4 cups fish stock (see following recipe)
3/4 pound monkfish (sometimes called
  ocean blowfish)
3/4 pound firm fish such as shark, tuna,
  or swordfish
1 bunch parsley
1 28-ounce can Italian plum tomatoes, crushed
1/2 cup red wine
Freshly ground white pepper
Juice of 1 lemon
Salt
1/2 pound bay scallops

1. Scrub clams, steamers, and mussels, and reserve. Clean crabs. Remove head parts and apron, and chop in half with cleaver.

2. In a large casserole, heat the oil and sauté the garlic and chorizo for 2 to 3 minutes. Add shellfish and fish stock. Simmer over low heat, covered. Add

the crab on top of the shellfish and steam until the crabs have turned red, and the shells have opened. Remove and reserve.

3. While shellfish are cooking, cut the fish into 2-inch chunks. After shellfish have been removed, add the fish to the stock. Chop parsley stems (reserving the leaves) and add with the tomatoes and wine. Simmer gently, covered, for 10 to 15 minutes, or until they test fork-done.

4. Add pepper, lemon juice, and salt if needed; taste and correct seasonings.

5. Return cooked and reserved seafood and the scallops to the pot, with minced parsley leaves, and heat to serving temperature, about 3 minutes. Serve in large soup bowls with crusty bread. If the shells crowd the bowls, second helpings may be in order.

Makes 4 to 6 servings.

Fish Stock

1 cod head and collar
2 small whitings, about 1 pound
Clams, crabs or any inexpensive seafood,
  optional
4 cups water
2 ribs celery, with leaves
1 carrot
1 medium onion
1 bay leaf
1 cup white wine

1. Place all ingredients in a soup pot and simmer very gently, uncovered, for 1 hour, or until bones are soft and stock tastes strong.

2. Line a colander with a towel or muslin cloth and strain the stock into a large bowl. Discard the bones and vegetables but retain the larger chunks of fish or seafood for the soup, if desired.

3. Store in refrigerator in covered container for 2 or 3 days. This stock freezes well for 3 months.

Makes 4 cups.

Evelyn Wilkinson's Hassle-Free Turkey Chili

Each year *Newsday* looks to its readers for interesting recipes in an annual contest. The following chili recipes shared kudos one year.

1 tablespoon vegetable oil
1 pound ground raw turkey
1 large onion, chopped fine
1 large red pepper, chopped
1 teaspoon ground cumin, or more to taste
1 teaspoon oregano
1/4 teaspoon salt
1 tablespoon chili powder
1 dried chili pepper, seeded and crumbled
1 8-ounce can tomato sauce

1 tablespoon tomato paste
1/4 cup light rum
1 cup chicken stock, approximately
1/2 ounce unsweetened baking chocolate
Chopped raw onion, red kidney beans or black beans, optional

1. In a large skillet heat oil. Add turkey and onions and sauté until meat loses its raw color.

2. Add red pepper, cumin, oregano, salt, chili powder, chili pepper, tomato sauce, tomato paste, rum, and chicken stock. Simmer for 45 minutes, adding additional chicken stock if necessary.

3. Add the chocolate and stir until dissolved; simmer 5 minutes. Top with chopped raw onion and serve over cooked kidney or black beans, if desired.

Makes 4 servings.

Ron Fischer's Melville Fire and Gas Co. Chili

8 cloves garlic, minced
6 tablespoons olive oil
2 tablespoons unsalted butter
2/3 cup tomato paste
1 cup red wine
2 cups peeled plum tomatoes, whole
1 cup peeled plum tomatoes, puréed
3 pounds boneless chuck roast,
    in 1/2-inch cubes
1 pound ground beef chuck
1 pound ground pork
2 tablespoons salt
3 tablespoons chili powder
1 tablespoon cumin
1 teaspoon cayenne pepper
1 teaspoon Tabasco sauce
1 teaspoon basil
1 teaspoon oregano
4 bay leaves
1 16-ounce bottle beer
4 large onions, chopped
4 green peppers, chopped
2 inner ribs celery, with leaves, diced
3 jalapeno peppers, diced
3 heaping tablespoons chopped fresh coriander
1 tablespoon grated Romano cheese

1. In a large 6-quart pot, lightly brown the garlic in the olive oil and butter. Add tomato paste and wine; simmer for 10 minutes; add tomatoes.

2. Working in batches, lightly brown meat in skillet. Reserve rendered fat when done. Add meat to sauce pot with the salt, chili powder, cumin, cayenne, Tabasco, basil, oregano, and bay leaves.

3. Stirring occasionally, let pot simmer for 2 hours, thinning with beer as required. Return 2 tablespoons reserved fat to skillet and sauté onions, green peppers, and celery. Add vegetables to pot along with jalapenos and coriander; simmer for 1 hour. Chili cooks about 3 hours in all.

4. Add cheese and stir thoroughly. Remove bay leaves. Serve with saltines or oysterettes and copious amounts of cold beer.

Makes 8 servings.

Michael Townsend's Chili Con Cervesa

1 pound pinto beans
1 12-ounce can beer
6 tablespoons chili powder
2 tablespoons hot chili powder
2 teaspoons cumin
1 tablespoon oregano, preferably Mexican
1 tablespoon paprika
1/2 teaspoon cayenne pepper
1/2 teaspoon freshly ground black pepper
2 tablespoons cider vinegar
1 bay leaf
2 pounds hot Italian sausage
3 pounds coarsely ground beef chuck
3 medium onions, chopped coarsely
4 medium cloves garlic, finely chopped
1 pint tomato sauce
2 cups water

1. Wash and pick over beans; cover with water and soak overnight.

2. In a medium bowl, combine beer, both chili powders, cumin, oregano, paprika, cayenne, black pepper, vinegar, and bay leaf. Cover and refrigerate overnight.

3. Slice the sausage into 1/4-inch pieces. Brown in a heavy skillet until the fat is rendered. Drain and transfer to a heavy Dutch oven or pot. Reserve fat. Brown the chuck, in 2 batches, in a little of the sausage fat. Drain and add to the sausage meat in the Dutch oven. Add the onions and garlic to the meat and cook until the onions are translucent, about 5 minutes.

4. Stir in the beer/spice mixture, tomato sauce, and water. Simmer uncovered for 3 to 4 hours, stirring occasionally. Add additional water, if necessary, to achieve desired consistency. Remove bay leaf.

5. About 1 hour before serving, rinse the beans and cover with water in a heavy pot. Bring to a boil and simmer for 1 hour, or until the beans are tender. Serve chili over drained beans.

Makes 8 servings.

Spinach Salad with Yogurt Dressing

For dressing:
1 cup plain yogurt
$^1/_3$ cup crumbled blue cheese
$^1/_2$ teaspoon salt
$^1/_2$ teaspoon celery seed
$^1/_2$ teaspoon dried basil or 1 teaspoon
   chopped fresh basil

For salad:
2 cups torn romaine lettuce
4 cups torn fresh spinach, about $^1/_2$ pound
1 cup sliced fresh mushrooms
1 small red onion, sliced in rings
2 tomatoes, cut in eighths

1. Combine yogurt, cheese, salt, celery seed, and basil for dressing. Cover and chill to blend flavors.

2. Place salad ingredients in bowl. Cover and refrigerate until ready to serve. To serve, pour dressing over greens and toss.

Makes 6 servings.

Vegetable Salad Augello

$^1/_2$ cup *each:* green beans, cauliflower, broccoli,
   eggplant, and zucchini,
   cut into pieces
2 large potatoes, peeled and cubed,
   boiled until tender
2 large tomatoes, chopped
1 large Spanish onion, sliced
$^1/_2$ cup green or black olives, pitted
$^1/_2$ cup shredded red cabbage
2 medium cucumbers, sliced
2 green peppers, chopped fine

For dressing:
3 cloves garlic, chopped
1 tablespoon drained capers
1 teaspoon oregano
4 tablespoons chopped fresh basil or
   2 tablespoons dried

$^1/_4$ teaspoon chopped fresh mint or
   $^1/_8$ teaspoon dried
Vinegar and oil to taste
Salt and pepper to taste

1. Blanch vegetables separately in boiling salted water. Drain, cool, and pat dry with paper towels. In a large bowl, combine vegetables and toss.

2. Combine garlic, capers, oregano, basil, and mint, adding vinegar and oil to taste, about 2 tablespoons vinegar to 1 cup oil. Season with salt and pepper. Adjust seasoning of dressing as desired. Toss with dressing and chill.

Makes 6 servings.

Tomato and Cucumber Salad

1 large cucumber, sliced
1 pound sliced fresh tomatoes, about
   2 or 3 tomatoes
1 medium red onion, diced
$^2/_3$ cup olive oil
$^1/_4$ cup red wine vinegar
1 clove garlic, mashed
Salt and pepper to taste
About 15 mint leaves, minced

1. Arrange cucumber and tomatoes attractively on a serving platter. Sprinkle red onion on top.

2. Combine oil, vinegar, garlic, salt, pepper, and mint leaves and pour over salad just before serving.

Makes 4 to 6 servings.

Marinated Cauliflower and Broccoli

The colors of the cauliflower and broccoli in this marinade are accented by flecks of red pepper. This salad could double as part of an antipasto tray.

    1 medium head cauliflower, cut into
        flowerettes
    1 large head broccoli, cut into flowerettes
    1 cup olive oil
    1/4 cup white wine vinegar
    2 bay leaves
    10 black peppercorns
    3/4 teaspoon ground cumin
    1/4 teaspoon red pepper flakes
    Salt to taste
    3/4 teaspoon oregano

1. Steam cauliflower and broccoli for 5 minutes.
2. Meanwhile, in a small bowl combine oil, vinegar, bay leaves, peppercorns, cumin, red pepper flakes, salt, and oregano. Pour into a large skillet and bring to a boil. Add partially cooked cauliflower and broccoli, and return to the boil.
3. Remove from heat and let stand until cool, stirring occasionally. Refrigerate overnight to blend flavors.

Makes 6 to 8 servings.

Romola and Sam Kaplan's Famous Coleslaw

    1 2-pound head cabbage
    1 large green pepper, seeded and sliced thinly
    1 large onion, sliced thinly
    Salt
    1/4 cup sugar
    1/3 cup hot water
    1/3 cup white vinegar
    1/4 cup vegetable oil

1. Remove outer leaves of cabbage and shred thinly on a hand shredder, not in a food processor.

Combine with green pepper and onion and spread in a shallow pan, such as a 9-by-13-inch baking pan. Salt heavily. Let stand 20 to 30 minutes. Squeeze moisture out of cabbage handful by handful. As cabbage is squeezed dry, place in a bowl.
2. To prepare dressing, dissolve sugar in hot water and blend in vinegar.
3. Toss cabbage with sugar-vinegar mixture and the oil, and refrigerate for at least an hour or two before serving. Refrigerated, covered, this will keep about 1 week.

Makes 6 to 8 servings.

Fresh Bean and Red Onion Salad

    1/2 pound *each* green and yellow beans
    6 sprigs fresh savory or 1 teaspoon dried
    1 1/2 teaspoons Dijon mustard
    1/2 teaspoon coarse salt
    Freshly ground pepper
    3 tablespoons tarragon vinegar
    1 tablespoon minced shallot
    2/3 cup olive oil
    1 red onion, thinly sliced
    1 hard-cooked egg, finely chopped for garnish

1. Snip off tiny stem end of beans. Bring 3 to 4 quarts water to a boil, and salt if desired. Cook beans with 3 sprigs of savory or 1/2 teaspoon dried in the boiling water, uncovered, for 4 to 5 minutes. Do not overcook. Immediately run under cold water to stop cooking.
2. While beans are cooking, whisk mustard, salt, pepper, and vinegar in a bowl. Add the shallots. Slowly pour in oil while whisking continuously. Fold red onion, remaining savory and dressing into beans. Taste and adjust seasoning. Place on lettuce leaves and garnish with egg.

Makes 4 to 6 servings.

Marinated Vegetable Sticks

The combination of colors is so stunning that I like to serve this as a centerpiece.

2 pounds carrots
1 1/2 pounds green beans
3 zucchini
3 red peppers

For dressing:
1/3 cup red wine vinegar
1 cup oil (half olive, half vegetable)
1 to 2 tablespoons Dijon mustard
Salt and pepper
Pinch sugar
2 cloves garlic, minced
1/4 teaspoon caraway seeds
1/2 teaspoon dill weed
1/2 teaspoon ground cumin
1 teaspoon dried basil

1. Peel carrots and cut in matchsticks, about 2 1/2 inches long. Cut ends off beans. Scrub zucchini and cut the same size as the carrots. Cut peppers into strips, roughly the same size as the carrots.

2. Combine vinegar, oil, mustard, salt, pepper, sugar, and garlic. Divide among four bowls. Add caraway to one portion, dill weed to second, cumin to the third, and basil to the fourth.

3. Cook the carrots in boiling salted water briefly, until just slightly tender—do not overcook. Remove, drain briefly under cold running water. Pat dry with paper towels and while still warm, toss with dressing seasoned with caraway seeds. Cook beans in boiling salted water briefly, until just slightly tender. Remove, drain briefly, pat dry and toss with dill weed dressing. Repeat procedure with zucchini, tossing with cumin-flavored dressing. Do not cook peppers, merely toss with basil-flavored dressing.

4. To serve, mound vegetables on a platter. Serve as a salad course or vegetable accompaniment to barbequed poultry or meat.

Makes 8 servings.

Broccoli and Potato Salad

There's a natural affinity of broccoli, potatoes, and basil in Italian cooking; this is especially good in the summer.

2 heads broccoli
2 pounds potatoes
1/2 cup chopped onion
2 cloves garlic, chopped
2 tablespoons capers, rinsed
4 to 6 anchovy fillets
3/4 cup olive oil
1/4 cup lemon juice
1/2 teaspoon salt
1/4 teaspoon pepper
1/2 cup packed fresh parsley
1/2 cup packed fresh basil
2 tablespoons chopped pimiento for garnish

1. Cut flowerettes from broccoli and save for another use. Peel stems and cut into 1/4-inch slices. Steam for 5 minutes or until crisp-tender. Place in colander and rinse with cold water until cool. Drain well and set aside.

2. Wash potatoes and cook in salted water until tender. Rinse with cold water until cool. Peel and cut into chunks. Set aside.

3. In blender or food processor, place onion, garlic, capers, anchovies, olive oil, lemon juice, salt, pepper, parsley, and basil. Process until smooth.

4. Place broccoli and potato slices in a large bowl. Pour dressing over vegetables and toss lightly. Garnish with pimiento.

Makes 6 servings.

French-style Potato Salad

The key to this salad is dressing the potatoes with the vinegar-wine mixture while they are still warm so they can absorb the flavors fully.

8 medium new potatoes
3 tablespoons minced shallots
Salt
Freshly ground black pepper
1/4 cup white wine vinegar
1/4 cup dry white wine
1 teaspoon tarragon
1 tablespoon chopped fresh parsley
1/4 cup vegetable oil
Fresh chives for garnish, chopped

1. Cook potatoes in their skins until tender. Peel, if desired, then cut into 1/2-inch chunks while still warm; place in a large bowl. Sprinkle with shallots, and salt and pepper to taste.
2. Heat vinegar and wine and pour over potatoes. Let stand about 30 minutes. Drain off excess vinegar.
3. Season with tarragon and parsley. Dress with enough oil to coat. Refrigerate.
4. Remove 30 minutes before serving, and sprinkle chives on top. Serve cold.

Makes 6 servings.

Potato Sausage Salad from Jonathan's

For a main course or as part of a buffet spread, this potato and sausage combination from Jonathan's, the popular gourmet food shop in Huntington, is a winner. Developed by chef Cindy Pierce, this recipe is shared by owner John Randall.

6 pounds new potatoes, well cleaned
but not peeled

For dressing:
2 tablespoons Dijon mustard
1 teaspoon salt
1/2 cup white wine
1/2 cup chicken broth
1 cup olive oil

1 1/2 pounds kielbasa or chorizo, cooked
1 cup chopped scallions
Chopped fresh dill to taste

1. Simmer potatoes in a large pot of boiling water until tender.
2. Meanwhile, combine mustard, salt, wine, and broth in a food processor or blender. Blend, then add oil slowly.
3. Cool potatoes, slice, and mix with dressing. Gently fold in sausage, scallion, and dill.

Makes 12 to 16 servings.

Green Potato and Chicken Salad

2 pounds russet potatoes
1 whole boneless chicken breast
1 pound fresh green beans
8 cherry tomatoes
1/4 cup water
1/4 cup olive oil
2 tablespoons red wine vinegar
1/4 cup fresh basil or 2 tablespoons dried
1/2 teaspoon finely minced garlic
1/2 teaspoon salt
1/4 teaspoon freshly ground pepper
1/2 cup chopped fresh parsley
1/2 cup grated Parmesan cheese

1. Peel potatoes and cut into 1/2-inch cubes. Cut chicken breast in half. Cook potatoes and chicken in salted water until tender. Drain well. Cut chicken breast into same size pieces as the potatoes. Cook green beans in boiling salted water until tender. If cherry tomatoes are bite-size, leave whole; otherwise

cut in half. Combine vegetables and chicken in a medium bowl.

2. In a blender or food processor combine water, oil, vinegar, basil, garlic, salt, pepper, parsley, and cheese. Process until smooth. Pour over vegetables and chicken and toss lightly.

Makes 4 to 6 servings.

Duck and Spinach Salad

Should you ever have leftover Long Island duck, serve it in a salad, tossed with a creamy, mustard-spiked dressing. This salad is good enough that I have roasted a duck specially for it.

For the dressing:
1 egg yolk
3 hard-cooked eggs
1 clove garlic, chopped
2 teaspoons Dijon mustard
3 tablespoons sugar
3 to 4 tablespoons red wine vinegar
Salt and pepper
1/2 cup oil
1/2 cup cream

2 cups shredded cooked duck
2 pounds fresh spinach, washed, dried and
   torn into pieces
1 red pepper, cut into slivers
1 bunch scallions, minced, including some
   of the green

1. Prepare the dressing: in a food processor or blender, blend yolk, hard-cooked eggs, and garlic. Add mustard, sugar, vinegar, salt and pepper, and blend again. With the machine running, slowly pour in oil, and then the cream.

2. To serve, combine the duck, spinach, red pepper and scallions in a large bowl and toss with the dressing.

Makes 6 to 8 servings.

Cold Pasta with Green Beans and Basil

The basil vinaigrette that dresses this simple pasta salad also is delicious over potatoes or in a tossed green salad.

1 pound ziti or fusilli
1 1/2 pounds fresh green beans
2 red bell peppers
2 or 3 ripe tomatoes
Salt and pepper to taste
1 cup tightly packed fresh basil leaves
2 cloves garlic
1/4 to 1/3 cup fine red wine vinegar
1 to 2 teaspoons Dijon mustard
3/4 cup olive oil
1/2 cup vegetable oil

1. Bring 4 to 6 quarts of water to a boil. Cook the ziti or fusilli until al dente. Rinse with cold water and drain well.

2. Meanwhile, wash beans, trim ends, and cut into 1-inch pieces. Cook in boiling water until crisp-tender. Drain and rinse in cold water. Set aside.

3. Cut red peppers into strips and set aside. Peel and seed tomatoes, cut into chunks, and set in a colander to drain. Sprinkle with salt and pepper. Reserve.

4. Put basil in the bowl of a food processor or blender, and process. Drop the garlic through the feed tube and using on/off motions, process or blend until smooth. Add vinegar and mustard and process again. Slowly pour in oils and process until smooth. Add salt and pepper to taste.

5. Toss beans with most of the vinaigrette. Fold in the cold pasta, adding additional vinaigrette if necessary. An hour before serving, toss in peppers and tomatoes, adding more vinaigrette as needed. The salad should be moist but not soupy.

Makes 6 to 8 servings.

Peach harvesting at Wickham Farm, Cutchogue

Nicola Zanghi's Lobster and Peach Salad

Nicola Zanghi, chef and proprietor of Restaurant Zanghi in Glen Cove, combines two of Long Island's finest products—lobster and peaches.

For the dressing:
1/2 cup olive oil
1/4 cup walnut oil
2 tablespoons lemon or lime juice
1 tablespoon honey
2 tablespoons Dijon mustard
2 tablespoons fruit vinegar
1/2 bunch scallions, sliced
2 tablespoons freshly grated, peeled ginger
About 1/2 teaspoon salt
1 teaspoon freshly cracked peppercorns

8 to 12 medium peaches
2 1-pound lobsters
1 teaspoon olive oil

For salad: Approximately 4 cups of field and slightly bitter salad greens—dandelion, mâche, arugula, watercress or Belgian endive, well washed, drained, and reserved

1. The day before serving, whisk together salad dressing ingredients. Refrigerate. Or, prepare ahead and let stand at room temperature for several hours. Strain before serving.

2. If peaches are young and thin skinned, it will not be necessary to peel them; otherwise, do so. Cut peaches in half, avoiding bruising the flesh of the skin. Slice into 1/4-inch-thick slices. Place on a plate and moisten with some of the salad dressing. Allow to marinate 2 to 4 hours in the refrigerator.

3. Divide the salad greens among four large plates or platters. Mound lightly in center. Reserve in refrigerator.

4. Preheat oven to 425 degrees. Rub lobsters with oil, place in oven for 15 minutes. Remove and when cool enough to handle, remove meat from claws and tail sections, leaving meat intact. Slice tail meat into 1/4-inch medallions.

5. When ready to serve, arrange alternating slices of lobster meat, with peaches in a crescent around salad greens. Dribble dressing on top.

Makes 4 servings.

VEGETABLES

Asparagus with Parmesan

1 pound asparagus
1 tablespoon butter
1¹/₂ tablespoons olive or vegetable oil
Salt and pepper to taste
¹/₄ to ¹/₃ cup grated fresh Parmesan cheese

1. Wash asparagus well. Break off tough bottom of asparagus and peel if they are thick. Steam briefly, just until tender, about 5 to 8 minutes.
2. In a skillet, heat the butter and oil together over medium-high heat. Add the asparagus and season lightly with salt and pepper. Stir, then toss with Parmesan cheese and serve.

Makes 4 servings.

NOTE: Cooked asparagus could be topped with equal parts of cheese and bread crumbs and run under broiler briefly.

Hot Beans Vinaigrette

2 pounds green beans, ends trimmed
4 quarts boiling water
2 tablespoons olive oil
3 tablespoons finely chopped ham
3 medium onions, sliced thin
4 tablespoons cider or white vinegar
2 tablespoons sugar
¹/₂ teaspoon freshly ground pepper
1 tablespoon chopped fresh dill
Salt to taste

1. Place beans, a few at a time, in the rapidly boiling water. Allow water to return to a boil and add more beans. Cook beans at a rolling boil for 3 minutes; then lower heat so that the vegetables cook partially covered at a simmer for 8 to 10 minutes. Drain.
2. Meanwhile, heat the oil in a skillet and fry ham until light brown. Remove and set aside. Add onions and slowly sauté until golden brown, adding more oil, if needed. To onions add vinegar, sugar, and pepper and stir to mix. Allow to cook for a few minutes. Return ham to dish and cook until reheated.
3. Place hot green beans in a serving dish; top with the onion mixture. Season with salt. Toss to coat. Top with dill.

Makes 6 to 8 servings.

Steamed Broccoli and Cauliflower with Herbed Butter

The elegance of this dish is in the presentation. Ring the outside of a large bowl with broccoli flowerettes, then mound the cauliflower in the center.

12 tablespoons unsalted butter, softened
1 teaspoon ground cumin
1¹/₂ teaspoons oregano
¹/₂ teaspoon ground coriander
2 tablespoons chopped fresh parsley
1 small clove garlic, very finely minced
1 head broccoli
1 small head cauliflower
2 shallots, minced

1. Combine softened butter, cumin, oregano, coriander, parsley, and garlic until herbs are evenly dispersed. Place butter on wax paper and using the

paper, shape it into a log. Freeze. Before serving, remove from freezer to thaw.

2. Cut broccoli and cauliflower into flowerettes; place in top of steamer basket and top with shallots. Steam until tender. Slice butter in rounds and place on top of vegetables.

Makes 4 to 6 servings.

Broccoli Soufflé

4 cups broccoli flowerettes, chopped
2 tablespoons butter
2 tablespoons flour
1/2 cup milk
1/2 cup heavy cream
2 tablespoons grated Parmesan cheese
Salt and pepper to taste
Pinch grated fresh nutmeg
4 egg yolks
5 egg whites, stiffly beaten

1. Bring a pot of salted water to a boil. Add broccoli, cover, and boil for about 5 minutes. Drain well, mince the broccoli and drain again.

2. Melt butter in a saucepan, stir in flour and cook while stirring for 2 or 3 minutes. Do not let brown. Mix cream and milk, add to the flour mixture, stirring constantly, and cook until thickened and smooth. Stir in cheese, season with salt, pepper, and nutmeg. Remove from heat and cool slightly.

3. Place egg yolks in a bowl, add 1/3 of the cream sauce, and stir to combine. When well blended, add this egg mixture to the rest of the cream sauce in the saucepan, stirring constantly over medium-low heat. Add broccoli and mix well. Remove from heat. Fold in about 1/3 of the beaten egg whites, then fold in the rest.

4. Butter a 6-cup soufflé dish, dust the sides with flour, and pour the mixture into the dish. Place dish in a pan with hot water coming halfway up the side. Bake in a preheated 350 degree oven for about 30 minutes until well set.

Makes 4 to 6 servings.

Long Island Broccoli with Potatoes

Bob Crayne, *Newsday*'s executive chef, is an intuitive cook, one who scans recipes then creates his own version from a little of this, a little of that. For this book, however, he was prevailed upon to measure and time the recipes so they could be reproduced. Proud to work with all Long Island ingredients, he created this simple dish for broccoli and potatoes.

1 head broccoli
2 pounds potatoes
3 tablespoons vegetable oil
1/2 teaspoon minced garlic
10 tablespoons chicken broth
1/4 teaspoon red pepper flakes
Salt and pepper to taste

1. Prepare broccoli by trimming the flowerettes from the stems. Peel stems and slice into thin rounds. Peel and thinly slice potatoes. Heat oil in a large frying pan. Add potatoes and cover pan. Cook 10 minutes over medium heat, stirring once or twice.

2. Add broccoli stems, stir and cook, covered, 10 more minutes. Add garlic, broth, and red pepper flakes. Add flowerettes and cook 10 more minutes. Season with salt and pepper.

Makes 6 to 8 servings.

Browned Brussels Sprouts

2 pints fresh Brussels sprouts (or 2 10-ounce packages frozen)
3 tablespoons butter or margarine
2 tablespoons lemon juice
2 teaspoons caraway seeds
Salt and pepper to taste, optional

1. Cook fresh Brussels sprouts in boiling water until just tender, about 7 to 8 minutes; drain.

2. Heat butter until lightly browned in a large skillet and add lemon juice, sprouts, caraway seeds, and seasoning. Heat and stir for 2 minutes, turning sprouts to coat.

Makes 4 servings.

Mapled Acorn Squash Rings (recipe, page 89) and Sweet and Sour Stuffed Cabbage (recipe, page 146)
with Brussels Sprouts with Chestnuts (recipe below)

Brussels Sprouts with Chestnuts

Brussels sprouts still on the stalk not only look dramatic, but the sprouts tend to keep better this way; store them in a dark, cool spot.

　　1 pound small firm Brussels sprouts
　　4 slices lean bacon, diced
　　2 tablespoons butter
　　1 tablespoon minced shallots
　　1 pound fresh chestnuts, cooked and peeled
　　　　(see page 147 or note below)
　　Salt and pepper to taste

　　1. Trim wilted or yellow leaves of sprouts and stem end. Put sprouts in a saucepan, cover with boil-ing water, and boil about 4 to 5 minutes or until tender. Drain.

　　2. In a skillet, sauté bacon until browned. Drain bacon; discard fat and wipe out skillet. Add butter to skillet; sauté shallots until light golden. Add well-drained sprouts, chestnuts, and salt and pepper. Mix well, heat through, and serve.

Makes 4 to 6 servings.

NOTE: Canned unsweetened chestnuts can be used, about $1/2$ pound drained weight.

OPPOSITE ABOVE *Farmer John Keller, Riverhead*

Brussels Sprouts au Gratin

2 pounds Brussels sprouts, well-trimmed
3 tablespoons butter
Salt and pepper to taste
2 cups béchamel (white sauce, see note)
1/2 cup grated Gruyère cheese
2 tablespoons fine dry bread crumbs,
  unseasoned

1. Cook Brussels sprouts in a large pan of boiling water for about 6 minutes. Drain well. Place sprouts in a buttered baking dish; add salt and pepper. Cover with béchamel sauce; sprinkle with the cheese and bread crumbs.

2. Bake in a preheated 350 degree oven for 15 to 20 minutes until brown.

Makes 4 to 6 servings.

NOTE: Prepare standard white sauce by melting 4 tablespoons butter. Stir in 4 tablespoons flour and cook about 1 minute. Add 2 cups milk and cook, stirring constantly, until thickened. Season with salt, white pepper, and grated nutmeg.

Creamed Cabbage

1 medium-sized firm green cabbage,
  finely shredded
3 tablespoons butter
1 clove garlic, crushed
2 tablespoons flour
3/4 cup of the water the cabbage was boiled in
Salt and ample pepper to taste
1/3 cup heavy cream

1. Boil cabbage in about 1 1/2 cups of water for about 10 minutes until partially cooked; it should still be firm. Drain well; reserve cooking water.

2. In a saucepan, heat butter, add garlic, then add flour; stir. Sauté for 2 minutes; do not let brown. Stir in enough of the cabbage cooking water to make a thick white sauce. Add the cabbage, salt and pepper. Mix well, cover, and simmer until cabbage is soft and cooked. Stir in cream, heat through, and serve.

Makes 4 servings.

Savoy Cabbage and Bacon

Serve this with any roast pork dish or roast game hen.

1 firm Savoy cabbage, about 2 pounds
1/4 pound slab bacon, diced
3 large white onions, thinly sliced
2 large cloves garlic, minced
Pinch of grated fresh nutmeg
Salt and pepper to taste
Kielbasa, optional

1. Trim any wilted cabbage leaves. Quarter cabbage and cook in ample boiling water for 20 minutes. Drain well. Remove and discard cores; chop cabbage.

2. Sauté bacon in a skillet over medium heat for 5 minutes, stirring frequently. Add onion and garlic, continue to sauté a few minutes more until onion is limp. Add chopped cabbage, nutmeg, salt and pepper. Mix well. Cover tightly, cook gently for about 15 minutes until cabbage is tender.

Makes 6 servings.

NOTE: If you want to serve this cabbage as a main dish, add thickly sliced sausage, such as kielbasa, for the last 15 minutes of cooking.

Sautéed Cabbage

Sylvia Carter adapted this simple cabbage sauté from a recipe from Ida Cerbone of Manducatis fame. It was designed as an accompaniment for whole roast pig, but probably would taste just as good with a less elaborate pork roast.

1/3 cup vegetable oil or part olive oil
1 clove garlic, minced
1 teaspoon capers, drained and smashed
4 ounces oil-cured Italian olives, pitted and
  cut in half (about 1/2 cup)
1 small head cabbage, cut in wedges
Salt and black pepper to taste
1/4 teaspoon dried, crushed red pepper

1. Heat oil in a large skillet. Add garlic, capers, olives, and toss to sauté briefly. Add the cabbage, season to taste with salt and black pepper, toss to coat with oil.

2. Cover and let steam for about 15 minutes, until tender but still crunchy. Remove cover and stir occasionally. During the last few minutes of cooking, add the crushed red pepper.

Makes 4 to 6 servings.

Red Cabbage Cooked in Red Wine

Guy Reuge and his wife, Maria, own Mirabelle, a charming restaurant in St. James. In keeping with the philosophy of a French country inn, Reuge buys fresh local products whenever possible. He serves this red cabbage as an accompaniment to his duck, page 136.

1 small head red cabbage (about 2½ pounds)
2 carrots
1 Granny Smith apple
1 medium onion
3 cups red wine
1 bay leaf
Salt and pepper to taste

1. Shred the cabbage and rinse it. Drain. Peel the carrots and cut them into 2-inch sticks, ¼ inch by ¼-inch. Peel and core the apple and slice thinly. Peel the onion and slice thinly.

2. Combine the cabbage, carrots, apple, and onion in a casserole with the wine, bay leaf, salt and pepper.

3. Bring the wine to a boil, cover, and simmer mixture over low heat, stirring occasionally, for 1½ hours.

Makes 8 servings.

Smothered Cauliflower

1 medium to large head cauliflower
2 tablespoons butter
2 tablespoons olive oil
3 medium onions, sliced thin
Pinch salt
1 tablespoon sugar
½ cup raisins
¼ cup pine nuts

1. Trim the cauliflower into flowerettes and parboil for 5 minutes.

2. In a large skillet, heat the butter and oil. Sauté onions about 2 minutes over medium-high heat.

3. Add the cauliflower to the onions and stir. Add salt, sugar, raisins, and stir well.

4. Adjust heat to low, cover skillet and let mixture steam for 20 minutes, stirring occasionally. Stir in pine nuts.

Makes 4 to 6 servings.

Cauliflower Neapolitan

1 head cauliflower, about 2½ pounds
8 tablespoons butter (1 stick)
1 cup plain bread crumbs, preferably homemade
Salt and pepper to taste
8 ounces mozzarella, diced or shredded

1. Separate cauliflower into flowerettes and cook in boiling salted water about 5 minutes or until tender but still firm. Drain.

2. Butter a casserole generously with half of the butter. Dust casserole with half of the bread crumbs. Add cauliflower, season with salt and pepper, sprinkle with remaining bread crumbs and dot with remaining butter. Top with mozzarella. The casserole may be done ahead to this point and refrigerated.

3. Bake, uncovered, for 25 minutes at 350 degrees.

Makes 4 to 6 servings.

A Variety of Vegetables

Summer and fall on Long Island are the seasons to indulge, to buy two dozen ears of corn picked that morning, to go home with quarts of tomatoes ripened on the vine, to stagger under the weight of a head of cauliflower brought to sweet perfection.

For too many months during the long winter and even early spring, we have to rely on vegetables trucked across the length of the United States, forced into early maturity and toughness to withstand the rigors of the trip. We recognize that those vegetable producers do the best they can, saving us from a winter of root vegetables alone. But we don't confuse the substitute with the freshly picked real thing direct from the farms on Long Island.

The taste is different, of course; fresh is sweeter, purer. And the cooking times frequently will change because fresh foods cook far quicker. Besides, fresh vegetables just look better; who can resist Brussels sprouts on the stalk or fresh beets with the earth still clinging to them. At the farm stand, cucumbers won't have that greasy wax coating, eggplant will shine, and spinach will be crisp, dark green, and inviting.

When they're in season, there's no need to consult a guide to select vegetables at their peak. They're fresh by definition. In fact, what you're more likely to need is restraint to keep from buying the lot.

Yet, should you find yourself standing unaided in front of a Long Island farm stand in full swing, a few guidelines are in order. Always look for rich colors, whatever the vegetable; any that look dried out or cracked should be avoided. Tough or discolored leaves are always a sign that the poor vegetable has seen better days. Fresh vegetables will always have a nice fresh smell.

The biggest vegetable crop on Long Island is the humble potato, but much of the supply is grouped together with other Eastern potatoes and sold as such. Of course, on the farm stands they're available, with a hint of the earth letting you know they are fresh. Also, look for firm, well-shaped potatoes with a relatively smooth skin.

The number two vegetable here is cauliflower; the best is the fall variety—huge, creamy white, sweet, and tender. Summer cauliflower is also good, it just doesn't have the intensity of flavor that the fall variety produces. To get the pure white color, workers have to tie the leaves of each head of cauliflower together for a few days before harvest. If not tied properly and some light does get in, the flowerettes get a purplish cast on the stem; it's not as attractive but it tastes pretty good. If the flowerettes are starting to spread apart, look for another head; that's a sign that the cauliflower is old.

Corn is grown on Long Island strictly for the farm stand trade; it's not a commercial crop. And when those first ears start appearing on stands, it's a true sign that summer has arrived. People take strong positions on the matter of fresh corn. Some vow they won't eat any unless the pot of water is boiling in the field and the corn comes directly from the stalk. Others maintain the corn must be picked only in the early morning, while some hold that late afternoon is prime time. The biggest killer of corn is time; make sure it's picked the day you buy it, and go home and cook it that night. If you can't resist and you buy extra, cook all of it; then you have corn ready to use in corn bread or corn oysters.

Don't pull back the husk of the corn to see if it's fresh; that starts the deterioration process. Better, shop at a reliable stand. Fresh corn has husks that are not parchment dry; the pale part of the silk will feel slightly moist. Don't worry about the occasional worm, just cut off the offending end or spot, or forget it.

Cabbage has always been a big East End crop, and a good head of cabbage is easy to spot. Look for a firm or hard head that is heavy for its size. When Brussels sprouts are sold on the stalk, you can tell if the outer leaves fit tightly and the sprouts are firm and free from small holes. The better the broccoli, and its cousin, the purple cauliflower, look, the better it probably will taste. The color should be a dark or sage green; the purple cauliflower, which looks quite similar to broccoli, should have a slight, not surprising purplish cast. As soon as the buds start to open or bright yellow flowers appear, the broccoli has aged; go on to something else.

When the season has been good, lots of sun, not

too much rain, a Long Island tomato can make you forget all those pallid wintertime imitations. Juicy, intensely flavored, a ripe tomato can be eaten out of hand, just like an apple. That's the time to plan a fresh tomato sauce for pasta, or slice them and serve them with mozzarella, basil leaves, and a drizzle of olive oil. If you come across a lot of fresh, ripe plum tomatoes, make sauce and then sun dry the extra, one of the best ways to savor the flavor in winter. A truly ripe tomato will have a deep red color and a slight softness.

However, the best way to assure consistently superior vegetables is to cultivate a relationship with the grower, or at least the workers at the farm stands. They'll be able to tell you if you should wait because the tomatoes are just beginning to ripen and will taste even better next week. They can steer you away from yesterday's corn that didn't sell out. Jules Bond has honed this skill to a fine art; he knows the best farmer for potatoes, and someone else down the road who has the tastiest asparagus, the first of the spring harvest. One dinner alone could require four stops, but such is the pursuit of the dedicated vegetable cook.

ALL ABOUT CORN

Kathy Rau, cooperative extension specialist for Nassau County, believes these are the two best ways to cook corn on the cob—one of Long Island's major vegetable crops.

The Best Way to Cook Corn on the Cob

Have ready a kettle with 3 to 6 quarts boiling water. Shuck corn just before cooking. Add shucked corn to boiling water. Do not add sugar or salt. When the water returns to the boil, remove kettle from heat. Cover and let corn stand in water from 5 to 10 minutes, although it can stand as long as 20 minutes without great damage. Drain corn and serve immediately.

Cooking Corn by Microwave

Place 4 ears unshucked corn on a tray in the microwave oven. Microwave on high for 8 to 9 minutes. Remove ears and shuck before serving. Be careful when shucking—ears will be very hot.

Cooking Corn on the Grill

Turn back corn husks and remove silk, but do not remove husks. Place corn in their husks in enough water to cover for about 1 hour. Have coals in outdoor grill white-hot. Tie husks at top and center of each ear, then place on grill. Turn every 5 minutes to expose all surfaces to the heat. Cook about 20 minutes total.

Long Island Cauliflower with Fresh Pea Purée

1 medium Long Island cauliflower
1 pound fresh peas or 1 10-ounce package
  frozen
1/2 small onion, finely chopped
3 tablespoons butter, melted
2 tablespoons heavy cream
Salt and white pepper to taste
3 tablespoons Romano or Parmesan cheese
1 tablespoon plain bread crumbs

1. Core cauliflower, leaving just a little of the core to hold the cauliflower together. Cook in boiling water, covered, for 4 to 6 minutes until cauliflower tests fork-tender, but not mushy. Cool immediately under cold running water.

2. Poach peas in boiling water for 2 minutes. Cool under cold running water. Sauté onion in 1 tablespoon butter until wilted. Add peas and sauté for 2 more minutes. Put peas and onion in a blender or food processor. Add the cream, salt, pepper, and 2 tablespoons of the cheese. Blend until a fine purée.

3. Place cauliflower in a buttered round casserole, stem down. Dribble 1 tablespoon of butter on top. Season lightly with salt and white pepper. Cover cauliflower with purée mixture. Blend crumbs and remaining cheese and sprinkle over. Dribble remaining butter on top.

4. Bake in a preheated 400 degree oven for 12 minutes or until top is bubbly. To serve, slice as one would slice a high pie.

Makes 6 to 8 servings.

Long Island Cauliflower with Mozzarella

1 Long Island cauliflower
1 tablespoon butter
Salt and pepper to taste

Enough thinly sliced mozzarella to cover
  top of cauliflower, about 1 pound
Thick Italian tomato sauce
3 tablespoons grated Romano or
  Parmesan cheese

1. Core cauliflower, leaving enough core to hold cauliflower together. Cook in boiling water, covered, for 4 to 6 minutes until cauliflower tests fork-tender but not mushy. Cool immediately under cold running water.

2. Place cauliflower in round casserole. Dribble butter on top and season with salt and pepper to taste. Cover head with mozzarella cheese; cover cheese with tomato sauce. Sprinkle cheese on top and bake for 15 minutes at 400 degrees. Slice as one would a pie.

Makes 4 to 6 servings.

Curried Vegetables

Cauliflower also pairs well with the flavors of India; this is one of my favorite vegetarian meals, filled out with brown rice.

1 small head cauliflower, cut in
  bite-size pieces
2 medium potatoes, peeled and chopped
3 carrots, peeled, sliced 1/4 inch thick
2 cups fresh peas
1 tablespoon oil
4 tablespoons butter
1 cinnamon stick
2 bay leaves
1 or 2 dried hot peppers, minced
4 cloves garlic, minced
1 tablespoon minced fresh ginger
2 tablespoons chopped cilantro
  (fresh coriander)
3 cardamom pods
1 to 2 teaspoons curry powder
1 to 2 teaspoons turmeric

½ teaspoon powdered coriander
½ teaspoon cumin
1 onion, sliced
1 tablespoon tomato paste
1 tablespoon chutney
1½ cups plain yogurt

1. Separately parboil cauliflower, potatoes, carrots, and peas until tender but not thoroughly cooked. Refresh under cold water, drain, and set aside.

2. Heat oil and butter in a large sauté pan. Add the cinnamon stick, bay leaves, hot peppers, garlic, ginger, cilantro, cardamom, curry powder, turmeric, coriander, cumin, and onion. Cook until onion is limp, about 5 minutes.

3. Blend tomato paste and chutney and combine with the spices. Add reserved vegetables and toss thoroughly in mixture. Stir in yogurt and cook, partially covered, over medium heat for about 15 minutes. Remove bay leaves and cinnamon sticks before serving.

Makes 4 servings.

Carrot, Parsnip, and Orange Pudding for Passover

5 carrots (1 bunch with green leaves), peeled
4 parsnips (about 1 pound)
½ cup water
Pinch salt
3 oranges
4 tablespoons butter, at room temperature
½ cup ground almonds mixed with
   2 tablespoons sugar
3 eggs
⅓ cup sugar
¼ cup matzo cake meal

1. Roughly grate carrots and parsnips in a food processor. Place in a saucepan with water and a pinch of salt. Cover and simmer until barely soft,

about 7 to 10 minutes. Peel and segment the oranges over a bowl to catch their juice. Add more orange juice, if necessary, to make ½ cup; add juice to the pot with vegetables.

2. Grease an 8- or 9-inch shallow ovenproof dish with 1 tablespoon butter. Sprinkle half of the almond-sugar mixture over bottom of dish.

3. Beat eggs lightly. Add sugar and beat again for 1 minute; stir in cake meal.

4. Strain carrots and parsnips but do not press them. Reserve ½ cup strained juice. Fold in carrots, parsnips, and orange slices with egg mixture; add 2 tablespoons of the softened butter and reserved juice. Spread in baking dish. Top with bits of remaining butter and remaining almond mixture. Bake in a preheated 375 degree oven for 45 minutes.

Makes 6 to 8 servings.

Carrot and Pear Purée

This vegetable purée is simple, but versatile enough that you may wish to flavor it with a little nutmeg or ginger, cream, or even a splash of sherry. It goes nicely with so many things.

3 pounds sweet young carrots
1 large pear
Salt and pepper to taste
1 tablespoon butter (optional)

1. Peel carrots and slice in circles, ¼ inch thick. Peel pear, remove core, and cut into chunks. Add carrots and pear to a saucepan of boiling water; simmer uncovered until carrots are very tender and pear is cooked, 20 to 30 minutes. Drain well.

2. Purée in food processor or blender. Add salt, pepper, and butter, if desired. Can be made in advance and reheated.

Makes 4 to 6 servings.

Corn Oysters

Once you've tasted them, you'll know these corn oysters are worth all the trouble of grating the fresh ears.

2 cups grated fresh corn on the cob
1/4 cup heavy cream
3 tablespoons flour
1 teaspoon baking powder
2 large eggs, well beaten
1 tablespoon butter
Salt and pepper to taste

1. Blend corn and cream, then add flour and baking powder, stir until smooth. Add eggs, butter, salt, pepper, and mix.
2. Grease a cast iron griddle, drop the mixture by spoonfuls and cook until browned. The oysters can also be deep fried.

Makes 4 servings.

Alice's Corn and Clam Soufflé

2 frying peppers, minced
1 large onion, minced
3 tablespoons butter
4 tablespoons flour
2 cups milk
1 cup cooked chopped clams
3 egg yolks, beaten
2 cups fresh corn kernels scraped from the cob
1 teaspoon salt
1/2 teaspoon black pepper
3 egg whites, stiffly beaten
Butter

1. Using a heavy saucepan, fry peppers and onion in butter until wilted. Add flour and stir to mix completely. Gradually add milk, stirring to prevent lumps. Stir in clams.
2. Mix beaten egg yolks with a small amount of hot milk mixture. With flame on low, return egg-milk mixture to pan, stirring briskly to prevent egg from curdling. Add the corn, salt, and pepper. Remove from heat. Beat egg whites and fold into corn mixture.

3. Grease a soufflé dish with butter. Pour mixture into dish and bake in a preheated 350 degree oven for 30 minutes or until firm. Serve immediately.

Makes 6 servings.

Fresh Corn Bread

4 ears corn, husked and cleaned of silk, or
    1 cup corn kernels
1 cup flour
1 cup yellow cornmeal
2 teaspoons baking powder
3 tablespoons sugar
1 teaspoon salt
1/2 cup milk
1 small onion, finely chopped
2 eggs, beaten
1/4 cup melted butter

1. If using fresh corn, cut the kernels off the cobs with a sharp knife. Set aside.
2. In a mixing bowl, combine the flour, cornmeal, baking powder, sugar, and salt. Mix well. Add corn kernels, milk, onion, eggs, and butter. Stir just until blended.
3. Spread in a greased 8-inch square pan. Bake in a preheated 425 degree oven about 20 minutes. Mixture can also be spooned into 12 muffin tins, and baked for about 15 minutes.

Makes about 12 squares or muffins.

Corn Pancakes

Serve this with the duck recipe, Le Canard en Deux Services, on page 136.

7 fresh young corn on the cob
3/4 cup all-purpose flour
6 eggs
Salt and pepper to taste
Corn oil for frying pancakes

1. Remove the corn from the cobs and cook the kernels in a saucepan of boiling water until they are just tender. (Cooking time depends on the age of the corn; the older the corn, the longer it needs to be cooked.) Drain the corn, let it cool, and reserve ²/₃ cup of the kernels.

2. In a food processor purée the remaining corn with the flour, eggs, and salt and pepper to taste. Transfer the batter to a bowl, add the remaining kernels and stir well. Let the batter rest for 1 hour.

3. In a crêpe pan, add corn oil to coat the bottom of the pan and heat until it is hot. Fill a ¹/₄-cup measure with the batter and pour into the pan. Cook the pancake, turning it, for 45 seconds to 1 minute, or until it is golden. Repeat using all of the batter.

Makes about 16 pancakes.

Eggplant Rollatini

This eggplant dish is hearty enough to stand on its own as a main course.

    2 1-pound eggplants
    Olive oil
    1 15-ounce container ricotta
    ¹/₃ cup grated Parmesan cheese
    1 tablespoon chopped fresh parsley
    1 egg
    Salt, pepper, and nutmeg to taste
    2 tablespoons olive oil
    1 small onion
    1 clove garlic, crushed
    1 28-ounce can crushed tomatoes
    ¹/₂ teaspoon oregano
    1 tablespoon fresh chopped basil or
        ¹/₂ teaspoon dried
    Pinch sugar

1. Peel eggplant and cut lengthwise into 8 even slices. Brush both sides with olive oil and arrange on a baking sheet. Bake in a preheated 400 degree oven for 15 minutes or until softened. Cool.

2. In a bowl combine the ricotta, Parmesan, parsley, egg, and salt, pepper, and nutmeg to taste.

3. In a saucepan, heat 2 tablespoons olive oil. Sauté onion and garlic for 5 minutes. Add the toma-toes, oregano, basil, sugar, salt, and pepper. Bring to a boil, lower heat, cover, and simmer 20 minutes.

4. To assemble, cover bottom of 9-by-13-inch ovenproof baking dish with 1 cup of the sauce. Place 2 tablespoons ricotta mixture on the narrow edge of each eggplant slice. Roll up each slice and place it seam side down in a single layer in the baking dish. Cover with remaining tomato sauce. Bake in a preheated 350 degree oven for 20 minutes or until eggplant is tender.

Makes 6 servings.

Eggplant in Garlic Sauce

This Chinese-style eggplant dish has a bit of a Mideastern influence; eggplant blends well with strong flavors. Pick eggplant that is deep purple, shiny without wrinkles, firm to the touch.

    2 medium eggplants, about 3 to 3¹/₂ pounds
        total
    1 to 2 tablespoons vegetable oil or just enough
        to coat the pan
    2 large cloves garlic, minced, or more if desired
    1 medium onion, quartered, and thinly sliced
    ¹/₂ teaspoon hot sesame oil, or more to taste
    1 tablespoon soy sauce
    1 teaspoon sugar
    ¹/₄ teaspoon white pepper
    1 teaspoon cornstarch dissolved in
        1 tablespoon cold water

1. Prepare eggplant by placing it on a charcoal grill or gas flame and rotating slowly until the skin is partially burnt. Do not overcook. Set aside to cool. Peel off skin and slice mostly cooked eggplant into 1-inch cubes or sticks.

2. Heat oil in a sauté pan over medium-high heat. Add garlic, cook briefly, then add onion and sauté until golden. Do not allow to burn. Add the hot sesame oil, and the eggplant. Stir-fry, coating the eggplant, for a couple minutes. Stir in the soy sauce, sugar, white pepper, add cornstarch mixture, tossing continuously, until the sauce thickens. Cornstarch gives the vegetables a nice shine.

Makes 4 servings.

Easy Eggplant Stew

In France it's ratatouille, in Italy, caponata. Each glorifies the natural affinity of these vegetables.

 1 medium eggplant, about 1½ pounds
 Coarse salt
 2 zucchini, cut in ½-inch chunks
 3 Italian frying peppers, cut in 1-inch pieces
 2 red onions, thinly sliced
 Olive oil
 1 bay leaf
 ¾ teaspoon thyme
 1 teaspoon basil
 3 tomatoes, peeled, seeded, and diced

1. Cut eggplant in chunks, about 1-inch square; do not peel. Place on paper towels, sprinkle with salt, cover with more paper towels and let stand 30 minutes. Press to remove liquid.

2. In a large pan, sauté eggplant, zucchini, peppers, and onions in enough oil to film the bottom of the pan. Cook over medium heat, stirring constantly, adding more oil as needed. When onions are limp, add bay leaf, thyme, basil, and tomatoes, cover partially, and cook for about 20 minutes, or until vegetables are tender. Remove bay leaf before serving.

Makes 4 to 6 servings.

Eggplant and Tomato Fontina

Adding the cream and Fontina cheese to fried eggplant slices gives them a rich flavor.

 2 medium eggplants, about 2½ to 3 pounds
 Coarse salt
 Olive oil
 Fresh pepper
 4 ripe tomatoes
 ¾ teaspoon cumin
 1 teaspoon oregano
 1 garlic clove, finely minced
 ½ cup heavy cream
 1 cup shredded Fontina cheese

1. Cut eggplant in ¼-inch slices. Spread on paper towels and cover generously with coarse salt. Top with paper towel and press gently to draw out the moisture. Let sit for 1 hour, changing towels as they become wet.

2. Heat enough oil to film the bottom of a large frying pan. Dry eggplant, sprinkle with pepper, and sauté slices on both sides until golden; do not let brown. Let drain on paper towels. Fry remaining slices, adding oil as necessary.

3. Meanwhile, peel, seed and chop tomatoes. Press all the juice out of tomatoes, letting them hang in strainer to get as much liquid out as possible. Combine chopped tomatoes with the cumin, oregano, and garlic.

4. In an ovenproof baking dish, lightly oil the bottom, then spread half the eggplant in overlapping rows, covering the bottom. Spread the tomatoes on top, then place remaining eggplant slices in attractive overlapping rows on top. Pour cream around side of dish. Top with cheese. Bake in a preheated 350 degree oven for 20 to 30 minutes, or until top is golden and most of cream is absorbed.

Makes 4 to 6 servings.

Orange Parsnips

If you haven't tried parsnips in a while, be sure to give this version a whirl; you will be pleasantly surprised how well they adapt to a bit of sweetness.

 2 tablespoons butter
 1 tablespoon oil
 1 pound parsnips, peeled and cut into coarse
  julienne strips
 2 tablespoons brown sugar
 3 tablespoons white wine
 Grated rind of ½ orange
 Juice of ½ orange
 Fresh mint leaves for garnish, optional

1. Heat butter and oil in a heavy skillet. Add parsnips and sauté, stirring occasionally, until they begin to brown lightly. Stir in brown sugar and continue to sauté until parsnips are coated and slightly glazed.

2. Add the wine, orange rind, and orange juice. Cover and simmer over low heat, stirring occasionally, until the liquids have been absorbed, about 15 to 20 minutes. Serve hot, garnished with mint leaves if desired.

Makes 4 to 6 servings.

Peas with Mint

A classic combination.

> 2 tablespoons butter
> 1/2 cup chopped scallions
> 3 cups shelled young green peas
> 4 tablespoons water
> 2 tablespoons chopped fresh mint
> 1 teaspoon granulated sugar
> 1 teaspoon lemon juice

In a medium skillet melt butter, and sauté scallions for 2 minutes. Add the peas, water, mint, sugar, and lemon juice. Cover tightly and simmer about 5 minutes or until peas are tender.

Makes 6 to 8 servings.

Peas, Italian-style

> 2 tablespoons minced Italian parsley
> 2 cloves garlic, minced
> 2 thin slices prosciutto, chopped
> 3 tablespoons olive oil
> 2 cups shelled fresh peas
> 3/4 cup beef broth
> Salt and pepper

Sauté parsley, garlic, and prosciutto in oil briefly. Add peas, broth and sugar and cook until peas are tender. Season with salt and pepper to taste.

Makes 4 servings.

Fried Potatoes My Way

As anyone who reads her regularly will know, Sylvia Carter is in love with potatoes. Any style. In fact, one year the staff surprised her on her birthday with an all-potato luncheon—salad, mashed, boiled, and fried. This is her version of fried potatoes.

> Grease rendered from 8 slices bacon
> 2 to 3 pounds potatoes, well scrubbed, peeled and thinly sliced
> 2 to 3 onions, thinly sliced
> Salt and pepper

1. Heat grease in a 9- or 10-inch skillet and layer potatoes and onions in skillet, generously peppering each layer.
2. Brown bottom layer of potatoes over fairly high heat, and turn bottom potatoes to the top. When the potatoes on the bottom start to brown, repeat process. This should take about 15 minutes.
3. Cover skillet, lower heat, and cook until the potatoes are tender, another 15 to 20 minutes. Scrape crispy parts from the skillet when serving.

Makes 4 servings.

Oven-fried Potatoes

> 6 russet potatoes
> 1/4 cup vegetable oil
> Salt and pepper to taste
> 1/2 teaspoon oregano
> Paprika

1. Scrub potatoes and pat dry with paper towels. Cut into circles 1/4 inch thick. Place them in a large mixing bowl and add vegetable oil, salt, pepper, oregano, and paprika. Mix well. (Hands work just fine.)
2. Place potatoes in a single layer on a lightly greased aluminum foil-covered jelly roll pan. Bake in a preheated 350 degree oven for 30 to 40 minutes, or until potatoes are tender.

Makes 6 servings.

Perfect French Fries

Marie Bianco went out on assignment to find the method for perfect French fries. This is the result; the secret is in "double cooking" the potatoes.

8 large russet potatoes
48 ounces vegetable oil for frying
1/2 teaspoon freshly ground kosher salt

1. Scrub potatoes well. Peel if desired. Using a sharp knife or mandoline, slice lengthwise into slices 1/4- to 3/8-inch thick. Cut slices lengthwise into strips the same width. As each potato is cut, place immediately into a bowl of very cold water. Do not soak potatoes for more than 10 minutes after the last potato has been prepared.

2. When ready to fry, remove potatoes from water and pat dry, using paper towels or tea towels.

3. Heat oil in a large heavy electric skillet or deep-fat fryer. Otherwise, use a heavy skillet and a deep-fry thermometer. Heat shortening to 375 to 380 degrees. Slowly add potatoes to oil. If you dump them in all at once, the temperature will drop and the potatoes will absorb too much oil. The oil should never stop bubbling. Depending on the size of your pan, the potatoes will have to be fried in 3 to 4 batches.

4. Once the potatoes have cooked for about 5 minutes, remove them from the pan with a slotted spoon or flat strainer and spread them out to drain on a single layer of paper toweling. Pat the tops with an additional paper towel to remove as much grease as possible. Continue frying potatoes until all are done. The potatoes can remain at room temperature for several hours until the second cooking.

5. Just before serving, reheat oil to 390 to 400 degrees. Cook potatoes again in batches, until crisp and golden brown, about 2 minutes. As potatoes are cooked, spread in a single layer on a baking sheet lined with paper toweling and keep warm in a pre-heated 300 degree oven.

6. Just before serving, sprinkle with freshly ground kosher salt. Salting them too soon breaks down some of the crispness.

Makes 8 servings.

Elaine Blech's Potato Latkes

6 medium potatoes, peeled and grated
1 small onion, grated
2 eggs
3 tablespoons flour
1 teaspoon salt
Pepper to taste
1/2 teaspoon baking powder
Oil

1. Let the potatoes sit briefly in a colander, then strain off the liquid. Mix potatoes, onions, eggs, flour, salt, pepper, and baking powder.

2. Drop the potato mixture by the tablespoonful into the hot oil; brown on both sides, then drain on paper towels. Eat with apple sauce and gusto.

Makes 6 servings.

Potato Frittata

Perfect for a hot lunch.

3 tablespoons butter
2 tablespoons vegetable oil
2 cups thinly sliced, peeled potatoes
1 medium onion, sliced
1 red pepper, cut into strips
6 eggs
2 tablespoons water
Salt and pepper to taste
1 cup shredded Cheddar cheese
2 tablespoons chopped parsley

1. In a large skillet, heat butter and oil. Sauté potatoes for 5 minutes, turning frequently. Add onion and red pepper, and cook until vegetables are tender.

2. In a medium bowl, beat eggs with water, salt and pepper. Pour mixture over vegetables and cook over medium heat without stirring until the edges are set and slightly browned. Sprinkle with cheese, cover, and cook over low heat for 2 minutes or until eggs are cooked to desired firmness. Remove cover and sprinkle with parsley. Cut into wedges.

Makes 4 servings.

New Potatoes and Peas with Bacon and Scallions

1/2 pound bacon, preferably slab, diced
1 bunch scallions, including green parts, diced
3 pounds new potatoes
2 pounds fresh peas (before shelling), shelled
Salt and pepper to taste
1/2 cup butter, melted

1. In a heavy skillet, fry diced bacon until crisp. Remove with a slotted spoon and drain. Add scallions to pan and sauté a minute or two, just until wilted. Set aside.

2. Scrub new potatoes, halve or quarter them depending on size, and place in saucepan with lightly salted water to cover. Cover tightly, bring water to a boil, reduce to a simmer and cook for 10 to 15 minutes, or until potatoes can be pierced with a fork. Drain.

3. While the potatoes are cooking, steam peas in a steamer basket over hot water, until barely tender.

4. Return the bacon to the scallions, and add the potatoes, peas, salt and pepper, and melted butter. Toss together. The recipe may be done half an hour or so up to this point. When ready to serve, cover and reheat very gently.

Makes 8 servings.

Mapled Acorn Squash Rings

Instead of acorn squash halves, try rings as in this recipe for a lovely autumn meal.

2 acorn squash, unpeeled
4 tablespoons butter, melted
1/4 to 1/2 cup maple syrup
Juice of 1/2 lemon
1/2 to 1 teaspoon ground cardamom

1. Cut the squash in half crosswise. Set in a steamer pan and steam for 10 minutes. Squash should test a bit tender but still quite firm.

2. Immediately plunge into cold water to stop the cooking. Drain and pat dry. Cut in 1/2-inch rings, discarding ends. Leave peels on for firmness and color contrast.

3. Brush butter on a 10-by-15-inch jelly roll pan or cookie sheet with sides. Coat both sides of squash with butter. Arrange in a single layer in the pan and drizzle with syrup and lemon juice. Sprinkle with cardamom.

4. Bake in a preheated 375 degree oven for about 25 minutes. Turn rings, add water as needed, and continue baking another 20 minutes or until rings are tender but still firm. Arrange on a platter.

Makes 4 servings.

Pattypan Squash Bake

Be sure to cook the pattypan squash enough so that the skin is tender.

2 pounds pattypan squash
2 eggs, lightly beaten
1 cup milk
1 1/2 tablespoons sugar
Tabasco sauce
3 scallions, finely chopped
Salt and pepper
3/4 cup grated sharp Cheddar cheese
1/2 cup bread crumbs

1. Cut out stem end and opposite end, if tough, of pattypan squash. Cut into chunks, about 1/2 inch thick. Cook in a large pot of boiling salted water for 5 to 8 minutes, or until tender. Drain.

2. Combine eggs, milk, sugar, Tabasco to taste, scallions, salt and pepper. When squash has cooled slightly, place in an ovenproof casserole. Pour egg mixture over. Combine cheese and bread crumbs, and sprinkle on top. Bake in a preheated 350 degree oven for 20 minutes, or until top is lightly browned.

Makes 4 to 6 servings.

Gratin of Squash

1 2½-pound butternut squash
2 tablespoons butter
2 tablespoons flour
1 cup milk
1 bay leaf
Freshly ground nutmeg to taste
Salt and pepper to taste
¼ cup grated cheese
Dash Tabasco sauce
Lemon juice
2 eggs
3 scallions, chopped, including part of
    the green
½ cup dry bread crumbs
½ cup grated Parmesan cheese

1. Peel squash, remove seeds, and cut in chunks. Steam until tender, 15 to 20 minutes.

2. Prepare white sauce: melt butter, stir in flour and cook 1 minute. Remove from heat and let stand 5 minutes. Return to heat and slowly add milk, stirring constantly until thickened. Add bay leaf, nutmeg, salt and pepper and simmer 10 minutes. Stir in ¼ cup cheese. Let cool. Season with Tabasco and lemon juice to taste.

3. When squash is cooked, drain thoroughly, then purée in a food processor or blender. Add squash to white sauce, and combine. Remove from heat and add eggs to squash mixture. Pour into a greased casserole. Combine scallions, bread crumbs, and cheese and sprinkle over top. Bake in a preheated 350 degree oven for 20 to 25 minutes, or until golden brown on top. Let stand 5 minutes before serving.

Makes 6 servings.

Yellow Squash with Black Olives

Cooking teacher Diane Morello brings an Italian sensibility to this recipe for tender summer squash.

¾ cup olive oil
2 medium onions, thinly sliced
4 tablespoons minced garlic, divided (about
    5 to 6 cloves)
1 pound yellow squash, sliced ¼-inch thick
¼ cup minced Italian parsley
½ teaspoon oregano
½ teaspoon basil
Salt and pepper
¼ cup wine vinegar
1 cup pitted black olives, drained, sliced
Fresh parsley for garnish, minced

1. In a large skillet, heat ½ cup oil. Add onion and 2 tablespoons garlic. Sauté until soft; do not brown. Add sliced squash, parsley, oregano, basil, salt and pepper. Simmer partially covered, 5 minutes. Stir in vinegar. Simmer 10 minutes uncovered. Heat remaining ¼ cup oil in another pan. Add olives and sauté 2 minutes. Add remaining garlic, cook until limp. Refrigerate 2 hours.

2. Arrange squash on a serving platter. Scatter olives over squash and sprinkle with minced parsley. Serve chilled.

Makes 4 servings.

Zucchini Campagnola

¼ cup olive oil
3 pounds of zucchini, peeled and cut into 2-
    inch square chunks
3 large potatoes, peeled and quartered
3 large onions, peeled and cut into
    ½-inch slices
1 35-ounce can Italian peeled tomatoes,
    crushed
2 tablespoons sugar
Salt and pepper to taste
6 large basil leaves

1. Pour the oil into an 8-quart saucepan and heat over a moderate flame. Add the zucchini, potatoes, and onions, stirring constantly and adjusting the flame if necessary so that the onions turn golden brown but do not burn.

2. Add the tomatoes, sugar, and salt and pepper to taste. Raise heat and bring the mixture to a boil.

Reduce to a slow simmer, cover, and cook, stirring occasionally until the potatoes are fork-tender (approximately 40 minutes). Add basil the last 10 or 15 minutes of cooking. Serve at once.

Makes 6 servings.

Windows on the World French-fried Zucchini

From the lofty heights of Windows on the World in the World Trade Center in Manhattan comes this version of French-fried zucchini.

2 1/2 pounds unpeeled zucchini, washed
1 1/4 cups all-purpose flour
6 eggs beaten, seasoned with salt and pepper
3 cups bread crumbs, unseasoned
Peanut oil, about 4 cups
Salt and pepper

1. Trim zucchini ends. Cut zucchini into lengthwise slices 3/8 inch thick; then cut each slice into fingers 3/8 inch thick.
2. Place the flour, beaten eggs, and bread crumbs into three shallow bowls. Place the zucchini fingers, a handful at a time, into the flour. Shake off any excess. Dip them one at a time into the egg and then into the bread crumbs. Gently pat the zucchini to help the bread crumbs adhere. Place on paper towels.
3. Heat about 4 cups oil in a deep-fat fryer or deep, heavy pot to 325 degrees. Fry zucchini in small batches—just as much as will make a single layer in the fryer. Fry until golden brown, and remove with slotted spoon. Drain on paper towels. Serve hot sprinkled with salt and pepper.

Makes 4 to 6 servings.

Zucchini and Eggplant on the Grill

4 small zucchini
2 small, firm eggplants
Salt
Olive oil
Black pepper

1. Wash zucchini and cut in lengthwise or crosswise slices, about 1/4 inch thick. Wash the eggplants and cut in 1/4-inch slices lengthwise. Sprinkle salt on eggplants and drain on paper towels for 30 minutes. Rinse and pat dry.
2. Brush the zucchini and eggplants with olive oil and place over a hot fire. Grill, turning and basting with more oil, until eggplants are lightly browned and zucchini are tender and lightly browned. Serve immediately with freshly ground pepper.

Makes 4 to 6 servings.

Zucchini Pancakes

Here is another vegetable dish suitable for Passover.

1 1/2 pounds zucchini
1 small onion, grated
Oil for frying
1 egg, beaten lightly
1/4 cup matzo meal
1/2 teaspoon salt
1/8 teaspoon pepper

1. Scrub zucchini; peel but leave a few thin strips of green for color. Grate onion by hand or in food processor, then grate zucchini. Heat 1/2-inch depth of oil in a large electric skillet or in a large skillet on moderately high heat (350 degrees). Mix the zucchini, onion, egg, matzo meal, salt and pepper.
2. Add by tablespoons into hot oil. Cook for 2 minutes on each side. Serve immediately.

Makes 25 to 30 tiny pancakes.

Zucchini Nut Bread

3 cups all-purpose flour
1½ teaspoons cinnamon
1 teaspoon baking soda
1 teaspoon salt
¼ teaspoon baking powder
3 eggs
2 cups sugar
1 cup vegetable oil
1 tablespoon vanilla extract
2 cups grated zucchini (use small zucchini or
    scoop seeds out of large ones), do not peel
½ cup chopped walnuts

1. In a large bowl place the flour, cinnamon, baking soda, salt, and baking powder. Toss lightly with a fork to mix.

2. Beat eggs well in bowl. Gradually add sugar and oil, mixing well. Add vanilla and dry ingredients. Stir well and add zucchini and walnuts.

3. Spread batter in a well-buttered 9-by-5-inch loaf pan.

4. Bake in a preheated 350 degree oven for 80 to 90 minutes or until bread tests done. Or use 2 buttered 8-by-4-inch loaf pans and cook for 60 minutes.

5. Cool bread in pan 10 minutes. Remove from pan, and cool on a rack. Don't cut until completely cool.

Makes one 9-by-5-inch loaf or two 8-by-4-inch loaves.

Hot Tomatoes with Anchovies and Cheese

Tomatoes prepared this way can be expanded easily to serve a crowd, and are especially delicious late summer.

6 ripe plum tomatoes
4 to 6 fillets anchovy fillets
About ⅓ cup grated Romano or
    Parmesan cheese
About ⅓ cup toasted bread crumbs
Olive oil

1. Slice tomatoes in half lengthwise and arrange on a baking sheet, cut side up. Place a small bit of anchovy (about ¼ to ½ fillet) on each. Sprinkle each with about ½ tablespoon grated cheese, and over that ½ tablespoon toasted bread crumbs. Drizzle oil sparingly over the top.

2. Bake in a preheated 375 degree oven for 10 to 12 minutes or until tomatoes are heated through and top is crispy. Do not overcook or the tomatoes will collapse. They should retain their firmness. Serve hot.

Makes 4 servings, 3 halves per serving.

Pasta with Uncooked Tomato and Basil Sauce

When the tomatoes are at the peak of their season, serve them in this uncooked sauce.

2½ pounds tomatoes, preferably
    plum tomatoes
½ cup olive oil
1 tablespoon balsamic vinegar
5 to 6 large fresh basil leaves, chopped
4 scallions, chopped
Salt and freshly ground pepper
1 pound fresh pasta

1. Peel tomatoes, seed and chop fine. In a bowl, combine tomatoes with the oil, vinegar, basil, scallions, salt and pepper. The mixture can be refrigerated until ready to serve or can be used immediately.

2. Cook pasta until al dente. Place in a heated bowl and pour tomato mixture on top. Toss lightly.

Makes 4 servings.

Fettuccine Primavera

From the many approaches to pasta primavera, this one remains my favorite. If you prepare the vegetables in advance, the actual sauce won't take much longer to prepare than the pasta takes to cook.

1½ cups fresh peas
1½ cups chopped carrots
1 cup chopped green beans
1 pound fettuccine
1 tablespoon olive oil
4 tablespoons butter
¼ pound prosciutto, chopped
1 to 1½ cups heavy cream
1 tomato, peeled, seeded, and chopped
¾ to 1 cup freshly grated Parmesan cheese
1 to 2 tablespoons Dijon mustard
Salt and freshly ground pepper to taste

1. Separately parboil peas, carrots, and green beans until each is just tender but not thoroughly cooked. Refresh in cold water and set aside.

2. Cook fettuccine in boiling salted water until al dente.

3. While pasta cooks, heat the oil in a large sauté pan, add butter, then quickly sauté the prosciutto, peas, carrots, and beans. Drain pasta thoroughly; add to pan along with the cream, little by little, and some of the cheese. Add the tomato, more cream and cheese until the sauce is of desired consistency and flavor. Add mustard, salt and pepper to taste.

Makes 6 appetizer or 4 main course servings.

Stefano Morel's Spaghetti with Salsa Tricolore (tricolor sauce)

For besciamella sauce:
3 tablespoons butter
3 tablespoons flour
Salt
1½ cups milk

For pomodoro sauce:
1 28-ounce can crushed tomatoes
2 tablespoons olive oil
1 clove garlic
½ small onion
Salt and freshly ground pepper

For pesto:
3 cups fresh basil leaves (clean and pat dry)
Pepper to taste
2 tablespoons olive oil
3 cloves garlic
Salt
1 pound regular spaghetti or linguine
Parmesan cheese

1. For besciamella sauce: melt butter in small pan over medium-high heat. Add flour and mix well; sprinkle with salt. Keep on fire for one minute while stirring constantly. Remove from heat; slowly add milk and stir mixture, making sure not to form lumps. Put on medium-high heat and stir constantly until mixture thickens; it should take 5 minutes. Remove from pan and pour sauce in a bowl. Let stand until ready to use it.

2. For pomodoro sauce: blend tomatoes in blender or food processor. Coat bottom of small pan with olive oil; place over medium-high heat. Add minced garlic and onion; brown very lightly. Add blended tomatoes; season with salt and pepper. Let sauce come to a boil, then simmer for 30 minutes or until sauce thickens; keep hot until ready to serve.

3. For pesto sauce: place basil and pepper in blender or food processor. Add oil, garlic, salt. Combine until finely minced. Remove and put into a glass jar until ready to serve. (Pesto can only be prepared in season when basil is fresh. It may be put in containers and frozen. When needed, take jar out of freezer, defrost, use portion of pesto needed and keep the rest in refrigerator filmed with oil, tightly covered.)

4. Cook spaghetti until al dente. Drain and place spaghetti in a large bowl. Pour besciamella sauce over spaghetti, then pour on an equal amount of pomodoro sauce. Add 1 cup pesto sauce. Sprinkle generously with freshly grated Parmesan cheese. Mix spaghetti until all the sauces and cheese are blended well.

Makes 4 servings.

FISH & SHELLFISH

Bluefish Livornese

A whole bluefish makes quite a show, topped in this recipe from Ida Cerbone at Manducatis with tomatoes, capers, and olives. A dry Italian white wine such as Bolla Trebbiano or a young Chianti—try Castellare or Ruffino—would go well with this bluefish.

    1 3-pound bluefish, cleaned
    1/2 cup plain bread crumbs
    1 pound fresh tomatoes, chopped
    2 cloves garlic, chopped
    2 tablespoons capers
    10 Gaeta olives, pitted and halved
    1 tablespoon oregano
    2 tablespoons minced fresh parsley
    1/4 cup light olive oil
    Salt and pepper to taste

    1. Place bluefish in a large, ovenproof pan. Sprinkle crumbs over it, then the tomatoes, garlic, capers, olives, oregano, and parsley. Drizzle with oil.
    2. Pour 1 cup of water around the fish in pan and bake in a preheated 400 degree oven, uncovered, for 30 minutes. Season with salt and pepper to taste.

Makes 6 servings.

Bluefish Cooked over Hot Coals

As it cooks, the bluefish juices combine with the tomatoes and lemons to create a wonderful sauce. Make sure your oregano is fresh and aromatic.

    4 bluefish fillets, about 1 1/2 to 2 pounds total
    Oregano
    Salt and pepper
    1 green pepper, chopped
    1 large onion, chopped
    1 to 2 tomatoes, thinly sliced
    1 to 2 lemons, thinly sliced
    Butter

    1. Place each fillet, skin side down, on a separate sheet of aluminum foil, large enough to enclose it. Sprinkle generously with oregano, salt, and pepper. Top each with some green pepper and onion, then cover with tomatoes. Season tomatoes with salt and pepper. Top with lemon slices. Dot with pieces of butter and sprinkle with a bit more oregano.
    2. Seal foil tightly. Place on a barbecue over hot coals, or high heat if gas, cover, and cook for 15 to 20 minutes. Remove cover, open top of foil packet and let cook a few minutes more. Serve in foil packets.

Makes 4 servings.

Grilled Bluefish with Mustard and Onions

Bluefish and outdoor cooking are meant for each other; this version uses mustard and onions that seem to mellow the flavor of the fish. Serve with grilled zucchini and eggplant, page 91.

    4 bluefish fillets, about 2 pounds
    2 tablespoons Dijon mustard, or to taste
    1 onion, very thinly sliced
    Salt and pepper

1. Prepare a charcoal fire. When the coals are hot, grease grill with oil, then add fillets, flesh side down. Spread mustard on skin of fillets, top with onion slices and season with salt and pepper.

2. Cook, covered about 10 minutes, or until fish flakes easily when tested with a fork. Cooking time will depend on size of fish.

Makes 4 servings.

Bluefish Epicure

A real delicacy at the Bond household can be found when Jules cooks the fish that his wife, Marjorie, catches on her boat. This is one version using bluefish; Bond likes to cut off the darker pieces of meat.

8 tablespoons butter
3/4 pound fresh mushrooms, chopped
1 medium onion, chopped
1/2 cup tomato purée
1/3 cup dry vermouth
1 large clove garlic, minced
1 cup chopped boiled ham
1 teaspoon tarragon, crushed
Salt and pepper to taste
4 medium bluefish fillets, about
    1 3/4 pounds total
1 cup fresh white bread crumbs
2 tablespoons minced fresh parsley
Butter

1. Heat 5 tablespoons of the butter in a saucepan. Add mushrooms and onion. Sauté gently for 5 minutes until onions are soft. Add tomato purée, vermouth, garlic, ham, tarragon, salt and pepper; mix well and cook over low heat for 10 minutes or until sauce is quite thick.

2. Place fillets in a buttered baking dish, cover with sauce. Mix bread crumbs and parsley, sprinkle on top. Dot with a few pieces of butter and bake in a preheated 400 degree oven for 15 minutes. Just before serving, brown for a minute under the broiler.

Makes 4 servings.

Fish Fillets with Béarnaise Sauce

Serve this with a big California Chardonnay such as Mt. Eden, Freemark Abbey, or Grgich Hills.

1/4 cup minced shallots
1 1/2 pounds fish fillets, such as flounder
White wine, about 1 1/2 cups
Salt and pepper

For the Béarnaise Sauce:
3 tablespoons white wine vinegar
2 teaspoons minced shallots
1/2 teaspoon tarragon
1 teaspoon green peppercorns, crushed
3 egg yolks mixed with 1 tablespoon water,
    at room temperature
8 tablespoons butter, very cold
1 tablespoon heavy cream, room temperature

1. Place the 1/4 cup of shallots in a shallow baking dish just large enough to hold the fillets. Place fillets on top. Salt and pepper to taste. Bring the wine to a boil. Pour enough wine around fillets just to cover. Bake in a preheated 350 degree oven for 8 to 10 minutes, or until done.

2. Meanwhile, prepare the sauce. Reduce the vinegar with the shallots, tarragon, and peppercorns over high heat until almost all of the liquid has evaporated. Reduce heat to very low and stir in the yolk-water mixture. Add 1 tablespoon butter and whisk until melted, do not overcook. Add remaining butter, 1 tablespoon at a time, whisking vigorously. If pan gets too hot, remove from stove. If butter separates, add 1 tablespoon very cold water and whisk vigorously to emulsify mixture. Stir in cream. Taste and adjust seasonings as desired.

3. To serve, place fillets on heated plates and spoon sauce along the side. Serve extra sauce in sauceboat.

Makes 4 servings.

Anthony Barbera's Stuffed Flounder

2¹/₂ pounds flounder fillets, about 10 fillets
¹/₂ cup cooking oil
2 carrots, roughly chopped
2 ribs celery, roughly chopped
2 medium onions, roughly chopped
1 medium onion, thinly sliced
¹/₂ pound mushrooms, roughly chopped
2 tablespoons raisins
2 tablespoons white wine
2 tablespoons butter
2 slices white bread, crust removed and
    cut up
Salt and pepper to taste
1 egg yolk
2 tablespoons grated Romano cheese
1 cup Marinara Sauce (see recipe below)
Oregano

1. Wash flounder and drain.
2. Heat ¹/₄ cup cooking oil in a skillet and add carrots, celery and the 2 chopped onions to the pan. Sauté about 10 minutes, stirring often.
3. In a small pan, sauté thinly sliced onion in remaining ¹/₄ cup oil until translucent. Remove onions from oil; reserve onions. Drain oil and add to the other skillet.
4. Add mushrooms to skillet. Sauté another 10 minutes, tossing vegetables with a wooden spoon. Add raisins and sauté for a few minutes. Remove vegetable and drain oil from skillet. Return skillet to the heat and add the white wine and butter. When butter is melted, return vegetables to skillet; add bread and 4 small flounder fillets. Cook just until fish is tender.
5. Put mixture through a meat grinder or chop, not too fine, in a food processor. Let cool.
6. Add salt and pepper, egg yolk, and cheese to mixture. Taste for seasoning and adjust.
7. Put a heaping tablespoon of the mixture in the center of each remaining flounder fillet. Fold sides over filling slightly. Roll from end to end and place in an oiled baking pan.
8. Mix reserved onions with 1 cup marinara sauce and baste the tops of the fish. Sprinkle with oregano. Bake, uncovered, in a preheated 350 degree oven for 30 minutes.

Makes 6 servings.

Marinara Sauce

¹/₄ cup olive oil
6 cloves garlic
2 28-ounce cans Italian plum tomatoes
1 teaspoon freshly ground black pepper
1 teaspoon salt
1¹/₂ teaspoons oregano
2 tablespoons minced fresh parsley

1. Heat olive oil in a large skillet. Hit cloves of garlic with the flat side of a knife, then mince. Add to the skillet and when garlic is just on the verge of browning, add tomatoes. Add black pepper, salt, and oregano. Keep heat high until the sauce begins to bubble. Then turn heat down and simmer, uncovered, for 25 minutes. Turn heat off. Add parsley.
2. Taste for seasoning and correct.

Makes 1 quart sauce.

Oven-fried Flounder

3 tablespoons flour
3 tablespoons cornmeal
¹/₂ teaspoon dry mustard
¹/₄ teaspoon rosemary
2 tablespoons oil
2 pounds flounder fillets
3 tablespoons milk
¹/₃ cup grated Parmesan cheese
Paprika
Salt and pepper

1. Mix flour, cornmeal, mustard, and rosemary.
2. Heat oil in shallow baking dish and set aside.
3. Dip fillets in milk, then in flour-cornmeal mixture. Turn fillets in the hot oil, then lay flat in baking dish without crowding. Sprinkle with half of the Parmesan cheese, some paprika, salt and pepper.
4. Bake uncovered in a preheated 475 degree oven for 4 to 5 minutes. Turn fish, sprinkle with remaining Parmesan and more paprika, salt, and pepper. Bake another 4 to 5 minutes or until fish flakes with a fork.

Makes 4 servings.

Flounder Stuffed with Feta and Spinach

It is crucial to use a sharp, tangy feta to give the fish a needed zing. All you need to complete the menu is plain boiled potatoes, Long Island, of course. This is one of my favorites.

2 pounds fresh spinach or 2 10-ounce
    packages frozen chopped spinach
1/2 pound feta cheese
1 bunch scallions, chopped, including part of
    the green
2 cloves garlic, minced
6 tablespoons butter
2 1/2 teaspoons oregano
Pinch ground nutmeg
Freshly ground black pepper
2 pounds flounder, about 8 to 10 fillets
1/4 cup white wine
2 tablespoons minced fresh parsley

1. Rinse fresh spinach leaves in water to remove grit. Shake dry, then cook in a deep saucepan in the water that clings to the leaves about 8 to 10 minutes, or until spinach is tender. Remove, squeeze spinach dry, then chop coarsely with a knife. Do not use a food processor or blender. If using frozen spinach, cook gently until tender. Squeeze dry, then chop with knife. Combine spinach and feta in a bowl, stirring to combine.

2. In a small sauté pan, briefly cook the scallions and garlic in 2 tablespoons butter. Cool slightly, then stir into spinach mixture. Add 1 teaspoon oregano, nutmeg, and pepper. Spread out flounder fillets and divide spinach mixture among them. Roll fillets and place seam side down in a 9-by-13-inch baking dish. The fish can be made in advance up to this point.

3. Heat remaining 4 tablespoons butter just until melted. Stir in wine, 1 1/2 teaspoons oregano, and parsley. Pour over fish. Bake in a preheated 350 degree oven for 15 minutes, basting twice with pan juices. Cook under broiler briefly, about 3 minutes, to brown slightly.

Makes 4 to 6 servings.

Rolled Flounder Fillets

When I was developing recipes for a low-calorie story, these rolled flounder fillets became a favorite. They're good even when you're not dieting.

2 16-ounce cans stewed tomatoes, drained
1 green pepper, chopped
1 medium onion, chopped
1 1/2 teaspoons ground cumin
3/4 teaspoon red pepper flakes, or more
    to taste
Salt and pepper to taste
8 flounder or grey sole fillets, about
    1 3/4 pounds

1. In a saucepan, cook drained tomatoes, green pepper, onion, cumin, and red pepper flakes and reduce until thickened, about 20 minutes. Season with salt and pepper to taste. Pour a little sauce on the bottom of a baking dish. Roll fillets and place seam side down on top. Top with remaining sauce. Dish can be prepared in advance to this point and refrigerated 2 hours before serving.

2. Bake in a preheated 350 degree oven about 15 to 20 minutes, or until fish flakes easily. If the fillets are thick, the cooking time will be longer.

Makes 4 servings.

Baked Fish and Potatoes with Basil

1 1/2 pounds potatoes, pared and thinly sliced,
    about 5 cups
2 pounds firm-fleshed fish steaks such as cod
1 tablespoon lemon juice
4 tablespoons chopped fresh basil leaves
1 teaspoon salt
1/4 teaspoon pepper
3/4 cup grated Parmesan cheese
4 tablespoons olive oil
2 ripe tomatoes, sliced
1 tablespoon chopped fresh parsley
    for garnish

1. Parboil potatoes in boiling salted water until almost tender, about 5 minutes. Drain well and set aside.

2. Moisten fish with lemon juice and rub 1 tablespoon basil, 1/4 teaspoon salt and pepper onto both sides of the fish.

3. Place the potatoes in a shallow baking dish. Sprinkle with 1 tablespoon basil, 1/4 teaspoon salt, 1/4 cup Parmesan, and 1 tablespoon olive oil. Cover with fish, sprinkle on salt, 1/4 cup Parmesan cheese and 1 tablespoon olive oil.

4. Cover with aluminum foil and bake in a preheated 400 degree oven for 15 minutes. Uncover, top with tomato slices, remaining basil, Parmesan, and olive oil. Return to oven and bake until fish flakes easily when flaked with fork. Sprinkle with parsley.

Makes 4 to 6 servings.

Beer-batter Fried Flounder

2 1/2 cups sifted flour
1/2 cup flat beer or ale
1/2 cup lukewarm water
1 teaspoon oil
1/2 cup lemon juice
1/4 cup minced fresh parsley
1 teaspoon tarragon
Salt and pepper to taste
2 pounds flounder fillets, cut in half
2 egg whites
Oil, about 1 cup

1. Prepare the batter. Mix flour, beer, water, and oil until quite smooth and soft.

2. Blend the lemon juice, parsley, and tarragon. Season with salt and pepper. Mix well and coat the flounder fillets with the mixture; let stand for 10 minutes before cooking.

3. Beat the egg whites until firm, and fold into the batter.

4. In a large skillet, add oil to a depth of 1/2-inch and heat. Sauté the fillets, 2 or 3 at a time, until browned and crisp on both sides. Serve with tartar sauce and lemon wedges.

Makes 4 servings.

Fish and Potato Cakes

Serve this with a fresh green salad and you have a perfect winter meal.

8 flounder fillets, about 1 1/2 pounds
1 1/2 to 2 cups milk
8 potatoes, grated coarsely
1 cup cornstarch
3 cups flour
2 tablespoons baking powder
2 tablespoons chopped onion
4 eggs, slightly beaten
6 scallions, minced
1/2 teaspoon thyme
1 teaspoon salt
1/2 teaspoon white pepper
1/2 teaspoon cayenne pepper, optional
1/2 teaspoon turmeric, optional
1/2 to 1 cup white wine
1/2 to 1 cup milk
Vegetable oil or shortening for frying
Lemon Butter Sauce (see page 100)

1. Cut fillets in half lengthwise and cut again the short way in 1/4-inch strips. Soak in 1 cup of the milk for 1 hour.

2. Meanwhile, rinse grated potatoes under cold running water in a fine mesh strainer. Combine cornstarch, flour, baking powder, onion, eggs, scallions, thyme, salt, pepper, cayenne and turmeric if using. Add enough wine and milk to make a batter with the texture of heavy cream.

3. Let mixture rest for 1 hour in the refrigerator. When ready to assemble, remove fish from refrigerator and drain. Combine fish and potatoes with batter and mix carefully.

4. Heat oil in a large frying pan to 360 degrees. Dip a large serving spoon in hot oil. Pick up one spoonful of the mixture, trying to get fish pieces in each spoonful. Add mixture to frying pan by pushing it off the spoon with another spoon. Turn when the cakes are golden brown. Place on paper towels to drain.

5. Place in a preheated 250 degree oven for 30 minutes before serving. Serve with lemon butter sauce.

Makes 4 to 6 servings.

Bluefish Cooked over Hot Coals (recipe, page 94)

Lemon Butter Sauce

Shark Kebobs

6 tablespoons butter
2 tablespoons flour
1 cup chicken broth
1 cup white wine
½ cup lemon juice
Pepper to taste
Cayenne pepper or ¼ teaspoon Tabasco
    sauce, optional

Melt butter in a sauté pan over medium heat. Add
flour and stir until golden. Add broth, wine, and
lemon juice. Bring to a simmer and cook for 5 minutes. Add pepper, cayenne or Tabasco.

Grilled Bluefish with Mustard and Onions (recipe, page 94)

Shark Kebobs

The firm, moist shark has a delicate flavor. Don't be put off by its bad press, try it.

1 1/4 pounds mako shark or swordfish
2 tablespoons vegetable oil
4 tablespoons lemon juice
6 tablespoons dry white wine
1 tablespoon water
1/2 teaspoon dill weed
1/4 teaspoon oregano
1 clove garlic
1 tablespoon finely minced onion
Freshly ground pepper to taste
2 medium zucchini, cut in small chunks
8 red cherry tomatoes
2 green peppers, cut into squares
Paprika
Lemon wedges

1. Cut fish into 1-inch cubes and rinse well with water. Pat dry. In medium-sized shallow glass dish, combine the vegetable oil, lemon juice, white wine, water, dill weed, oregano, garlic, onion, and pepper.

2. Place fish cubes in marinade; cover and refrigerate at least 2 hours.

3. Thread fish cubes on skewers alternating with zucchini, tomatoes, and peppers; sprinkle lightly with paprika.

4. Prepare a charcoal fire. Grill over hot coals for 10 minutes, turning occasionally. Baste frequently with marinade. Serve with lemon wedges.

Makes 4 servings.

Barbequed Shark Steaks

We've used shark again, here in a tasty marinade that also serves as a basting sauce. A dry Sauvignon Blanc or a white Graves suits the tangy marinade.

   2 pounds shark steaks or other fish steaks
      such as swordfish
   1/4 cup orange juice
   1/4 cup soy sauce
   2 tablespoons ketchup
   2 tablespoons vegetable oil
   2 tablespoons chopped Italian parsley
   1 tablespoon lemon juice
   1/2 teaspoon oregano
   1/2 teaspoon black pepper
   1 clove garlic, crushed

1. Place fish in a single layer in a shallow dish. Combine orange juice, soy sauce, ketchup, oil, parsley, lemon juice, oregano, pepper, and garlic and pour over fish. Marinate for 30 minutes, turning once. Remove fish, reserving marinade.

2. Place fish in a well-greased, hinged wire grill and cook over hot coals for 5 minutes. Baste with marinade, turn and cook for another 5 minutes or until done. Steaks may also be placed in a shallow broiler pan and placed 4 inches from source of heat for 5 minutes, basted with marinade, turned and broiled for another 5 minutes.

Makes 4 to 6 servings.

Codfish Gratin

Jean Arondel, chef at the American Hotel in Sag Harbor, enjoys putting his French imprint on local ingredients, as in this codfish soufflé, a popular fall and winter dish.

   1 1/2 pounds potatoes
   1/2 cup olive oil
   1 pound codfish fillets
   4 to 6 cloves garlic, mashed
   Pinch salt and pepper to taste

   1/2 cup crème fraîche or heavy cream
   1 tablespoon grated Parmesan cheese
   Toast points

1. Peel and quarter the potatoes. Cover with water, add a pinch of salt and bring to a boil. Cook until very tender. Drain.

2. While the potatoes are cooking, heat the olive oil and cook the codfish gently until it flakes easily in the pan. Add the garlic, salt and pepper, and continue cooking for 2 to 3 minutes.

3. Purée the potatoes, fish, and garlic. Add crème fraîche or heavy cream and mix again until well blended.

4. Place mixture in a soufflé dish or ovenproof dish, top with the Parmesan cheese and place under the broiler until top is golden brown. Serve with toast points.

Makes 4 servings.

Chinese Steamed Fluke

The Chinese way of steaming is in a bamboo steamer set in a wok—but you can improvise with a rack placed in a large pan.

   1 2- to 3-pound whole fluke, dressed with
      head, tail, and fins left on
   1 tablespoon fresh ginger, cut in tiny slivers
   1 bunch scallions, cut in 1-inch pieces
      and shredded
   2 teaspoons oil
   2 cloves garlic, crushed
   2 tablespoons fermented black beans, soaked
      in hot water 20 minutes
   3 tablespoons soy sauce
   1/4 cup dry sherry
   1 tablespoon hoisin sauce
   2 teaspoons white vinegar
   1/2 teaspoon sugar

1. Place fish on top of a large sheet of cheesecloth. Lower fish onto a rack over 1 inch of water in a pot just large enough to hold the fish (a covered roasting pan or large wok works well). Cut diagonal

slashes in the top of the fish down to the bones but not through them; the cuts should be about 1 inch long and 1½ inches apart. Place a couple of slivers of ginger in each gash. Sprinkle half of the scallions on top. Cover and steam fish 12 to 15 minutes or until just cooked. Look into the center of the cuts to see if the flesh is white; if it is not done, the flesh will look raw in the center.

2. Meanwhile, in a saucepan stir-fry garlic briefly in the oil. Drain black beans well, mash slightly with the back of a spoon, then stir into the garlic and cook another minute or two. Add soy sauce, sherry, hoisin sauce, vinegar, and sugar and let cook over low heat about 5 minutes.

3. When fish is cooked, lift gently out of pot, using the cheesecloth and set onto a heated platter. Slide cheesecloth out from under the fish. Taste the sauce and add a little bit of the fish cooking juice from the platter and cooking pot to sauce to thin slightly. Pour a small amount of the sauce over the fish, scatter remaining scallions on top and serve remaining sauce separately.

4. To serve: using a thin spatula or spoon, cut gently down the center backbone of the fish. Slide the spatula flat along the bones to lift off the flesh. After serving the top of the fish, lift the center bone off, scraping the bottom flesh down off the bones as you lift. Serve remaining portion.

Makes 4 servings.

Fried Porgies with Mustard Sauce

Porgies are one of the prolific fish off Long Island, and relatively cheap. This method, inspired by food writer Charles Pierce, is quick, especially if you make the sauce in advance.

1 clove garlic, cut in half
8 tablespoons Dijon mustard
¼ cup sugar
¼ cup white wine vinegar
6 tablespoons plus 1 teaspoon finely chopped fresh dill
½ teaspoon fennel seeds, crushed
¾ cup vegetable oil
Salt and pepper

4 1-pound porgies, cleaned, scaled but with head and tail left on
Flour
Vegetable oil for frying

1. To prepare the mustard sauce, place garlic, mustard, sugar, vinegar, the dill less 1 teaspoon, and fennel in a food processor or blender. Blend until smooth. Slowly add the oil, drop by drop, with the machine running until mixture begins to resemble mayonnaise. Taste and add salt and pepper as needed.

2. To cook porgies, make 3 diagonal cuts in the fish, about ¼-inch deep. Dust with flour, and sprinkle with salt, pepper, and 1 teaspoon dill. In a large skillet heat 2 to 3 tablespoons oil. Sauté a couple minutes in hot oil, then turn and sauté another few minutes, or until fish flakes easily. Serve with mustard sauce on the side.

Makes 4 servings.

Poached Salmon with Dill–Cucumber Sauce

Every once in a while, fishermen catch a North Atlantic salmon swimming by the tip of Long Island. Then, be sure to serve it with this dill-cucumber sauce from Joseph Melluso, owner of Joseph's, a fish specialty shop in Oceanside.

4 6-ounce salmon steaks
1 quart boiling water
1 cup white wine
1 small onion, sliced
8 sprigs fresh parsley
8 whole peppercorns
1 teaspoon salt

Dill-Cucumber Sauce:
1 cucumber
1 cup sour cream
½ cup mayonnaise
1½ tablespoons grated onion
3 dashes Tabasco
½ teaspoon salt
1 heaping tablespoon finely chopped fresh dill

1. Place salmon in a large skillet. Add the boiling water, wine, onion, parsley, peppercorns, and salt. Liquid must cover salmon. Bring to a boil. Cover; reduce heat and simmer, allowing about 10 minutes per inch of thickness of salmon measured at its thickest part, or until salmon flakes easily when tested with a fork. Carefully remove from liquid. Cool and chill until ready to serve.

2. For sauce: peel cucumber, cut in half lengthwise and scoop out seeds. Whisk together sour cream and mayonnaise. Add onion, Tabasco, salt, and dill. Grate cucumber into sauce.

Makes 4 servings.

Swordfish with Salsa

This recipe would also work well with weakfish.

Olive oil
1 small onion, sliced
2 cloves garlic, minced
1 1/2 pounds swordfish steaks or
 2 pounds weakfish fillets
1 lemon
1/2 teaspoon ground cumin
1/2 teaspoon oregano
Salt and pepper to taste

For salsa:
3 ripe tomatoes, peeled and seeded
1 small fresh hot pepper
1 clove garlic
1/2 onion
Salt and pepper to taste
2 tablespoons minced fresh cilantro

1. Brush the bottom of an ovenproof baking dish with oil. Spread onion slices on bottom of dish and sprinkle with garlic. Add bass and squeeze juice of half a lemon over the fish. Season with cumin, oregano, salt and pepper. Cover and cook in a preheated 350 degree oven for 15 minutes. Remove cover and bake another 5 minutes or until fish flakes.

2. Meanwhile, prepare the salsa. Combine tomatoes, hot pepper, garlic, and onion in a blender or food processor. Blend briefly, just until mashed. Add salt and pepper to taste and sprinkle with cilantro. If desired, add a little lemon juice to taste. Serve alongside bass.

Makes 4 servings.

Grilled Swordfish

Often when I grill the swordfish, I'll garnish it simply with fresh tomatoes. Or, I'll precook sweet potatoes and finish them on the grill. Brush 1/2-inch slices of sweet potatoes with butter and grill them a few minutes on each side.

4 swordfish steaks, about 1 3/4 pounds
Olive oil
Balsamic or red wine vinegar
1 tomato, chopped
6 basil leaves
2 to 3 cloves garlic, smashed

1. Place swordfish in a ceramic or glass dish. Cover with olive oil. Add a small amount of vinegar, just to flavor. Add tomato, basil and garlic, cover and let stand 1 hour, or refrigerate 4 to 5 hours or overnight.

2. To cook, remove swordfish from marinade and cook over hot coals, or high heat on a gas grill, about 5 minutes per side. Brush with marinade occasionally.

Makes 4 servings.

OPPOSITE *Robert Lipinski's Steamers (recipe, page 34), Grilled Swordfish (recipe above), and Gerard's Fra Diavolo (recipe, page 118)*

Teriyaki Swordfish

Swordfish, tilefish, or any other firm fish could be used in this easy recipe with a Japanese accent.

1/2 cup mirin (available in Oriental
   specialty stores)
1/4 cup soy sauce
1 tablespoon minced ginger
1 clove garlic, minced
1 tablespoon cornstarch
4 swordfish steaks, about 1 3/4 pounds

1. Combine mirin, soy sauce, ginger, and garlic in a saucepan and bring to a boil. Add cornstarch gradually, stirring often. Simmer 2 minutes.

2. Place swordfish on broiler rack and brush with sauce. Broil about 5 minutes per side, brushing with sauce when turning.

Makes 4 servings.

Sole with Champagne Sauce

When I'm feeling festive, I like to prepare an elegant sauce for fish. After a visit to Champagne, I was inspired to create this sauce, using, not surprisingly, champagne; the local version of sparkling wine or a dry white wine will substitute. Continue the champagne into the meal with a California dry sparkling wine such as Domaine Chandon or Gold Seal's Fournier Brut from New York State.

Champagne Sauce:
1 onion, chopped
1 tablespoon butter
1 1/2 pounds fish bones and head
1 bay leaf
1 teaspoon thyme
3 cups nonvintage champagne
1 cup cream

For fish:
16 tablespoons butter
3 pounds fresh spinach, washed
1/2 lemon

3 pounds lemon or grey sole fillets,
   or flounder
Flour
Salt and pepper

1. For sauce, sauté onion in butter over low heat until soft, about 10 minutes. Add fish bones and heads, bay leaf, thyme, and champagne. Simmer for 20 to 25 minutes, uncovered. Strain and cook over high heat until reduced by half. Add cream and reduce again until thick enough to coat a spoon, about 15 minutes. This can be done in advance. To hold, butter a piece of wax paper and place it, buttered side down, on the sauce.

2. Melt 8 tablespoons butter in a large saucepan. Shake excess water off spinach and add to saucepan. Squeeze lemon juice on top and season with salt and pepper. Cook over low heat until soft and tender. Remove spinach and chop finely by hand. Do not use a food processor. Discard liquid in pan, return spinach and add 2 tablespoons butter. Dish can be prepared in advance to this point.

3. To serve, dust the sole in flour seasoned with salt and pepper. Fry gently in 3 tablespoons butter until cooked through, turning once. Add more butter, as needed. Reheat spinach if needed. Reheat sauce and swirl in remaining 3 tablespoons butter. Taste and correct seasoning as needed. Mound spinach on heated dinner plates, place sole on top and pour sauce over the fish. Serve with boiled potatoes.

Makes 6 servings.

Grey Sole on Red Pepper Sauce

By cooking the fish in muffin tins, you can serve the sole in tight spirals on top of the red pepper sauce. I discovered that the secret is to wedge the fish tightly into each muffin tin; then the fish will hold its shape.

2 pounds grey sole fillets
2 cloves garlic, finely minced
Dry vermouth
1 pound plum tomatoes, peeled, seeded, and
    chopped, about ½ cup
2 tablespoons pitted, chopped oil-cured
    black olives
½ cup minced Italian parsley
1 teaspoon anchovy paste
2 teaspoons capers, drained and crushed
Salt and pepper to taste

Red Pepper Sauce:
4 large red peppers
2 tablespoons olive oil
2 to 3 cloves garlic, peeled
Dash red pepper flakes
Juice of ½ lemon

1. Cut fillets in half lengthwise. Place in a large pan, sprinkle with garlic and cover with vermouth. Refrigerate 2 hours. Combine tomatoes, olives, parsley, anchovy paste, capers, and salt and pepper to taste. Set aside.

2. Prepare sauce: Coarsely chop peppers. Place peppers in a saucepan with the oil, garlic, and red pepper flakes. Cover with a piece of waxed paper, then cover with lid. Cook over very low heat for 1 hour or until peppers are tender. Purée in blender or food processor briefly, leaving the mixture slightly lumpy. Add lemon juice.

3. Remove fillets from vermouth. Spread the tomato mixture very lightly on the fillets. Roll fillets in a tight roll and place in muffin tins, making 8 rolls. It is okay if fillets rise above top of tins. Add partial pieces of fish to each roll as needed to make rolls fit snugly in the tins. Dish can be prepared in advance to this point.

4. To cook, bake fish in a preheated 350 degree oven for 25 minutes. To serve, reheat pepper sauce gently. Spoon the sauce on 4 heated plates. Using 2 spoons, remove the fish rolls from the muffin tins and place 2 fish rolls on top of the sauce on each plate.

Makes 4 servings.

Fish Gratin

This gratin is extremely rich; serve with plain steamed broccoli as a balance. Tilefish tastes delicious, but is difficult to work with since it has a few, very stubborn bones to remove before you can cut the steaks into chunks. Cod or any other firm-flesh fish will work quite well.

1½ pounds tilefish, cod or other
    firm-flesh fish
Flour
3 tablespoons butter
Salt and pepper

For sauce:
2 tablespoons butter
2 tablespoons flour
1 cup half and half
1 tablespoon sherry
½ cup shredded Gruyère cheese
Dash Tabasco sauce
Salt and pepper
Nutmeg
Juice of ½ lemon

¼ cup bread crumbs

1. Cut fish in ¾-inch chunks. Toss in flour, shaking off excess. Melt 3 tablespoons butter in a large sauté pan; add the fish a few pieces at a time, and toss to cook briefly. Season with salt and pepper. Fish should be barely cooked. Remove to paper towels.

2. For sauce, melt butter in saucepan; stir in flour and cook for 1 minute. Add half and half, stirring constantly over medium heat until sauce thickens. Lower heat, stir in sherry, cheese, Tabasco, salt, pepper, and nutmeg to taste. The sauce should be highly seasoned and quite thick. Add lemon juice, and stir. Place fish in a buttered gratin pan, pour sauce over and sprinkle bread crumbs on top. Bake in a preheated 350 degree oven for 15 minutes. Place under broiler to crisp and brown top.

Makes 4 servings.

OVERLEAF *Trap fishermen from Rempe Fish Market, Greenport, in Gardiners Bay*

Baked Stuffed Squid

For dinner, have large portions with a salad; small squid, while a nuisance to stuff individually, are wonderful appetizers. Either way, these baked squid combine well with salads or sliced garden tomatoes.

    10 medium-to-large squid, or about
        1 1/2 pounds cleaned
    1 pound additional squid, tentacles, small
        squid, etc.
    7 tablespoons dry white wine
    Juice of 1 lemon
    6 to 8 tablespoons olive oil
    4 anchovy fillets
    4 cloves garlic, minced
    3/4 cup bread crumbs
    Freshly ground black pepper to taste

    1. Clean and dry squid; reserve.
    2. Chop tentacles and additional small squid in small dice. Set in bowl and cover with 2 to 3 tablespoons wine and 1/2 of the lemon juice.
    3. Heat 4 tablespoons oil in a heavy saucepan. Add anchovy fillets and garlic. Sauté slowly over low to moderate heat for 3 to 5 minutes or until anchovies have cooked down and the flavors have melded.
    4. Add bread crumbs and mix well. Remove from heat. Add chopped squid and mix to combine. When mixture is cool enough to handle, divide into 10 portions (or enough for the number of squid). Fill each cavity loosely.
    5. Using 1 tablespoon of oil, lightly grease an 8-by-11-inch casserole and arrange the stuffed squid in one layer. Cover with oil as needed, remaining wine and lemon juice, and black pepper. Bake in preheated 375 degree oven for about 30 minutes.

Makes 4 to 6 servings.

HOW TO CLEAN SQUID

Many fish stores sell squid already cleaned or will clean them on request. If not, don't worry, it is not really a difficult chore. Expect to get one pound of cleaned squid from 2 pounds uncleaned. The mantle or the body and the tentacles are the edible parts.

    1. Hold the mantle in one hand, and with the other, pull the tentacles firmly. All the contents of the body cavity should come out, leaving the mantle empty. If not, feel inside for the quill (also called pen) and pull it out along with the attached viscera.
    2. Cut the tentacles off the head and reserve. Discard the remainder of what has been pulled out.
    3. Clean out anything still in the mantle and wash thoroughly. It is now ready for stuffing.
    4. Make rings by cutting across mantle. If bite size pieces are desired, lay the mantle flat and cut down the center from top to tail. Spread open and wash thoroughly.

Squid Rings and Pasta

When purchasing fresh squid, try to get them all the same size and allow for shrinkage in cooking. Frozen squid will probably come in different sizes, in which case the larger ones can be sorted for stuffing, while the smaller ones can be used either to enrich the stuffing or can be reserved for another dish altogether such as these rings over pasta. Two pounds of uncleaned squid will result in a little over one pound, cleaned.

    1 1/2 pounds squid, weight after cleaning
    6 tablespoons oil
    2 cloves garlic, quartered
    2 pounds Swiss chard, cleaned, dried, and cut
        in 1-inch lengths
    1/2 teaspoon black pepper or to taste
    1/2 teaspoon red pepper flakes or to taste
    Salt to taste
    1 medium lime
    1/2 lemon
    1 pound linguine
    Lime wedges for garnish

1. Cut squid into ½-inch rings and towel dry. Reserve. Bring 5 to 6 quarts of water to a boil for the pasta.

2. Meanwhile, heat oil in a heavy saucepan just before smoking stage. Add garlic and cook briefly. Remove garlic before it burns and turns bitter; discard.

3. Add squid to oil and cook over high heat stirring constantly, for 2 to 4 minutes or until squid tests done but is still tender. Overcooking will make it rubbery.

4. Add chard and stir to mix thoroughly. Add black and red pepper and salt, if desired. Squeeze the juice of lime and lemon over squid mixture and simmer, covered, over low heat until chard is barely done. Remove chard and squid and keep warm.

5. Cook pasta until al dente while finishing squid sauté. Reduce remaining liquid over high heat until the remaining sauce is thickened and concentrated. Taste and correct seasonings. Return chard and squid to pan, stirring to reheat.

6. Drain pasta, and serve squid immediately over the linguine. Garnish with additional lime wedges.

Makes 4 to 6 servings.

Pan-fried Brook Trout

Surrounded by salt water, Long Island specializes, not surprisingly, in saltwater fish. But you can get fresh water trout from the Cold Spring Harbor Fish Hatchery and cook them simply as in this recipe. Just call the fish hatchery to check that trout are available before you run out there.

½ cup unsalted butter
4 9- or 10-inch brook trout, cleaned
  and dressed
Salt and pepper to taste

1. Heat butter gently in a 12-inch skillet or in one large enough to hold all of the fish. It should be quite hot. Pat fish dry, season lightly, and place in pan.

2. Cook just until brown on one side; turn and cook until brown on the other side, about 2 minutes on each side. Cover skillet, reduce heat and let fish steam gently for about 2 more minutes, to cook through. Serve with pan juices and crusty bread for mopping.

Makes 2 servings.

NOTE: For a different flavor, fry 8 slices of bacon, substitute the resulting bacon fat for the butter and serve the trout with the crisp, drained bacon.

Tuna à la Basquaise

Local fresh tuna is a rare and delightful treat; when you find it, try this recipe from Chef Jean Arondel at The American Hotel.

4 tablespoons olive oil
2 cups sliced onions
4 cloves garlic, crushed
2 cups sliced green peppers
6 medium-size tomatoes, peeled
  and quartered
Pinch thyme
1 bay leaf
Salt and pepper to taste
1 cup dry white wine
4 tuna steaks, about 2 pounds
Flour

1. Heat 2 tablespoons oil and cook onions until lightly golden. Add garlic and peppers. Stir and let cook a few minutes. Add tomatoes, thyme, bay leaf, salt, pepper, and wine. Let cook over low heat for 15 to 20 minutes. Remove bay leaf.

2. Dust tuna lightly in flour. In an ovenproof skillet, sauté tuna quickly in remaining olive oil on both sides. Pour tomato mixture over tuna and bring to a boil. Cover and put in a preheated 350 degree oven for 15 minutes.

Makes 4 servings.

Weakfish Boulangère

Jules Bond is a creative fish cook; here he combines a French technique for cooking potatoes with a favorite Long Island fish.

8 medium potatoes
12 small white onions, peeled
1 4-pound weakfish, scaled and cleaned
Salt and pepper to taste
Pinch thyme
1/2 cup chicken broth
6 tablespoons butter, melted
2 tablespoons minced fresh parsley
Lemon slices

1. Boil potatoes for about 6 minutes, peel, and slice 1/4 inch thick. Parboil the peeled onions for 5 minutes. Butter a shallow baking dish, line the bottom with sliced potatoes, place fish on top and arrange the onions around it. Season fish with salt and pepper, sprinkle with thyme; add broth. Place 2 or 3 lemon slices on fish.

2. Bake in a preheated 350 degree oven for about 30 minutes until fish and potatoes are done. Baste frequently with the melted butter. When fish is cooked, spoon some of cooking liquid over it, sprinkle with parsley, garnish with remaining lemon slices and serve.

Makes 4 servings.

Weakfish Fillets in Cream and Dill

2 pounds weakfish fillets
Salt and pepper to taste
Flour
2 eggs, beaten with 2 tablespoons milk and
    1 teaspoon oil
1/4 cup cooking oil
6 tablespoons butter
1 1/2 cups sour cream
2 tablespoons finely chopped fresh dill
    (or 1 1/2 teaspoons dried dill weed)
1 teaspoon paprika

1. Trim fillets and cut in serving pieces. Season with salt and pepper, dredge in flour and dip in egg mixture.

2. Heat oil and 4 tablespoons butter in a skillet. Fry fish until golden brown on both sides.

3. Place fish in a baking dish and dot with pats of butter. Blend sour cream and dill, spoon over fish, sprinkle with paprika, and bake in a preheated 375 degree oven for about 10 minutes until nicely browned.

Makes 4 servings.

Weakfish (Sea Trout) Stuffed with Lobster

While this lobster stuffing pairs well with weakfish, it could be used with other whole fish. I serve this when I want to make a dramatic presentation. The rich stuffing would be well balanced by a Chardonnay, such as New York's Hargrave Vineyard's Collector Series.

2 pounds cooked lobster meat
1 tablespoon oil
2 tablespoons butter or margarine
1 small zucchini, diced, about 1 generous cup
1 leek, cleaned, minced, with green part
    set aside
2 teaspoons tarragon
1/2 cup heavy cream
1/3 cup bread crumbs
1 whole 4- to 5-pound weakfish or sea trout,
    cleaned and dressed, with head and
    tail attached
White wine
Salt and pepper to taste
Juice of 1 fresh lemon for basting
Lemon slices to decorate

1. Chop lobster meat coarsely. Heat oil and butter in a sauté pan, then cook the zucchini, leek, and tarragon until very soft over medium heat, about 7 to 10 minutes. Add cream and cook until slightly thick-

Weakfish Stuffed with Lobster

ened, stirring with a wire whisk. Stir in lobster meat and bread crumbs. Set mixture aside.

2. Stuff fish with lobster mixture. Sew opening closed. Pour a little white wine in bottom of a large baking pan. Place fish in pan, season with salt and pepper, if desired. Squeeze lemon juice over fish.

3. Bake in a preheated 350 degree oven for 45 minutes or until fish flakes when tested with a fork. Add more wine as it evaporates and baste with lemon juice a few times during baking.

Makes 6 servings.

Baked Whiting in Sour Cream

4 large whiting fillets, about 2 pounds
1½ cups sour cream
¼ cup mayonnaise
Salt and pepper
Pinch thyme
1 teaspoon paprika
2 tablespoons diced pimiento
1 tablespoon butter, softened
2 teaspoons dill weed
Lemon wedges for garnish

1. Place fish in a shallow, buttered baking dish. Blend together sour cream, mayonnaise, salt, pepper, thyme, paprika, pimiento and butter. Spoon over the fish, and sprinkle with dill.

2. Bake in a preheated 350 degree oven for 20 minutes. Garnish with lemon wedges when serving.

Makes 4 servings.

Whiting in Caper Cream Sauce

Whiting is a frequently caught, less frequently cooked Long Island product. Here, its bland flavor, similar in consistency and taste to cod, is combined with piquant capers and mustard.

4 large whiting fillets, about 2 pounds
Salt and pepper to taste
1 tablespoon lemon juice
1/4 cup flour
5 tablespoons butter
1 teaspoon Dijon mustard
1 1/2 tablespoons drained capers
1/2 cup dry white wine
2 teaspoons cornstarch
1/4 cup heavy cream
Chopped fresh parsley

1. Season fish with salt and pepper, sprinkle with lemon juice, and dredge lightly in flour. Heat butter in a skillet and sauté the fish, turning very gently until lightly browned on both sides. Remove fish carefully to a serving plate and keep warm.

2. Add mustard, capers, and wine to the skillet, mix well, and bring to a boil. Lower heat and simmer for 2 to 3 minutes. Dissolve cornstarch in 2 tablespoons water, and blend it and the cream into the simmering sauce. Cook for 2 more minutes. Correct seasoning, top fish with sauce, and sprinkle with parsley.

Makes 4 servings.

Pan Roast of Clams in the Style of the Grand Central Oyster Bar

2 to 3 tablespoons butter
4 teaspoons Worcestershire sauce
1/2 cup bottled chili sauce
1 tablespoon sweet paprika
1/2 teaspoon Tabasco
4 dozen shucked littleneck or cherrystone
    clams, with their juice
1 quart milk (or half and half, or half heavy
    cream, half milk)
8 1/2-inch thick slices Italian or French bread,
    dried in the oven

1. In a large, heavy saucepan, melt the butter, then stir in the Worcestershire sauce, chili sauce, paprika, and Tabasco.

2. When the mixture begins to bubble, add the clams with their juice. Cook over medium heat, stirring constantly, until mixture begins to bubble again, about another minute.

3. Add the milk or half and half. Stir well. When mixture is heated through, remove from heat. In each of 4 bowls, place 2 slices of bread. Pour over clams and sauce, dividing the clams equally among the bowls. Serve immediately.

Makes 4 servings.

Clam Hash

5 tablespoons butter
1/2 cup minced onion
1 clove garlic, minced
2 cups coarsely chopped clams
2 cups diced cooked potatoes
2 tablespoons chopped pimiento
1 tablespoon chopped fresh chives
1 tablespoon chopped fresh parsley
2 dashes Tabasco, or to taste
1 tablespoon Worcestershire sauce
1 teaspoon paprika
Salt and pepper to taste
1/2 cup light cream
Lemon wedges and parsley sprigs for garnish

1. Heat butter in a skillet, add onion and sauté for a few minutes until onion is soft—do not let brown. Combine the garlic, clams, potatoes, pimiento, chives, parsley, Tabasco, Worcestershire sauce, paprika, salt and pepper, and add to the skillet. Spread out evenly and sauté over medium heat for about 10 minutes, shaking the skillet a few times to prevent sticking.

2. Add the cream, mix well, smooth mixture, and cook over a gentle heat for about 15 minutes, until the bottom is well browned. Shake pan a few times.

3. To serve, invert hash on a plate and garnish with lemon wedges and parsley.

Makes 4 servings.

NOTE: A Teflon-coated skillet is best for preparing the hash. The food won't stick and the hash will be attractive when inverted.

Long Island Clam Pie

Clam pie, an East End tradition, is best, fishermen's wives claim, when the filling is simple and doesn't detract from the flavor of the clam. This version is by Barbara Rader, former food editor for *Newsday*.

1 tablespoon finely minced salt pork
1/2 cup finely chopped onions
2 cups ground clams (about 2 dozen
    cherrystone clams)
1/4 cup clam juice
1/2 cup cracker crumbs
1/2 cup half and half
1/2 teaspoon freshly ground pepper
Double pastry crust for an 8- or 9-inch pie (see
    page 163)
1 tablespoon butter

1. In a heavy skillet, fry salt pork until light brown, but not burned. Remove salt pork and set aside, leaving fat in pan. Sauté onion in fat until light brown but not burned. Drain. In a mixing bowl, combine the salt pork, onion, clams, clam juice, crackers, half and half, and pepper.

2. Roll out pastry and place bottom crust in pie

shell. Pour in mixture and dot with butter. Fit top on the pie, make slits for air vents and crimp the edges tightly.

3. Bake in a preheated 400 degree oven for 40 minutes or until crust is browned.

Makes 4 to 6 servings.

Fresh Clam Sauce over Angel Hair Pasta

Clam sauce over pasta is a tradition; making it with fresh clams gives it a light, sweet taste. A green salad, and a dry medium-bodied Italian white wine (try Principessa Gavi or Vaselli Orvieto) would make this an easy meal for friends.

2 tablespoons olive oil
4 tablespoons chopped shallots
2 cloves garlic, minced
2 large ripe tomatoes, peeled, seeded and
    chopped
1/4 cup dry white wine
Salt and pepper to taste
2 dozen cherrystone clams
8 ounces capellini or other very fine pasta
4 tablespoons chopped fresh Italian parsley
Red pepper flakes, optional

1. In a large skillet, heat the olive oil; sauté shallots and garlic until soft. Add the tomatoes, wine, salt and pepper to taste. Clams are naturally salty so use a minimum of salt. Cook 3 minutes. Meanwhile, bring 5 to 6 quarts of salted water to the boil.

2. Scrub clams well; discard any open clams. Add clams to the skillet, cover, and cook for 5 to 8 minutes or until they open. Discard any that do not open. Remove and keep warm.

3. Cook capellini until al dente. Drain and place on a warm platter. Pour sauce over pasta, arranging clams on top. Sprinkle with parsley and red pepper flakes, if desired.

Makes 4 servings.

OPPOSITE *"Rafting up," a boater's way of socializing, Port Jefferson harbor*

FROM THE TOP, CLOCKWISE *Clamming, Mt. Sinai harbor; Trap fishing, Gardiners Bay; Chowder clams are gathered from the bay bottom with a long-handled clam rake*

Gerard's Fra Diavolo

This is the first dish that Gerard Jetter, then my date, now my husband, prepared for me.

    1/3 to 1/2 cup olive oil
    1/4 pound sweet or mixed sweet and hot Italian
      sausages
    4 or 5 large cloves garlic, coarsely chopped
    1 cup chopped fresh Italian parsley
    1 1/2 heaping teaspoons red pepper flakes
    1 small red pepper, coarsely chopped
    1 small green pepper, coarsely chopped
    2 or 3 medium onions, coarsely chopped
    1 teaspoon salt
    1 teaspoon black pepper
    1 cup dry Italian red wine
    2 tablespoons oregano
    1 tablespoon thyme
    10 leaves fresh basil, chopped, or 1 tablespoon
      dried
    2 35-ounce cans peeled Italian tomatoes
    3 bay leaves
    2 1/2 dozen littleneck or top neck clams
    3 1 1/2-pound lobsters, cooked, meat removed
      from shell and coarsely chopped (see page
      119)
    1 1/2 pounds linguine

1. In a large, heavy pot, heat enough oil to film bottom of pot. Chop sausage, add to oil and cook until browned. Remove sausage with a slotted spoon. Add the garlic, parsley, and red pepper flakes. Cook 5 minutes over high heat. Add the red and green peppers, onions, salt and pepper, and cook over medium heat until onions and peppers are soft. Add 1/2 cup wine, oregano, thyme, and basil, and cook over high heat 5 minutes. Add the tomatoes, another 1/2 cup wine, and bay leaves, and cook over medium heat for 15 minutes, breaking up tomatoes. Simmer 1 1/4 hours until sauce is thick. Can be prepared in advance to this point. Remove bay leaves.

2. Cook clams in sauce over medium heat until they open, about 15 to 20 minutes. Cook the linguine in boiling salted water until tender but still firm, about 8 to 10 minutes. Stir lobster into sauce and heat through. To serve, place cooked linguine on heated plates and top with the sauce, clams, and lobster. There will be extra sauce.

Makes 4 servings.

Navarin of Lobster

With homage to Paul Bocuse and Michel Guérard, Pat Lenz shares her version of navarin of lobster.

    1 1/2 cups peeled potatoes cut into chunks
    1 1/2 cups carrots, cut into matchsticks
    1 cup fresh turnips, cut into matchsticks
    3/4 pound green beans, trimmed at ends, cut
      into 1-inch lengths
    1 cup fresh peas
    3 to 4 1 1/2-pound live lobsters
    6 tablespoons butter
    1/4 cup olive oil
    1/3 cup chopped shallots
    8 to 10 small white onions, peeled, cut in
      quarters or eighths
    Salt and pepper
    4 ripe tomatoes, peeled, seeded, and chopped,
      or equivalent in purée
    3/4 cup dry white wine
    1 1/2 cups chicken stock (see page 47)
    3 tablespoons flour

1. Cook potatoes in boiling, heavily salted water, until cooked but still firm, 10 to 15 minutes. Combine carrots and turnips and cover with cold, salted water. Bring to a boil and cook about 10 minutes. Drain and rinse until cold; pat dry. Cook beans in salted, boiling water until barely tender, about 8 to 10 minutes. Drain and rinse under cold water. Dry. Simmer peas in salted, boiling water for 4 minutes. Rinse under cold water and dry. Set aside vegetables.

2. Kill lobsters and cut in half (see page 119). Remove intestinal vein. Cut each tail section into thirds. Remove sac near head and lungs. Leave body in 2 sections; crack claws. Reserve coral and liver.

3. Heat 4 tablespoons of the butter with the oil in a heavy casserole, and toss lobster pieces for 3 to 4 minutes. Add shallots, onions, salt and pepper and stir; cook 5 minutes. Add tomatoes, wine, and stock. Cover and cook 10 minutes. Drain off liquid into a large saucepan and simmer sauce for 15 minutes.

4. Meanwhile, combine coral, liver, remaining butter, and flour until well blended. Add to sauce off heat. Cook over low heat for a minute or 2, stirring constantly. Add vegetables. Stir, bring to a boil and cook, stirring constantly for 5 minutes. Add cooked lobster mixture to sauce, heat through, and serve.

Makes 4 servings.

Baked Lobster

2 1½-pound lobsters
2½ cups good quality white bread, crust
   removed, cubed
2 tablespoons melted butter
1 teaspoon tarragon
1 clove garlic, crushed
2 tablespoons grated onion
2 tablespoons sherry or 1 tablespoon Cognac
Pepper to taste
Dash Tabasco
Butter

1. Have your fishmonger split the live lobsters, remove the sac in the head and vein in the tail; reserve liver (tomalley) and coral, if any. Crack the claws.

2. Mix bread, butter, tarragon, garlic, onion, sherry, pepper, Tabasco, coral, and liver. Fill the body cavity of the lobsters with the mixture and spread it over the meat in the tail. Dot with a few small pats of butter.

3. Bake in a preheated 400 degree oven for about 15 minutes until the surface is lightly browned.

Makes 2 servings.

HOW TO SELECT AND COOK LOBSTER

Look for lobsters with hard shells; if the shells can be pressed slightly, that means the lobster has shed recently. The meat is flavorful, but the shells won't be filled out. You'll wind up with lots of claws and water but not much inside them. Also, look for lobsters that are active; sometimes, if they seem dull, it's because they've been on ice for a long time in which case they will be moving slowly.

Authorities do not always agree on the proper way to cook lobster, much less the cooking time. They also differ as to whether it is desirable to plunge the lobster into boiling water head first; some say this is the quick and merciful way resulting in tender meat while others claim quite the opposite. From my experience, I have not observed any difference in flavor, and I've cooked them every way; I prefer to steam them, taking the advice of the lobstermen I interviewed that this is the tastiest method.

It is crucial not to overcook lobsters or they will become tough and rubbery. James Beard and *The Joy of Cooking* advises cooking them 5 minutes for the first pound and 3 minutes for each additional pound. Other sources recommend as much as 7 to 8 minutes for that first pound, all the way up to 15 minutes. I opt for the shorter cooking time; the best advice I've been given, though, is to use the color as a guide. When the lobster is a bright deep red it is done; the color must be vibrant. If it is a light red, keep cooking.

Cooking Lobster

To Boil. Bring lots of salted water to the boil, using 1 tablespoon salt per quart of water. Seawater is good to use if you are fortunate to be cooking near a shore. You will want enough water to cover the lobsters by a few inches. When the water is boiling hard, add the lobsters, cover, and return to the boil. Cook 5 minutes for the first pound and 3 minutes per additional pound. Remove and place under cold running water to stop the cooking.

To Steam: Bring a small amount of water at the bottom of a fish steaming kettle to a boil. Add the lobster, cover and let steam for 15 minutes. Be sure the water does not boil away. It is still possible to steam lobster if you do not have the official pot. A vegetable steamer tray works as well; you simply may have to repeat the process if you are cooking a lot of lobsters. Remove and place under cold running water to stop the cooking.

Killing a Lobster

Several recipes here call for a cut-up lobster. To kill a lobster, insert the tip of a sharp heavy knife where the top of the tail and body are joined. This will sever the spinal cord.

If you are serving split broiled lobsters, be sure to remove the hard sac in the head and the intestinal vein.

Mirabelle's Poached Lobster in a Tomato Basil Cream Sauce

Vintage champagne is suited to this elegant dish. Choose among Tattinger or Bollinger, or Schramsberg from California.

    3 cups heavy cream
    1 1/2 cups chopped fresh tomatoes (blanch to
        remove skins)
    2 tablespoons chopped fresh basil
    Salt and pepper to taste
    4 1 1/2-pound lobsters

    For the poaching liquid:
    2 gallons water
    1/2 bottle dry white wine
    1 cup red wine vinegar
    2 onions, quartered
    2 carrots, sliced
    Green part of 2 leeks, washed well and coarsely
        chopped
    1 teaspoon black or white peppercorns
    1 bay leaf
    1 parsley sprig

1. First, prepare the sauce: cook the cream and tomato in a saucepan over moderately high heat until reduced by half or until it is thickened. Add the basil and salt and pepper to taste. The sauce should be prepared while the lobsters are poaching.

2. In a large kettle or lobster pot combine the water, wine, vinegar, onions, carrots, leeks, peppercorns, bay leaf, and parsley. Bring to a boil and add the lobsters. Poach the lobsters for 5 minutes from the moment they are added. Remove the lobsters, let them stand for 2 minutes, or until they are slightly cooled, and remove the claws. Separate the tail from the head and remove the insides from the head. Rinse the head in warm water and split the head shell in half. Remove the fan-shaped fin, rinse and reserve it. Remove the meat from the tail. Remove the meat from the claws as carefully as possible, keeping the meat intact. Rinse the tail shell in warm water and reserve it.

3. Slice the tail meat into 1/4-inch slices. Keep the claw tips in the poaching liquid to keep them

Mirabelle's Poached Lobster, served here with a spinach timbale

warm. Arrange the tail and head shells decoratively on a plate and arrange all of the tail slices in the head shells. Nap the lobster with the sauce and arrange the claw tips decoratively on the plate. Place fan-shaped tail fin decoratively at bottom of plate.

Makes 4 servings.

Lobster and Scallops over Rice

While seafood pairs wonderfully with pasta, it is also delicious over rice. This is a new favorite of mine; you could also prepare it with all lobster or scallops.

    3 cups chicken stock, preferably homemade
        (see page 47)
    1 1/2 cups rice
    1 cup fresh or frozen peas
    1 cup finely chopped carrots
    Salt and pepper
    1 1 1/2-pound lobster, cooked (see page 119)
    2 tablespoons butter
    1 pound bay scallops
    2 tablespoons minced fresh basil or 2 teaspoons
        dried
    2 cloves garlic, minced
    1/2 cup dry vermouth
    1 cup heavy cream
    Lemon wedges

1. Bring stock to a boil in a medium saucepan. Stir in rice, peas, and carrots. Season with salt and pepper. Cover, reduce heat, and cook over low heat for 20 minutes or until rice is done.

2. Meanwhile, remove lobster meat from shell and cut into bite-size pieces. Heat butter in a large sauté pan. Add lobster and scallops and toss over high heat for about 2 minutes; scallops will cook quickly. Remove and set aside. Add basil and garlic, cook briefly, then stir in the vermouth and heavy cream. Cook over high heat, stirring, until sauce is thick enough to coat back of a spoon. Return seafood to sauce and keep warm over very low heat.

3. When rice is done, spoon on heated plates and top with seafood mixture. Serve with lemon wedges.

Makes 4 servings.

Rosario's Scallops, Scampi style

Roy Dragotta, assistant Suffolk County attorney, is a lover of Long Island scallops. He shared his version prepared in the style of Italian scampi. Dragotta counsels that the best bay scallops are served as simply as possible, just a quick sauté with some lemon. However, should you want a change, this approach fits the bill.

4 tablespoons lightly salted butter
1/2 cup olive oil
3 cloves garlic, minced
1/4 cup dry white wine
2 tablespoons lemon juice, freshly squeezed
Dash Worcestershire sauce
Dash Tabasco sauce
1/2 teaspoon salt
1 to 1 1/2 pounds fresh scallops
3/4 cup plain bread crumbs
1/4 cup minced fresh parsley or 2 tablespoons
    dried
Lemon wedges

1. Melt the butter in a baking pan large enough to hold the scallops in a single layer. Stir in the oil, garlic, wine, lemon juice, Worcestershire sauce, Tabasco, and salt. Mix well, then add the scallops, spreading evenly over the bottom of the pan and tossing gently to coat. Marinate 2 to 3 hours.

2. After marinating, place on broiling pan in 1 layer, sprinkle with bread crumbs and broil on top rack for 2 to 3 minutes until just bubbly. Serve immediately, garnished with lemon wedges and parsley.

Makes 6 servings.

Deviled Scallops

1 1/2 pounds scallops (halved if using
    sea scallops)
4 tablespoons butter, softened
1/2 teaspoon dry mustard
Pinch cayenne pepper
1/2 teaspoon powdered ginger
1 1/2 tablespoons flour
Salt to taste
1/2 cup hot milk
1/2 cup half and half
1/2 cup fresh white bread crumbs
2 tablespoons melted butter

1. Place scallops in a saucepan and heat gently for a minute. Remove from heat; pour off any juice.

2. Beat the butter until creamy, blend well with the dry mustard, cayenne pepper, ginger, flour, and salt. Blend in hot milk and half and half; mix with the scallops.

3. Put the mixture into individual large scallop shells, ramekins, or in a baking dish. Sprinkle with bread crumbs and melted butter. Bake in a preheated 400 degree oven for 6 to 8 minutes until top is nicely browned.

Makes 6 servings.

Jules Bond's Best Scallops

Of all the good food I've enjoyed at Jules Bond's house, this is the best—the simplest and the sweetest bay scallops, ever. Scallops are delicious with a semi-dry German white such as a Spätlese from Deinhard, Anheuser, or Sichel.

1 1/2 pounds bay scallops
1/3 cup dry vermouth
1 small clove garlic, crushed in a garlic press
1 teaspoon salt
White pepper to taste
Fine white bread crumbs
8 tablespoons butter, approximately
Lemon wedges for garnish

1. Place scallops in a bowl; add the vermouth, garlic, salt, and pepper. Mix well and let marinate for 1 hour.

2. Drain scallops and pat dry with paper towels. Roll them in bread crumbs and shake loose excess crumbs. Heat butter in a skillet. Sauté the scallops over fairly high heat, not too many at a time, for 2 to 3 minutes until they are golden brown. Remove them with a slotted spoon; keep warm. Repeat, using remaining scallops.

3. When serving, garnish with lemon wedges.

Makes 6 servings.

Scallops in Garlic-Ginger Sauce

For sauce:
1 tablespoon sugar
3 tablespoons soy sauce
2 tablespoons sherry
1 tablespoon cornstarch
1 tablespoon water
1 tablespoon vinegar
2 teaspoons finely chopped fresh ginger
3 cloves garlic, mashed

To cook:
1 pound bay scallops
3 tablespoons cornstarch
Vegetable oil
1 pound broccoli, trimmed and cut
  into flowerettes
1 6-ounce can water chestnuts, sliced
1 tablespoon chili oil, optional
3 tablespoons chicken broth

1. Combine sugar, soy sauce, sherry, cornstarch, water, vinegar, ginger, and garlic in a small bowl. Let stand at least 15 minutes.

2. Dredge scallops in cornstarch. Heat a small amount of oil in wok and add scallops. Cook until golden, about 1 or 2 minutes. Add broccoli and water chestnuts and cook 30 seconds. Remove scallop mixture with slotted spoon and set aside.

3. If using chili oil, drain vegetable oil in wok. Heat chili oil, add scallop mixture. Stir-fry to coat well. Stir chicken broth into garlic sauce and add to skillet. Stir-fry for 1 to 2 minutes until sauce is bubbly and heated through.

Makes 4 servings.

Scallops with Tomatoes and Saffron

It is crucial to use only ripe, sweet fresh tomatoes, not the cottony winter variety. Otherwise, substitute canned Italian-style plum tomatoes.

1 1/2 pounds bay scallops
Flour
Pinch saffron
2/3 cup white wine
4 tablespoons olive oil
4 cloves garlic, minced
4 medium ripe tomatoes, seeded and diced or
  16-ounce can Italian plum tomatoes, drained
1 teaspoon thyme
1 teaspoon oregano
1 bay leaf
Salt and pepper to taste
Juice of 1/2 lemon

1. Pat scallops dry with paper towels, then dust lightly with flour. Shake off excess. Set aside. Moisten saffron in wine.

2. Heat oil in a sauté pan and sauté garlic briefly; add scallops and cook over medium heat, stirring often, about 2 minutes. Remove with slotted spoon and set aside. Add wine to pan and cook over high heat 1 minute. Add tomatoes, thyme, oregano, and bay leaf to pan. Cook over high heat until slightly thickened, about 10 minutes. Season with salt and pepper, and cook another 5 minutes.

3. Remove bay leaf. Add scallops and lemon juice and cook just long enough to reheat.

Makes 4 servings.

Scallops & Scalloping

For bayman Arnold Leo, the only good scallop is one that he catches that morning and cooks in his own kitchen that afternoon. "Freshness, that's what I'm talking about," says Leo, an East Hampton bayman and secretary for the association of same. "I'm eating scallops I caught the same day, it makes quite a difference."

"I'm not at all in favor of that bread-crumb-with-sauce kind of thing," he adds. "I cook them very simply in oil on a kind of medium heat stirring constantly only for a very few minutes until just done. Maybe a squeeze of lemon juice, maybe some salt and pepper."

The scallop out of Long Island's East End bays —Peconic, Gardiners, Shinnecock, and Napeague— deserves such tender loving care. Not to be confused with its cousin, the larger sea scallop, or distant relative, the smaller southern or calico scallop, the true bay scallop is one of the area's finest products, caught fresh only during the short season starting the third Monday in September through March 31st. Unlike stationary clams and oysters, bay scallops are able to move about by opening and closing their shells, lurching forward as they force water out of their body cavities. The muscle that does all this work is the part of the scallop that is eaten, and the longer into the season, the larger the muscle grows.

Most baymen work alone or with one other partner—the state limits the daily catch to ten bushels per person, or twenty for two working together; in town waters the limit for two is generally fifteen bushels. "You go to certain places that traditionally have the best places," says Leo. "But you do have to look. Believe me, the word gets around really fast—you can almost tell from a mile away if someone's putting scallops on board. If he's obviously busy and you're not catching anything, you head over his way. If he's standing up gazing around, you know he's looking as much as you are."

He is the correct pronoun; a few women join their spouses on the water, but most often they cull the scallops from the extraneous matter that the dredges pick up. "The wife is very rarely hauling dredges; it's extremely physical work," says Leo. The wet dredges, hopefully filled with scallops, are ex-tremely heavy, well over fifty pounds, and must be lifted on board where the contents are sorted. The legal scallop must be at least 2¼ inches, measured from the middle of the hinge to the middle of the outer curve. When a bayman works a scallop bed, he most often drops his dredges—from six to eight—off both sides of the boat. "The most efficient method is to circle on the bed," says Leo. "After one circle you pull up those dredges and drop them on the cull board. Then you reverse the direction and the other side catches while you cull."

Since the dredge brings up whatever is on the bottom, a variety of shells, a certain number of starfish, and just general debris need to be culled from the precious scallops. Baymen are obligated not to throw starfish back in, but to keep as many of the vicious predators away from the scallop beds as possible. "When a starfish gets those arms around a shellfish, then with the rasp-like tongue, partly saws through, partly pries it open, it simply sucks the life juices out," says Leo.

"The biggest nuisance is the various kinds of seaweed, like sputnik grass," adds Leo. Not the official name, Leo explains, sputnik grass is the local term for the type of seaweed that appeared in these waters the year the Russians sent up Sputnik. "Then there's eel grass—in some locales it can be extremely thick," he says. "It has the virtue of dying off later in winter so you have a clean bed of scallops."

Eel grass is important, though, in the life cycle of the bay scallop, a favorite spot for the tiny scallops to hide out. "Eel grass keeps the scallops out of the sediment," says Robert Malouf, shellfish biologist at the State University of New York at Stony Brook. "Late in summer they drop off to the bottom where they finish their life cycle." Scallops live for only twenty-four months, and consequently, are vulnerable to fluctuating environmental pressures. "Among hard clams, individuals may live twenty years, so you have some insulation against the bad years," says Malouf. "But for scallops, all of which are going to die after twenty-four months or so, you are totally dependent on the reproductive success of the last year. It's a high risk life."

Scallops haven't been studied much, certainly

Arnold Leo and Elizabeth Shaffner bringing in scallops

far less than Long Island's famous hard clam, says John Scotti of Sea Grant. "There's a general feeling that scallops are much more subject to environmental conditions. You have to have winter conditions that don't kill them," says Scotti. "The environment is much more critical than for other species. On the other side, scallops can recoup more quickly. That's why the numbers go up and down."

Zanghi's Peconic Bay Scallops with Pistachios

The pistachios add an interesting touch to these scallops.

1 1/2 pounds scallops
2 tablespoons olive oil
2 tablespoons unsalted butter
1/2 cup shelled pistachio nuts
1/4 cup white wine
1/2 teaspoon lemon juice
2 tablespoons heavy cream
1/2 teaspoon thyme or marjoram
Salt, pepper, and nutmeg to taste

1. Refrigerate scallops overnight in a stainless steel colander, allowing them to drain. If the accumulated juices are free from odors, reserve and set aside. If not, discard.

2. Heat a 15-inch skillet over high heat, add the oil and 1 tablespoon butter. When butter is melted, but not brown, toss in the scallops and sauté for 2 minutes, constantly shaking the pan. Season, shake the pan once or twice, and remove the scallops with a slotted spoon.

3. Pour off excess oil, leaving just a film. Add nuts and sauté until lightly brown. Add the wine and lemon juice to deglaze the pan, then add the cream and reserved scallop juices, if using. Bring to a rapid boil and reduce by half. Sprinkle with the herbs and season to taste with salt, pepper, and nutmeg. Return scallops to pan. Add remaining butter. Blend briefly but do not overcook. Transfer to slightly warmed serving dishes and serve immediately.

Makes 4 servings.

Scallops in Chili Sauce

Chili paste with garlic is a pungent Chinese seasoning that adds zing to any stir-fry; look for it in stores specializing in Oriental ingredients.

For sauce:
2 tablespoons chili paste with garlic
6 tablespoons ketchup
2 1/2 tablespoons sherry
2 tablespoons soy sauce
3 tablespoons sugar
1 tablespoon cornstarch

Peanut oil
1 dried hot chili pepper, minced
3 tablespoons minced ginger
3 cloves garlic, minced
1 bunch scallions, chopped
1 onion, finely chopped
2 8-ounce cans water chestnuts, sliced in half crosswise
1 1/2 pounds sea scallops, cut in half crosswise if large

1. Combine the sauce ingredients: chili paste, ketchup, sherry, soy sauce, sugar, and cornstarch. Stir thoroughly and set aside.

2. Add enough oil to a wok or bottom of deep sauté pan to generously film the bottom. Over high heat, add chili pepper, ginger, garlic, scallions, and onion and stir-fry a minute or two, adding more oil if needed. Add water chestnuts and cook, stirring, another 2 minutes. Add scallops, stir-fry 2 more minutes.

3. Stir in sauce and cook another minute or two. Serve over rice.

Makes 4 servings.

Long Island Fried Mussels

Instead of fried clams, try fried mussels.

3 dozen mussels
1 cup milk
1 cup flour
1/4 teaspoon pepper
1/4 teaspoon salt
2 eggs
1 tablespoon water
1 tablespoon oil
Pinch of cayenne pepper or Tabasco sauce
1 cup dry, unseasoned bread crumbs
1 cup vegetable oil

For sauce:
1 tablespoon oil
1/2 teaspoon chopped garlic
4 tablespoons chopped scallions
8 whole canned tomatoes, chopped
1/4 teaspoon Tabasco sauce
Salt and pepper to taste

1. Wash and debeard mussels. Insert knife between shells and pop open—mussels are quite easy to open. Remove mussels. Soak mussels in milk for 2 hours, stirring every 30 minutes.

2. Combine flour, pepper and salt. Beat eggs, blend in the water, tablespoon of oil, cayenne or Tabasco. Have bread crumbs ready.

3. Drain mussels and pat dry. In this order, dip them in the flour, egg mixture, and bread crumbs, patting the crumbs in place. Place mussels on waxed paper on a tray and refrigerate until ready to cook.

4. To cook, heat oil to 350 degrees in a large frying pan. Place mussels in oil, being careful not to overcrowd. Fry until golden brown, turn, then drain on paper towels. Put on a cookie sheet in a preheated 250 degree oven until all mussels are cooked and ready to serve.

5. For sauce: heat oil and sauté garlic and scallions briefly. Add tomatoes and sauté 5 minutes to blend flavors. Add Tabasco, salt and pepper. Use as sauce for fried mussels.

Makes 4 servings.

Raffaele Saccucci's Mussels Marinara

5 to 6 pounds mussels
2 to 3 tablespoons chopped prosciutto or
    salt pork
2 to 4 tablespoons olive oil
3 to 4 cloves garlic, minced
2 28-ounce cans whole Italian plum tomatoes
    in purée, coarsely chopped
1 28-ounce can crushed Italian plum tomatoes
1/2 cup loosely packed fresh basil, chopped, or
    1 tablespoon dried
1 bay leaf
1 teaspoon red pepper flakes, or to taste
1/2 cup red wine
1 large bunch Italian parsley, leaves and stems
    finely chopped separately

1. Clean mussels, soak, and reserve (see page 36).

2. Using a large Dutch oven or soup pot, sauté prosciutto or salt pork with oil until lightly browned. Add garlic and sauté for 2 to 3 minutes on low heat until golden.

3. Add the tomatoes and their purée, basil, bay leaf, red pepper flakes, and wine. Add the chopped parsley stems to tomatoes.

4. Simmer on low heat, uncovered, stirring occasionally until mixture starts to bubble. Add mussels and reserved parsley leaves. Cover and continue simmering until mussels open. Ladle immediately into large soup bowls. Serve with lots of crusty bread, an empty platter for the shells, and extra napkins.

Makes 4 to 6 servings.

POULTRY & MEAT

PERFECT ROAST DUCK

It was inevitable, the search for the perfect method to roast a duckling. Even though sautéed duck breasts are chic and, indeed delicious, a basic roast duckling is one of the best ways to present the bird. That is, *if* you succeed in getting a crisp skin and *if* you manage to cook the legs without drying out the breast meat or cook off most of the fat, and yet leave enough for flavor.

Borrowing a technique from Karen Lee, Chinese cookbook author and a great cook, makes the process a cinch: she separates the skin from the duckling breast with a knife and lets the bird dry out. While I've simplified her approach somewhat, the essential idea remains. Pull the skin up, and away from the breast meat, shoving your fingers as far as you can into the bird. Then, turn the duck over. Remove any bits of fat or other material so that the underside flap of skin is smooth. This allows the fat to pour out when the duck is cooking. Scientific, or not, it works.

The Chinese hang their ducklings so that the skin gets very dry and after cooking remains very crisp. I have found that refrigerating the duckling uncovered overnight accomplishes the same thing. Granted, this approach takes time and requires some advance planning, but it certainly isn't hard. I have also hung a couple of ducklings on strings from a two-by-four placed across my kitchen counters, put a fan on them, and dried them out in a couple hours.

When the skin is as crisp as this method provides, I don't think a sauce is necessary. However, a chutney, as in the recipe on page 130, makes a fine accompaniment, setting off the flavor of the duckling with its slightly sweet/sour tang.

Long Island Duck with Fall Vegetables

2 large ducks, about 5 pounds each
2 tablespoons brown sugar
1/4 cup dry vermouth
1/2 cup duck or chicken broth
1 teaspoon rosemary
1 large yellow turnip (rutabaga)
3 carrots
2 ribs celery
3 large potatoes
1 teaspoon rosemary
Salt and pepper

For sauce:
1/2 cup dry vermouth
1 teaspoon rosemary
1 cup heavy cream

1. Prepare ducks for roasting (see at left). Combine sugar, vermouth, broth, and rosemary in a small saucepan; cook over medium heat about 5 minutes. Reserve. Place ducks on roasting rack and roast in a preheated 375 degree oven for 1 hour, basting occasionally with sugar-broth mixture.

2. Meanwhile, prepare vegetables. Peel turnip and cut into chunks, about 3/4 inch. Peel carrots and cut approximately the same size as the turnip. Do likewise with the celery. Peel potatoes and cut in 3/4-inch chunks. When duck has cooked 1 hour, remove 3 to 4 tablespoons of duck fat and place in another roasting pan. Add vegetables and toss to combine.

3. Reduce oven to 350 degrees. Add vegetable pan and roast another hour with duck. Continue basting duck occasionally. The vegetables will cook in 1 to 1 1/2 hours, the duck will take about 2 1/2 hours total cooking time. When the vegetables are cooked,

season with salt and pepper and add about 1 table-spoon basting sauce.

4. When ducks are done, remove to a carving platter. Pour off duck fat and place roasting pan on burner. Prepare the sauce over high heat: pour in vermouth and cook, scraping the bottom to incorporate browned bits. Add remaining basting sauce, rosemary, and cream. Cook over high heat until thickened enough to coat the back of the spoon. Serve sauce separately. Cut ducks in half and remove the backbones. Serve ½ duck per person with a spoonful of roasted vegetables.

Makes 4 servings.

Perfect Roast Duck with Pear Chutney

Zinfandel, California's unique varietal, will round out the fruit flavors inthe chutney and cut through any traces of fat in the duck. Try Sutter Home, Sonoma Vineyards, or Round Hill.

> 2 4- to 4½-pound ducks
> Salt and pepper to taste
> ¼ cup pear brandy, optional
>
> *For chutney:*
> ⅔ cup white vinegar
> 1 cup sugar
> 2 cups peeled, chopped pears (2 large firm
>   pears, about ¾ pound)
> ¼ cup golden raisins
> 2 cloves garlic, minced
> 1 medium onion, chopped
> 1 rib celery, chopped
> 1½ tablespoons minced ginger
> ½ teaspoon ground coriander
> Pinch cayenne pepper
> Salt and pepper to taste
> Juice of ½ lemon

1. Begin preparations for duck 24 hours before serving, longer if duck is frozen. Remove liver, heart, and gizzard from duck; rinse inside and out and dry with paper towels. Use a sharp knife to separate the skin over the breast from the meat. Using your hand, push between the skin and the breast as far as you can, about 4 to 5 inches. This allows the fat to drip out during cooking. If the skin breaks, sew with needle and thread.

2. Let duck sit on a rack in the refrigerator for at least 8 hours or overnight to dry the skin. Or, hang in front of a fan or in a cool spot for a few hours.

3. Preheat oven to 350 degrees. Season duck with salt and pepper and place on rack over pan in oven. Bake for 1 hour breast side up, turn, let fat run out to pan, and bake another hour breast side down. Turn breast side up and brush with pear brandy if desired. Bake another 20 to 30 minutes. Serve plain or with pear chutney on the side.

4. To make chutney, combine vinegar and sugar in a saucepan. Bring to the boil; add pears, raisins, garlic, onion, celery, ginger, coriander, and cayenne. Cook over low heat, uncovered, stirring occasionally for 1½ hours or until very thick. Season with salt and pepper to taste. Add lemon juice to taste. Makes 1 cup.

Makes 4 servings.

Roast Duck with Apples

A dry Alsace Riesling wine brings harmony here.

> 2 4½-pound ducks
> Salt and pepper to taste
> 5 tablespoons butter
> 3 firm apples, peeled, cored, and cut into thick
>   wedges
> 1 cup dry white wine
> ½ cup apple brandy or Cognac
> 1 cup heavy cream

1. Prepare duck for roasting (see page 129). Season cavity and outside of each duck with salt and pepper. Set on a rack, and roast breast side up in a preheated 350 degree oven for 1 hour. Turn breast side down and roast another hour. Turn breast side up and roast another 20 to 30 minutes, or until the juices run clear.

2. Meanwhile, heat butter in a sauté pan and sauté the apples in 3 tablespoons butter until golden and tender. Set aside; reheat just before serving.

3. Remove duck from oven and place on carving platter. Pour off duck fat in pan; place pan on

burner. Add wine to pan and cook over high heat, stirring constantly, until reduced by half. Lower the heat, stir in the brandy and heavy cream. Simmer over medium heat until thick enough to coat the back of a spoon.

4. To serve, gently reheat apple slices. Cut the ducks in half, cutting away the backbones. Arrange the apple slices on a platter, top with the sauce and duck halves.

Makes 4 servings.

Roast Long Island Duck with Beach Plum Sauce

John C. Ross also shared this approach for roast duckling as served at his restaurant, Ross' in Southold.

2 4½-pound ducks
1 onion, unpeeled
Salt
2 tablespoons honey

For sauce:
2 cups duck or chicken stock
   (see page 136 or 47)
⅔ cup red wine vinegar
¾ cup brown sugar
2 tablespoons flour mixed with
   2 tablespoons butter
1 orange
1 lemon
1 cinnamon stick
2 whole cloves
Freshly ground black pepper
2 to 3 tablespoons wild beach plum jam or
   other good fruit jam

1. Remove giblets from each duck cavity and rinse duck thoroughly. If desired, follow directions to roast duck, page 129. Cut off tail, flap, and wing tips. Place half of the onion and a teaspoon of salt in each cavity. Tie duck tightly with butcher's twine so that wings and legs are held against body. Place duck on a rack in a roasting pan with the breast facing up. Puncture skin with a sharp fork. Brush honey over outside of ducks.

2. Turn duck to one side and place in a preheated 500-degree oven. Cook until lightly browned, about 15 minutes. Turn duck to other side and brown another 15 minutes. Reduce heat to 425 degrees and turn duck breast side up. Cover loosely with foil and cook exactly 1½ hours. Remove from oven and cool at room temperature.

3. Meanwhile, prepare sauce. Heat stock in a heavy saucepot. Combine vinegar and brown sugar in a separate pan and reduce to a syrup. Add flour/butter mixture by bits to stock, stir, and bring to a boil. Cook until stock is slightly thickened. Squeeze juice of orange and lemon into thickened stock. Peel rinds and add. Add the cinnamon, cloves, and pepper; simmer for 30 minutes. Add reduced syrup and jam. Taste for seasoning. Strain before serving.

4. After duck is cool enough to handle, about 30 minutes, take a sharp heavy knife and pierce the top of the duck. Run the knife down the center of the breasts and to the side of the backbone until it is split in two halves. Cut along other side of backbone and remove. Using your fingers, remove rib bones and cartilage. Twist out thighbone, if desired. Reheat at 425 degrees for about 15 minutes. Serve with sauce.

Makes 4 servings.

Orange-Honey Barbequed Duck

2 5-pound ducks
Salt and pepper
2 6-ounce cans concentrated orange juice
1 cup water
2 8-ounce jars honey

1. Cut duck into leg and breast portions. Pat duck pieces dry and sprinkle both sides with salt and pepper. Place in an open roasting pan, skin side up, and cook for 1 hour over hot coals on grill.

2. Place orange juice, water, and honey in a blender or food processor and process until smooth.

3. After 1 hour turn duck skin side down. Do not pour off drippings. Pour orange and honey mixture over ducks and bake for 90 minutes, turning twice. Remove duck parts from pan, discard drippings, and brown on barbeque for 4 to 5 minutes on each side.

Makes 4 servings.

The Ubiquitous Long Island Duck

According to legend, a Yankee sea captain carrying a load of ducks from Peking in the late 1800s is responsible for Long Island's famous product, white Pekin duckling. It makes for a nice story, anyway. Happily, these immigrants did wend their way to Long Island, where they flourished in the ideal growing conditions of abundant fresh air and water.

They still flourish, although fewer in number than in the heydays of the late forties and early fifties, now that farmers are succumbing to the lure of the developer and the high cost of pollution controls. But 3½ million ducklings a year have to be taken seriously, especially when they command a premium price over the off-Island competitors.

Long Island birds are better. "No question about it," says Joe Birk, majordomo for the Long Island Duck Farmers Cooperative, Inc., and a man unbounded in his love and admiration for his product. "If for no other reason than we've been at it, perfecting it for 105 years."

Such perfection begins in the hatchery—many of the twenty farms have their own—where for twenty-eight days the eggs are nurtured at 99.25 degrees in trays that gently turn automatically each hour. Breeders produce about 100 baby ducklings each year of their two- to three-year life. "These ducks will not lay on a nest; they sit on the eggs for a day or so, then they get bored and run around," says Douglas Corwin, who with his father Lloyd, runs the largest independent farm, Crescent Duck Farm in Aquebogue. Back in the early 1900s, Corwin's great grandfather kept a couple of buildings of chickens; abandoned duck eggs would then be hatched by willing hens.

"It's very simple, all mechanical now," Corwin says, "but I've got more frustrations in that darn hatchery trying to get the darn things to hatch out at a successful rate." It seems that ducks that grow bigger wind up laying fewer eggs and these eggs don't "hatch out" as well. Corwin's task is to find the precise genetic combination that matches skill in egg cracking with big meaty birds. He is also trying to increase the size of the breast which now accounts for about forty-one percent of the lean meat on a duckling (the leg and thigh account for forty-four percent, the rest is on the wings and carcass).

Once they pass the first crucial days of their lives, they spend the next seven weeks dining on a mix of corn and soybean meals, a little fish meal, some meat scraps, and maybe some bakery meal thrown in.

It takes about thirty acres for Louis Gallo and his brother Mike to raise about three hundred and fifty thousand ducklings and some turkeys on their Patchogue farm each year. The difference? Gallo says it's like a hothouse tomato compared to one that's vine-ripened. But Corwin, who has turned primarily to indoor sheds for the million ducklings he produces, says he finds no difference—"Except that outside the feathers bleach more."

In any event, the Long Island climate is kind to the duckling, a short squatty bird that can't fly, and, in fact, can barely walk. It is, to its credit, just a great swimmer. "White Pekin ducks, treated properly, are very very hearty and on Long Island, they just thrive," says Birk, heralding the relatively mild winters and temperate summers.

By the 49th day, give or take three, the ducklings have put on seven pounds, converting about 2½ pounds of feed into each pound of live weight. Virtually all of the feed is trucked in, mostly from the Midwest grain belt. "Our property here is too valuable for grain," says Gallo, who uses about four thousand tons a year, twenty pounds of feed per duckling. Growers aim for 4½ to 5 pounds dressed weight, smaller if the ducklings are destined as the featured roast on a restaurant menu.

From holding pen to blast freezer—about seventy percent are shipped frozen, although the move to shipping them fresh is growing—takes a little less than an hour. The ducklings move along overhead tracks at a rapid clip, passing through a rotary drum that beats the feathers off, then through two dips in wax to eliminate the fine down. Duck feathers, by the way, represent an important return for the growers, as do the feet which are shipped off to Hong Kong to be processed into favored delicacies.

Each bird is scrutinized for wholesomeness by a U.S. Department of Agriculture inspector, who rejects a mere one percent. "The inspector sees that the entire bird, the head, all the essential organs are there. It's like performing an autopsy on each and every bird," says Birk. Down the assembly line, the ducklings are then graded strictly on looks, with A the top grade for a perfectly shaped bird with no tears or parts missing.

The growers don't bother to differentiate between male and female ducklings even though the male ducklings grow a little bit larger and females a little bit faster; the males are a little leaner and females a bit fattier. "But it's very hard to say just from eating a bird if you have a male or female; I could speculate, that's all I could do," says Corwin. The male also converts feed into meat a little more efficiently since the female is busy producing more fat, a task that consumes more calories. On the whole, though, the average duckling has about twenty to twenty-five percent fat, or about one pound of fat per duck.

All that fat—baby fat, after all, for they're still young at seven weeks—means a tasty bird. It also means a cook has to know his or her way around a kitchen to retain the juices while siphoning off the fat. "It's as easy to prepare duckling as 1, 2, 3," says Birk. "It doesn't have to be intimidating to make." Indeed, not; roasted at 350 degrees for 2½ to 3 hours (see page 129 for our humble instructions for the perfect roast duck) virtually all fat cooks away. Save that fat, or render it from the duckling you cut up into parts, and you will have the best medium for roasting potatoes ever known to man.

Don't worry about the fat, urges Birk; an equal weight of duckling lean meat has about half the fat content of steak or spareribs. Another nutritional bonus—duckling has less sodium than turkey or chicken and slightly less cholesterol than the rest of the poultry group.

Duck with Oriental Sauce

2 4½- to 5-pound ducks
2 onions
2 carrots
2 ribs celery
Salt and pepper to taste
2 1-inch pieces fresh ginger, chopped

For sauce:
4 whole navel oranges, peeled and separated
    into segments
Whole segments from 1 lime
Whole segments from ½ lemon
6 to 8 slices fresh ginger
4 tablespoons soy sauce
4 tablespoons dark corn syrup
1 tablespoon Cognac
Dash of white pepper

1. Cut off wing tips and place in a roasting pan. Cut onions, carrots, and celery into 1-inch chunks, sprinkle with salt and pepper, and stuff into each duck cavity. Stuff 1-inch ginger pieces into cavity. Place ducks on top of the wing tips and roast in a preheated 350 degree oven for 60 to 70 minutes.

2. While duck is cooking, prepare sauce. In a heavy skillet combine orange, lime, and lemon segments, ginger, soy sauce, corn syrup, Cognac, and pepper. Cook until smooth, stirring constantly. After duck has cooked 60 to 70 minutes, baste duck once with sauce and cook 30 minutes longer.

3. Remove duck from oven and cut into serving pieces. Serve with sauce on the side.

Makes 4 servings.

Braised Duck with Almonds and Raisins

Libby Hillman developed this duck recipe for her cookbook, *New Lessons in Gourmet Cooking.* Inspired by a trip to Mexico, she combined flavorings there of orange, tomato, and nuts.

1 4 to 5-pound duck, cut into serving pieces
1 tablespoon coarse salt

½ teaspoon freshly ground black pepper
1 cup flour
1 cup tomato purée (preferably fresh if you
    have sweet ripe tomatoes)
1 cup fresh orange juice
1 onion, diced
2 cloves garlic, minced
¼ cup slivered almonds
¼ cup raisins
½ teaspoon oregano
¼ teaspoon thyme
1 bay leaf
¼ cup chopped fresh parsley
½ cup dry white wine
2 tablespoons flour, optional

1. Cut away any excess fat from duck; sprinkle with salt and let stand for 30 minutes. Dry duck very well. Season with pepper and dredge in flour. Heat a large heavy pot slowly over low heat. Brown the duck a few pieces at a time. Do not add fat, since the duck fat will melt as it browns. When all the pieces are crisp and brown, pour off all of the fat.

2. Return duck to pot along with tomato purée, orange juice, onion, garlic, almonds, raisins, oregano, thyme, bay leaf, parsley, and wine. Cover and simmer over low heat for 1½ to 2 hours or place in a preheated 325 degree oven for at least 2 hours.

3. Remove duck from sauce. Let the casserole cool. Take a cup of large ice cubes and throw on the sauce. The cubes will congeal the fat; pick up and throw out. If sauce is too hot, this won't work; the ice cubes will just melt. Or if you have time, set the sauce in the freezer; in about 2 hours the fat will come to the top and harden. It is then easily removed. To thicken sauce, mix 2 tablespoons flour with 2 tablespoons of duck fat and add it gradually to simmering sauce.

Makes 2 to 3 servings.

20/20/20 Duckling

Joe Birk of the Long Island Duck Farmers Cooperative is proud of this recipe, and rightly so. It demonstrates his main thesis that duck is very easy to cook. I added the seasonings to the original recipe from the cooperative. If desired, you could cut back on the cayenne pepper since it is quite potent when cooking; oddly, it becomes very mild when the duck is done.

1 tablespoon salt
1 teaspoon sugar
1 teaspoon cayenne pepper
2 teaspoons black pepper
2 4- to 5-pound ducks, cut into quarters

1. Combine salt, sugar, and peppers. Rub mixture onto duck skin (there will be extra) and let stand for 30 minutes.

2. Heat an electric frying pan to 350 degrees. Place duck pieces skin side down and cook, covered, for 20 minutes. Turn over and cook, covered, another 20 minutes. Turn and cook, covered, another 20 minutes.

Makes 4 servings.

Duck Breasts in Green Peppercorn Sauce

For sheer elegance and simplicity, it's hard to top these duck breasts in a rich green peppercorn sauce. You could also use the same approach for fillet mignon, substituting beef stock for the duck stock and cooking it slightly longer. I like to serve potatoes roasted in duck fat with this dish.

2 tablespoons butter
Breasts from 2 5-pound ducks
Salt and pepper to taste
1/3 cup Cognac
1 1/2 tablespoons green peppercorns, crushed
1/2 cup duck or chicken stock
1 cup heavy cream

1. Heat butter in a large sauté pan. Season breasts with salt and pepper to taste. Sauté over medium heat about 3 to 5 minutes each side, 3 minutes for rare. Remove breasts and keep warm.

2. Add Cognac and flambé. When flames subside, add the green peppercorns, stock, and heavy cream. Cook over high heat until reduced and thick enough to coat the back of a spoon. Pour any accumulated juices from the duck back into the sauce.

3. Slice the duck on the diagonal and flare pieces on a plate. Top with the sauce and serve immediately.

Makes 4 servings.

Duck Breasts in Orange Sauce

Instead of a whole roast duck à la orange, try duck breasts instead. This sauce is very intense, so you don't need to serve much of it.

For marinade:
1/2 cup lemon juice
1/2 cup orange juice
2 bay leaves
1 teaspoon fresh minced ginger
2 cloves garlic, minced
Breasts from 3 ducks
Duck fat or oil

For sauce:
2 tablespoons sugar
3 tablespoons red wine vinegar
1 1/2 cups duck or chicken stock, approximately
4 shallots, minced
1/2 cup Madeira
Juice of 2 oranges
2 teaspoons sugar, optional
3 to 4 tablespoons butter

1. Combine lemon and orange juices, bay leaves, ginger, and garlic. Cut away excess fat on the sides of the duck breasts. Score the skin down to the meat in 1/2 inch intervals down and across so that you have 1/2-inch squares. Marinate duck 2 hours.

2. In a small saucepan, combine the sugar and vinegar and cook over medium-high heat until a light caramel color; do not burn. Add stock, stir, and cook over high heat until reduced by half. Set aside.

3. Remove duck from marinade. Strain marinade and set aside. Add enough duck fat or oil to coat the bottom of a large sauté pan and cook duck breasts skin side down about 8 to 10 minutes until

skin browns; turn and cook another 3 minutes, depending upon desired degree of doneness. Remove duck and keep warm.

4. Pour off excess fat, leaving a thin film over the bottom of the pan. Add shallots to pan and sauté briefly. Stir in Madeira and cook over high heat to reduce. Add strained marinade, reserved duck stock, and orange juice. Cook over high heat until thick enough to coat the back of a spoon, about 10 to 15 minutes. Taste, and add sugar if oranges aren't very sweet. Season with salt and pepper to taste. Stir in butter just before serving.

5. To serve, slice duck breasts on the diagonal. Arrange on plates and pour sauce over, passing additional sauce at the table.

Makes 4 servings.

Le Canard en Deux Services

Guy and Maria Reuge of Restaurant Mirabelle find this is one of their most popular main courses, duck served two ways. First, they serve the duck breast with a baked apple (page 158) and corn pancakes (page 84), followed by the duck leg and red cabbage (page 77). The recipe is long, yes, but taken step-by-step, it is within reach of a home cook. Prepare one day in advance.

4 4¹/₂- to 5-pound Long Island ducks
¹/₃ cup kosher salt
1 bouquet garni (1 bay leaf, 1 branch fresh thyme, ¹/₃ cup diced celery tops, 1 clove garlic, 1 small shallot, 1 parsley sprig, 1 tablespoon cracked peppercorns, and 1 tablespoon dried sage wrapped in a cheesecloth)

HOW TO BONE A DUCK

Paula Wolfert, in her latest cookbook, *The Cooking of South-West France*, was an inspiration to me, giving me the confidence to bone a duck. Her directions are clear and believe me, once you've boned a duck or two, you'll find it's no big deal. With a boned duck, you have many options, including preparing a stock from the carcass and rendering the fat so you can prepare the best potatoes ever.

The following directions are adapted from Wolfert's text; for a more detailed explanation and other excellent recipes for duck, consult her book.

1. Place duck breast side down and cut away the large flap of skin around the neck. Turn duck breast side up, and using the tip of a sharp knife, cut out the wishbone. You can feel the bone with your fingers; guide the knife around it. When you've loosened it from the meat, you can pull the wishbone out easily.

2. Cut along the center of the breast down the breast bone to remove one of the breasts. As the knife slides down to the carcass, gently pull the meat back. You can scrape the meat away from the bones with the tip of the knife. When the breast is nearly removed, you will see a section of fat between the breast and the leg and thigh; cut through that to remove the breast.

3. Gently pulling the meat and prodding with the tip of the knife, remove the leg and thigh from the carcass. Repeat on the other half.

4. Remove and reserve all excess fat and skin. If you want to render the fat, place all of the fat and skin in a large saucepan; add a few tablespoons water and simmer over medium heat for about 1 hour. Do not cook over high heat or the fat will not render properly. Strain into a clean container. Duck fat keeps 3 to 4 months refrigerated, and much longer in the freezer.

5. If desired, use carcass, neck, and wings to make a stock. Chop the carcass and add it with neck and wings to a large baking pan. Brown in a preheated 350 degree oven for 1 hour, turning occasionally. Place the browned bones along with 2 chopped carrots, 2 onions, halved, and a few black peppercorns in a stockpot. Cover with water, bring to a boil, then simmer 5 to 6 hours, skimming surface occasionally. Strain and refrigerate or freeze. If you reduce the strained stock even further, it can be frozen in ice cube trays. Then, to make a spectacular sauce, you just need to add a "cube" or two to the sauté pan.

For the stock:

Duck bones and carcasses from the ducks

3 pounds veal bones, browned lightly in a
   preheated 375 degree oven for 1 hour

2 onions, quartered

2 carrots, cut into chunks

1 bay leaf

Green part of 2 leeks, washed well

1/2 bottle dry white wine

For the sauce:

1 1/2 tablespoons honey

1 1/2 sticks sweet butter

Salt and pepper

1. Remove the breasts and legs from the ducks. (See page 136 for instructions.) Pat dry and arrange the breasts in a large roasting pan, uncovered, in the refrigerator for 24 hours. Spread the salt over the duck legs and arrange them in another large pan. Refrigerate for 24 hours.

2. Trim away excess fat from the duck after the breasts and legs have been removed. Add it to the carcasses and bones and roast them in a preheated 400 degree oven until the fat has melted and the bones are browned lightly, about 1 1/2 to 2 hours. Pour off the fat and reserve. Reserve the bones and carcasses for the duck stock.

3. Brown the duck legs skin side down in a frying pan over high heat, turn, and lightly brown the other side. The skin side should be well browned. Arrange the legs in the bottom of a large casserole and add the bouquet garni. Pour the reserved duck fat over the duck legs and bring the fat to a boil on top of the stove. When the fat is boiling, put the casserole in a preheated 250 degree oven and cook the duck legs for 2 hours. The duck fat should simmer but not boil. Remove the casserole from the oven and let the duck legs cool in the fat. Keep them refrigerated. (The legs will keep for up to 2 weeks if covered with the fat.)

4. Next, prepare the stock. In a large kettle, combine the reserved duck bones with the veal bones, onions, carrots, bay leaf, leeks, and white wine. Cover the bones with 4 to 5 inches of water. Bring the water to a boil and let the stock simmer over low heat for 3 to 4 hours, skimming the froth that rises to the top. Strain the stock into a large bowl; let cool and refrigerate.

5. To serve: Remove the fat from the top of the cooled stock. In a large saucepan, combine the stock with the honey and reduce the mixture over moder-

ately high heat until it is syrup-like. Add the butter 1 tablespoon at a time, stirring constantly, until the sauce is thickened. Add salt and pepper to taste.

6. Prepare the duck breasts. Grill them over hot coals about 5 inches from the heat, under a preheated broiler about 5 inches from the heat, or in a very hot frying pan over high heat for 3 minutes on each side for medium rare. Keep the breasts warm.

7. Meanwhile, remove the duck legs from the fat and arrange them in a roasting pan. Roast in a preheated 350 degree oven for about 15 minutes or until they release their fat and are crispy.

8. For the first service, slice the duck breasts thinly, fan each breast on a plate, and serve it with the baked apple and corn pancakes. Strain the sauce over the breasts, reserving half the sauce for the legs.

9. For the second service, arrange each leg on a plate and serve it with red cabbage. Nap the legs with the remaining sauce.

Makes 8 servings.

Grilled Duck Legs

This is a delicious way to use any extra legs left over after cooking duck breasts. Because the grill is covered, the legs get a lovely, smoky flavor; add mesquite or hickory chips to the coals, if desired. A lightly chilled Beaujolais goes nicely with the grilled duck.

2 cups heavy red wine

1/4 cup olive oil

4 cloves garlic, smashed

2 tablespoons chopped fresh basil or 2
   teaspoons dried

8 duck legs

1. Combine wine, oil, garlic, and basil and marinate the duck legs for 4 hours or overnight in refrigerator.

2. To cook, place legs in aluminum tray over very hot coals. Cover and cook for 45 minutes to an hour. Remove tray from grill, and place legs skin side down at edge of grill, away from the direct heat of the coals to crisp about 5 minutes.

Makes 4 servings.

Roast Chicken with Mushrooms and Herbs

Rather than stuffing the cavity of the bird, this method of slipping sautéed mushrooms and herbs under the skin makes for a particularly well-flavored chicken. Long Island's Lenz vineyards has a Pinot Noir you might do well to serve here.

1 4-pound roasting chicken
Kosher salt and freshly ground pepper
2 tablespoons butter or olive oil
$^1/_4$ cup minced shallots
1 tablespoon minced garlic
1 pound mushrooms, minced
1 tablespoon fresh thyme or $^1/_2$ teaspoon dried
2 tablespoons minced Italian parsley
$^1/_2$ teaspoon salt
$^1/_2$ teaspoon freshly ground pepper
$^1/_4$ cup toasted bread crumbs
2 tablespoons Madeira wine or sherry
$^1/_2$ cup white wine
$^1/_2$ cup chicken broth

1. Dry chicken; season with a sprinkling of salt and pepper.
2. Heat butter or oil in a skillet. Add shallots and garlic. Cook until wilted, about 2 or 3 minutes. Add mushrooms. Cook on high heat to reduce moisture, but do not let burn.
3. Add thyme, parsley, salt, pepper, and bread crumbs to form a paste. Set aside and cool thoroughly.
4. Starting at the neck of the chicken, separate the skin of the chicken from the flesh by gently working your fingers below the skin. Loosen the skin from the entire breast and legs. Preheat oven to 425 degrees.
5. Stuff the chicken with the prepared mixture, pushing it under the skin to cover legs and breast. Truss the chicken. Roast for 30 minutes. Reduce heat to 350 degrees. Baste chicken with white wine and broth and roast for another 30 minutes.

Makes 4 servings.

Broiled Chicken

When you hunger for a simple presentation, try a broiled chicken.

2$^1/_2$ pound broiler chicken
Salt and pepper

1. Split the chicken down the back by cutting it with a pair of sharp scissors. Cut on either side of the backbone. Freeze the backbone for future stocks.
2. Cut a slit in the skin just below the pointed tip of the breast. Push the ends of the leg bones into the opening; the legs are thus held fast. Place chicken flesh-side-up in a shallow pan. Sprinkle with salt and pepper.
3. Preheat oven on broil for 5 minutes. Set rack at least 4 or 5 inches below heat.
4. Broil chicken, flesh-side-up, for 20 minutes. Turn chicken over and broil for 5 to 7 minutes. Test by piercing between leg and second joint; the juices should appear clear. The oven may be switched from broil to bake, at 400 degrees, for 10 to 15 minutes, until ready to serve. This gives you a more flexible schedule for timing.

Makes 2 servings.

NOTE: You could coat the skin with Dijon mustard and bread crumbs 5 minutes before serving. Pop under the broiler to crisp. Or chicken could be served on a compote of rhubarb and strawberries, a seemingly odd but excellent combination.

Sylvia's Best Fried Chicken

After many attempts and copious research, Sylvia Carter concluded that this is the best way to make fried chicken. Trust her, you do need 2 tablespoons of pepper. The only way to serve this chicken, she says, is with mashed potatoes and cream gravy. Proper mashed potatoes, she adds, are made with heavy cream, butter, and pepper, and mashed with a hand masher.

1 quart milk

Juice of 1 lemon

1 3- to 3¼-pound broiler fryer, cut into
8 or 9 pieces, large pieces of fat and skin
removed

1½ cups flour

½ teaspoon baking powder

½ cup lard

½ cup solid vegetable shortening
(adjust amount as needed)

1½ tablespoons salt

2 tablespoons freshly ground black pepper

1. Begin preparation as much as 8 hours or at least 2 hours before you plan to fry the chicken: Combine milk and lemon juice in a pan or bowl that will hold chicken comfortably. Place chicken pieces in pan. If milk mixture does not cover them, turn them occasionally while they are soaking. If doing this more than 2 hours ahead, place chicken in refrigerator, covered, and remove about 1 hour before frying.

2. Remove chicken from milk and pat dry with paper towels. (Reserve milk if you are making gravy.)

3. Place flour on a plate and add baking powder. Fluff with a fork, combining well.

4. In a heavy, cast iron skillet, preferably at least 12 inches in diameter, heat lard and shortening.

5. On a second plate, combine salt and pepper. Roll and pat chicken in salt and pepper, being careful to season each piece evenly.

6. Dredge chicken in flour, being careful to flour all sides. Tap chicken pieces against each other to shake off excess flour.

7. Melted fat in cast iron pan should reach a level of about 1 inch. The fat should be nearly smoking, but not burning. Place chicken pieces in pan without crowding. Fry over moderately high heat until deep golden brown on one side, then turn and brown second side. The chicken should brown in about 7 minutes to a side. If it is browning more slowly, turn heat up. When chicken is nicely browned on both sides, cover pan most of the way, allowing some heat to escape. Reduce heat, cover, and fry for about 15 minutes longer. Turn chicken 2 or 3 times and lower heat if chicken is browning too quickly. If you must fry chicken in more than one batch to avoid crowding, keep fried pieces warm in a 225 degree oven.

8. Remove fried chicken to brown paper bags, which absorb grease best, drain briefly, and serve hot, with cream gravy and mashed potatoes on the side.

9. *To make cream gravy:* Remove all but 2 tablespoons of fat from cast iron skillet, making sure to leave some browned bits of chicken. Stir in 2 tablespoons flour and a little extra salt and pepper. Stir and cook for about 5 minutes until mixture is medium brown. Stir in 2 cups reserved milk a little at a time. Cook and stir until thickened; taste and adjust seasoning.

Makes 3 to 4 servings.

Ida Cerbone's Chicken with Mint

Fresh mint, available year-round, perks up this recipe for chicken.

2 cloves garlic, minced

¼ cup dry white wine

20 to 30 fresh mint leaves

1 4-pound broiler chicken, cut into
serving pieces

⅓ cup light olive oil

Salt and pepper to taste

Lemon slices for garnish

1. Early the day of the dinner or the night before, combine the garlic, wine, and half of the mint leaves. Marinate chicken in this mixture, covered and refrigerated. Turn chicken pieces occasionally.

2. To bake, place chicken pieces in a lightly oiled pan, brush with oil, and sprinkle with salt and pepper. Bake uncovered for 45 minutes in a preheated 350 degree oven. Garnish with lemon slices and remaining mint.

Makes 4 to 6 servings.

Libby's Baked Spicy Chicken

2 4-pound roasting chickens, cut into eighths
1 teaspoon coarse salt
2 teaspoons freshly ground pepper
1/2 teaspoon allspice
1/2 teaspoon red pepper flakes or
    1/8 teaspoon cayenne
1/2 teaspoon oregano
1/2 teaspoon thyme
1/4 cup minced garlic
1 bunch scallions, both green and
    white parts, diced
1 cup combined fresh orange and lemon juices

1. Dry chicken pieces well and set aside. Preheat oven to 375 degrees.

2. Mix salt, pepper, allspice, red pepper flakes, oregano, thyme, garlic, and scallions on a sheet of wax paper. Roll each piece of chicken in mixture and place in a jelly roll pan or other shallow baking pan. Bake for 30 minutes. Pour orange and lemon juice over all and bake another 15 minutes.

Makes 8 servings.

Marvin Krosinsky's Chinese-style Chicken

1 3 1/2-pound chicken
1/2 to 3/4 cup cornstarch
2 tablespoons light soy sauce
3 tablespoons sherry
2 or 3 green and red peppers
1 head broccoli or cauliflower
6 to 8 cloves garlic
1/2 cup peanut oil
Salt to taste
1/4 teaspoon white pepper
1/2 cup chicken broth
1/4 cup sherry

1. Rest the handle of a Chinese cleaver in the palm of your hand and place your forefinger over the top of the blade. Chop the chicken into bite-size pieces, cutting through the skin and bone. You may remove the meat from the bone if desired.

2. Combine cornstarch, soy sauce, and 3 tablespoons sherry—the marinade should be neither too thick or too thin, but should just coat the chicken lightly. Combine marinade with chicken pieces and stir thoroughly.

3. Meanwhile, cut peppers and broccoli or cauliflower in pieces the same size as the chicken. Set aside.

4. Prepare the garlic by pressing with the side of the cleaver until the skin is loosened. Remove skin, leaving garlic only slightly smashed.

5. In a wok or deep pan, heat oil until very hot, add salt. Add the garlic and cook briefly, then add chicken and cook, stirring until golden brown, about 5 to 8 minutes, and chicken is cooked through.

6. Remove chicken and let drain. Remove any burned pieces from oil. Using same oil, add the vegetables and stir-fry quickly. Add salt, pepper, broth, and sherry. Cover and steam vegetables until cooked but still crisp.

7. Place vegetables in the bottom of a serving dish; arrange over them the chicken. Reduce sauce in wok, using cornstarch to thicken if desired. Pour sauce over chicken and serve.

Makes 4 servings.

Chicken with Crumb Topping

The advantage of this recipe is that it can be prepared in advance, making it suitable as a main course for a large dinner party. Finish the dish through step two, then about a half hour before serving, pop it in the oven.

2 large whole chicken breasts
1 tablespoon Dijon mustard
2 tablespoons chutney or orange marmalade
1 tablespoon oil
3 tablespoons butter
1 small onion, minced
1/2 cup dry, unseasoned bread crumbs
1 1/2 teaspoons tarragon

1. Cut chicken breasts in half and remove the bone. Remove skin. Combine mustard and chutney. Spread over chicken breasts.

2. Heat oil and butter in a small pan. Add onion

and sauté until golden, adding more oil if needed. Add bread crumbs and tarragon and sauté briefly. Press the crumb mixture on top of the chicken, shaking off excess.

3. Place chicken in an ovenproof casserole in a single layer and bake in a preheated 350 degree oven for 20 to 30 minutes or until done. Run under the broiler briefly to get a crispy skin.

Makes 4 servings.

Rosemary Chicken with Pine Nuts and Raisins

½ cup raisins
8 chicken breast halves, skinned and boned
Flour
Salt and pepper to taste
8 sprigs fresh rosemary plus ½ teaspoon
    dried or 2½ teaspoons dried
¼ cup olive oil
2 tablespoons butter
1 cup dry white wine
½ cup pine nuts

1. Soak raisins in hot water for 15 minutes. Drain, squeeze dry.
2. Place each chicken breast half on a cutting board. Holding your knife parallel to the board, slice the chicken to make 2 thin cutlets. You will have 16 cutlets total. Dredge in flour; shake off any excess thoroughly. Sprinkle with salt and pepper to taste and ½ teaspoon dried rosemary.
3. Heat the oil and add the butter. When it has melted and is bubbling, add the chicken pieces and sauté very briefly on each side, just until golden—do not overcook. Remove to a heated platter and continue cooking until all pieces are used. Can be made in advance up to this point.
4. Pour out the remaining fat, add the wine and return pan to the heat. Cook over high heat, scraping up the browned bits from the bottom of the pan. Add the fresh rosemary or remaining dried, and cook over high heat until reduced and slightly thickened. Add raisins, pine nuts, and cooked chicken. Reduce heat and cover for a few minutes.

Makes 4 servings.

Chicken Breasts in Tarragon Cream

This is undoubtedly my favorite recipe for chicken, combining the flavors of tarragon and mustard with heavy cream. It nicely complements a sparkling wine, such as that from Krug or Sebastiani.

8 chicken breast halves, skinned and boned
Flour
Salt and pepper to taste
3 to 4 tablespoons sweet butter
2 tablespoons minced fresh tarragon or
    2 teaspoons dried
1 cup white wine
1½ cups heavy cream
1 to 2 teaspoons Dijon mustard

1. Place each chicken breast half on a cutting board. Holding your knife parallel to the board, slice the chicken to make 2 thin cutlets. You should end up with 16 cutlets total. Dust lightly in flour and shake to remove excess. Season pieces with salt and pepper. In a large sauté pan, heat butter and sauté chicken on each side until golden. As chicken is cooking, sprinkle with half of the tarragon. This goes very quickly, about 2 to 3 minutes per side. Remove chicken pieces to a heated plate and cover loosely with foil while sautéing remaining chicken. Chicken can be prepared ahead up to this point.
2. When the chicken is cooked, add white wine and cook over high heat until reduced by half. Add cream and remaining tarragon and cook over high heat to reduce until thick enough to coat the back of a spoon. Lower heat and stir in mustard. Do not let mustard boil. Add chicken back to sauce, stir to coat.

Makes 6 servings.

Peche Mignon's Poulet à l'Homard

A perfect Chardonnay candidate, particularly a label in the "big" California style or a white Burgundy. Select Chateau St. Jean for the former; and if you prefer France, opt for Meursault from Louis Jadot or Joseph Drouhin.

1 tablespoon finely minced shallots

4 tablespoons sweet butter

1 3½-pound Long Island grain-fed
frying chicken, cut into serving pieces or
6 chicken cutlets

1½ cups dry white wine

1 1½-pound live Long Island lobster, cut into
pieces—you may ask your fish supplier to
do this, or see page 119; reserve the coral

2 tablespoons Cognac

1 tablespoon Madeira

1½ cups heavy cream

½ cup reserved chicken poaching liquid

Salt and pepper to taste

1. Sauté shallots in 3 tablespoons of the butter until translucent. Add the chicken and brown lightly over medium heat on all sides. Add the wine, lower heat and cover to poach the chicken until done, about 10 to 15 minutes. Remove chicken and keep warm. Pour off half of the liquid and reserve.

2. In another sauté pan, heat remaining butter until the foam subsides. Add the lobster pieces and reserved coral and cook over high heat until the shells turn red. Flame with the Cognac, shaking the pan until the flame goes out. Add the Madeira, cream, and reserved chicken poaching liquid. Cook over medium heat until the lobster meat turns white and is done. This takes only a couple of minutes.

3. Remove the lobster. Reduce the sauce until large bubbles form. Taste for seasonings, adding salt and pepper to taste. Lower the heat, add the chicken and lobster and cook for just a minute.

Makes 4 servings.

Pheasant in Casserole

If there's a hunter in your family who bags pheasant, you might want to try this recipe for the bird in a casserole.

For brine:
½ cup coarse salt
¾ cup sugar
¼ cup vinegar
4 cups water
1 bay leaf, crushed

For casserole:
2 pheasants
2 cups dry red wine
Flour
14 tablespoons butter
2 tablespoons minced shallots
2 carrots, sliced thin
1 medium tomato, peeled, seeded, and
chopped
2 leeks, white part only, chopped
½ cup celery, white part only, chopped
1 bouquet garni: ½ teaspoon thyme,
½ teaspoon rosemary, a few sprigs parsley,
and 1 tablespoon juniper berries, crushed
1½ teaspoons paprika
2 cloves garlic, crushed
Salt and pepper to taste
3 tablespoons Cognac

1. Combine salt, sugar, vinegar, water, and bay leaf for brine. Marinate pheasants in the brine overnight in refrigerator. Remove from brine, rinse well, pat dry.

2. Skin the birds, remove breast, thighs, and legs. Marinate pheasant pieces in the red wine for 2 hours at room temperature. Remove from wine, pat dry. Reserve wine.

3. Dredge the pheasant pieces in flour. Heat 6 tablespoons of the butter and sauté the pieces, browning them on all sides. Remove the pieces and reserve. Pour off the butter, add about ¾ cup of the reserved wine and cook over high heat, scraping up browned bits from the bottom. Reserve this pan juice.

4. Heat remaining butter in a large saucepan; add shallots, carrots, tomato, leeks, and celery. Sauté for 10 minutes, stirring constantly. Add reserved pan juice, the bouquet garni tied together in a piece of cheesecloth, paprika, garlic, and salt and pepper. Cover and simmer for 1 hour.

5. Remove and discard bouquet garni, rub contents of pan through a sieve and return to pan. Add the pheasant pieces and enough wine to barely cover the meat. Cover and cook gently for 45 minutes to 1 hour or until meat is cooked. Correct seasoning. Add Cognac, flame and serve.

Makes 4 to 6 servings.

Walnut and Apple Game Hens

$1/2$ cup chopped celery
1 cup chopped, peeled, and cored apple
$1^1/2$ cups cubed toasted bread
$1/2$ cup walnuts, chopped
$1/2$ teaspoon thyme
$1/2$ teaspoon marjoram
$1/2$ cup chopped onion
Salt
Freshly ground black pepper
Milk
4 Cornish game hens
$1^1/2$ cups dry white wine
$3/4$ cup chicken stock
4 tablespoons orange marmalade

1. Combine celery, apple, bread, walnuts, thyme, marjoram, onion, and salt and pepper to taste. Moisten with milk. Wash cavity of game hens, sprinkle with salt and pepper. Divide stuffing among the 4 hens, and truss.

2. Place hens in a baking dish just large enough to hold them. Add wine and stock to dish. Bake in a preheated 350 degree oven about 1 hour, basting occasionally. During last 15 minutes of cooking, melt marmalade in small pan on the stove. Brush hens with marmalade to glaze.

3. Remove hens from oven, place on warmed serving platter. Reduce cooking liquid over very high heat until slightly thickened. Stir in remaining marmalade and taste, adding salt and pepper as needed.

Makes 4 servings.

Jules Bond's Turkey Dressing

There are those who believe that a turkey is just an excuse to eat the stuffing. However, you'll soon discover how good turkey can taste if you use one fresh from Long Island. You can then have the best of both worlds by making these two recipes for stuffings. And you might even want to make double portions: one to stuff the bird and one to cook separately.

3 tablespoons butter
$1/4$ pound lean smoked bacon, in small dice
1 cup finely chopped onion

$1/3$ pound chicken livers
$1/4$ pound sausage meat
$1/4$ pound ground veal
1 cup chopped fresh mushrooms
2 cups homemade croutons, preferably, or plain or onion-flavored commercial croutons
1 egg
1 pound cooked, shelled chestnuts, coarsely chopped (see note)
$1/2$ cup dry vermouth
$1/4$ cup Cognac
$1/2$ teaspoon rosemary, crushed
$1/2$ teaspoon chervil
$1/2$ teaspoon thyme
$1/4$ teaspoon grated nutmeg
Salt and pepper to taste

Heat butter in a skillet, add bacon and sauté until cooked, but not crispy. Add onion and sauté until onion is soft. Add chicken livers and sausage meat, mix and sauté over medium heat for 3 or 4 minutes. Add veal and mushrooms, mix well and sauté 2 more minutes. Remove from heat, blend with croutons, egg, chestnuts, vermouth, Cognac, rosemary, chervil, thyme, nutmeg, salt and pepper.

Makes enough to stuff a 14- to 15-pound turkey.

NOTE: You may substitute canned, unsweetened chestnuts or dried chestnuts, soaked in hot water for a few hours, then boiled until tender.

Oyster Stuffing

$1/2$ cup butter
1 cup chopped onion
1 green pepper, seeded and chopped
$1/4$ cup chopped celery, white part only
$3/4$ cup chopped boiled ham
6 slices bacon, diced
Pinch of sage, thyme, rosemary, and cayenne pepper
Salt to taste
6 cups unflavored croutons
18 oysters, drained and coarsely chopped (reserve the liquor)
Milk
3 eggs, lightly beaten

1. Heat butter, add onion, green pepper, celery, ham, and bacon and mix; sauté for about 5 minutes, stirring often.

2. Put mixture in a bowl and blend with the sage, thyme, rosemary, cayenne, and salt. Mix croutons with reserved oyster liquor and enough milk to just moisten them. Add to the mixture and combine lightly. Add beaten eggs, mix again, then add the chopped oysters. Blend lightly with a fork.

Makes enough stuffing for a 12-pound turkey.

Sylvia Carter's Barbequed Beef

Here's a barbeque easily prepared indoors. Just provide some warm buns or rolls, a little slaw, and you have a wholesome meal to serve a gathering of friends.

   4 pounds brisket, chuck, or bottom round
      beef roast
   2 medium onions, chopped fine
   1 1/2 cups water
   1/4 cup white vinegar
   1/4 cup dark brown sugar
   1 tablespoon molasses
   2 tablespoons prepared mustard
   1/4 teaspoon Tabasco sauce
   3 tablespoons Worcestershire sauce
   1 cup ketchup
   1/2 cup chili sauce
   1/2 lemon, sliced
   1 tablespoon salt
   1/4 teaspoon black pepper

1. The day before you plan to serve the barbeque, place meat, fat side up, in a roasting or baking pan. Cover with foil and cook in a preheated 325 degree oven for 3 hours or until well done. Uncover for the last half hour, to let meat brown.

2. Remove meat from pan and cool. Wrap in foil and refrigerate. Pour pan juices and fat into a bowl and refrigerate.

3. The day of the barbeque, remove meat from refrigerator and trim off fat. Using your hands, shred meat into pieces. Remove the layer of hardened fat from the pan juices.

4. In a large, heavy saucepan, melt about 3 ta-blespoons of the rendered fat and sauté the onions. Add the remaining ingredients and the pan juices from the roasted meat. Stir well, bring to a simmer, and simmer very slowly uncovered, for an hour or more, stirring often. Add more water if it gets too dry.

Makes about 10 servings.

NOTE: If you like a smoky flavor, pour liquid smoke around the meat while it is roasting.

No Salt Herbed Beef and Vegetable Kebobs

Bea Lewis, *Newsday's* nutrition columnist, makes these kebobs without salt, and no one seems to miss it.

   2 tablespoons vegetable oil
   2 tablespoons wine vinegar
   2 tablespoons water
   2 tablespoons minced onion
   1 tablespoon crushed basil leaves
   2 cloves garlic, finely minced
   1/4 teaspoon thyme leaves, crushed
   1/8 teaspoon black pepper
   1 pound boneless beef round,
      trimmed of fat and cut into
      1-inch cubes
   12 cherry tomatoes
   1 medium zucchini, cut into 1-inch cubes
   12 large mushrooms

1. To prepare marinade: combine oil, vinegar, water, onion, basil, garlic, thyme, and black pepper. Mix well. Place meat in a tight fitting bowl. Pour marinade over meat, toss to coat. Cover and refrigerate for 2 hours or more.

2. On four 13-inch skewers, alternately arrange meat with tomatoes, zucchini, and mushrooms. Place a mushroom at the end of each skewer. Brush with marinade.

3. Grill over hot coals for 8 to 10 minutes, turning occasionally and brushing with marinade often. Well-done meat requires longer cooking.

Makes 4 servings.

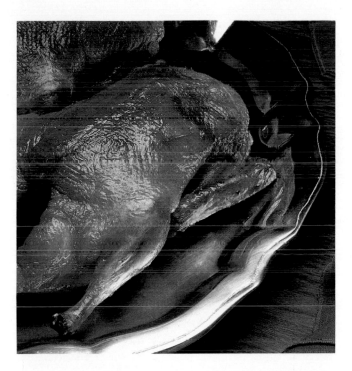

Perfect Roast Duck with Pear Chutney, Roast Duck with Apples, (recipes, page 130); Farmland in Riverhead

Sweet and Sour Stuffed Cabbage

Stuffed cabbage is a traditional way of serving spicy blends of meat, grains, and vegetables. Here are two versions—each delicious and inexpensive to make.

Large head of green cabbage, about
   3 to 4 pounds
3 cups water
1 cup brown rice
1 pound lean ground beef
1 egg
1/4 cup grated onion
1/4 cup grated carrot
1/3 cup grated raw potato
1 1/2 teaspoons salt
Freshly ground black pepper
1 large onion, sliced
1/4 cup seedless white raisins
1/3 cup brown sugar
3 cups canned crushed tomatoes
4 tablespoons fresh lemon juice or
   wine vinegar

1. Cook whole cabbage in a large pot of boiling water for 10 minutes. Remove cabbage from pot and detach as many outer leaves as possible without breaking them. Return the cabbage to the boiling water and cook 10 more minutes. Remove and again detach as many leaves as possible. You will need 18 leaves.

2. Bring 3 cups of water to boil, add the rice and cook for 15 minutes. Drain.

3. In a large bowl, mix the rice, ground beef, egg, grated onion, carrot, and potato, 1 teaspoon of the salt, and pepper to taste.

4. Place 2 heaping tablespoons of mixture in center of each cabbage leaf. Fold in sides of leaves and roll up tightly.

5. In the bottom of a shallow 3-quart baking pan, place a layer of sliced onions. Arrange cabbage rolls on top.

6. In a medium saucepan, combine the raisins, brown sugar, tomatoes, remaining salt, and lemon juice and bring to boil. Taste sauce and add more salt or brown sugar, if necessary.

7. Pour mixture over cabbage rolls, cover tightly and bake in a preheated 350 degree oven for 60 to 90 minutes, or until cabbage is tender.

Makes 8 servings.

Mon Petit Stuffed Chou

1 medium Savoy cabbage
2 tablespoons butter
1 pound lean ground pork
2 tablespoons chopped shallots
2 cloves garlic, minced
1 cup cooked rice
2 tablespoons minced fresh parsley
Salt and pepper to taste
3 cups beef stock (see page 47)
1 cup crushed tomatoes
1/2 teaspoon thyme
1 bay leaf

1. In a large pot of water cook cabbage for 5 minutes, if necessary weighting it to keep it down. Drain and rinse in cold water.

2. In a medium saucepan, melt the butter and in it cook the pork until it is no longer pink. Remove and set aside. Sauté shallots and garlic for 5 minutes. Return pork to pan and mix in the rice, parsley, salt and pepper to taste, and mix well.

3. Prepare the cabbage: starting in the center, carefully separate the leaves and spread tablespoons of stuffing in between. To hold the cabbage together, wrap it in cheesecloth, tie it with string, or secure it with toothpicks.

4. In a large pot heat the stock, tomatoes, thyme, and bay leaf. Add the cabbage and cook until tender, about 1 1/2 to 2 hours. Carefully turn cabbage once or twice during the cooking. Remove bay leaf. Remove cabbage and cut out wedges.

Makes 4 servings.

Junipered Acorn Squash

2 acorn squash
Melted butter
3 slices bacon, minced
1 pound ground beef
2 teaspoons juniper berries, slightly mashed
1 teaspoon dried rosemary or 1 tablespoon
   fresh
Salt and pepper to taste
1/4 cup dry bread crumbs
1 tablespoon brown sugar

1. Cut acorn squash in half, scoop out seeds and stringy pieces. Brush with butter and place cut side down on a baking pan. Add a small amount of water and bake in a preheated 350 degree oven for 30 minutes.

2. Sauté bacon and ground beef over low heat until beef loses its pink color and the bacon is cooked. Add juniper berries, rosemary, and salt and pepper. Remove from heat. Add enough bread crumbs to form a stiff mixture.

3. After squash has cooked 30 minutes, remove from oven. Brush cavities with more melted butter, sprinkle in brown sugar and fill with ground beef mixture. Return to oven and bake another 30 minutes or until squash is tender.

Makes 4 servings.

Veal Cutlets with Chestnuts and Apples

If you are using fresh chestnuts, make an X on the flat side of each one and bake chestnuts for 20 minutes in a 450 degree oven. The shell and skin should be easy to remove. Cook chestnuts in boiling water until tender, about 15 minutes. If you are using dried, soak overnight, then simmer until tender. The easiest solution is to buy chestnuts already roasted— just be sure not to get them in a sweet syrup.

> 1½ pounds veal cutlets
> Flour
> Salt and pepper to taste
> 3 tablespoons butter
> 3 tablespoons Cognac or apple brandy
> 1 teaspoon minced fresh ginger
> 1 Golden Delicious apple, peeled and very
>   thinly sliced
> 1½ teaspoons sugar
> ¾ cup dry white wine
> ¾ cup chicken broth
> ¾ cup roasted chestnuts, cut in half

1. Dredge veal in flour, shake off excess and season with salt and pepper. Heat butter in a large sauté pan and sauté veal on both sides until golden, about 5 to 6 minutes total. Remove and set aside.

2. Add Cognac and flame, then add ginger, apple slices, sugar, wine, and broth. Cook over high heat about 10 to 15 minutes, or until apples are tender and sauce is slightly thickened. Add chestnuts and cook 1 more minute. Return veal to pan, cover and heat briefly.

Makes 4 servings.

Barbequed Lamb Sonoma style

Victoria Sebastiani is a great cook and loves to pair her husband Sam's wine with her creations. This barbequed lamb calls for cabernet sauvignon, and not surprisingly, she believes Sebastiani Cabernet is the best choice.

> ¾ cup olive oil
> ½ cup red wine vinegar
> ½ cup cabernet sauvignon
> 1 4-ounce can chopped green chilies
> 6 cloves garlic, minced
> 4 teaspoons Italian seasoning
> 2 tablespoons hot mustard
> 1 6-pound leg of lamb, boned and butterflied
> 1 8-ounce can tomato sauce
> 3 tablespoons honey

1. Combine the oil, vinegar, wine, chilies, garlic, Italian seasoning, and mustard. Mix well. Place the lamb in a shallow dish and pour the mixture over it, coating all sides. Cover and keep refrigerated overnight, turning once.

2. To barbeque, remove the meat from the marinade and prepare a basting sauce by blending the marinade with the tomato sauce and honey, stirring well.

3. Barbeque the lamb over a double layer of hot coals for 8 to 10 minutes on each side, basting frequently with the sauce for medium rare lamb. Or, bake in a 375 degree oven for 10 to 15 minutes on each side.

Makes 6 servings.

LEFT *Marvin Krosinsky's Chinese-style Chicken (recipe, page 140)*

RIGHT *Ida Cerbone's Chicken with Mint (recipe, page 139)*

BELOW *Barbequed Lamb Sonoma Style (recipe, page 147) and Hot Beans Vinaigrette (recipe, page 72)*

OPPOSITE *Le Canard en Deux Services (recipe, page 136)*

Roast Fresh Ham

This fresh ham makes a spectacular main course for Easter dinner, or any dinner for that matter.

1 fresh ham, about 10 pounds
3 tablespoons oil
3 tablespoons grated onion
1 large clove garlic, crushed
1 teaspoon caraway seeds, crushed
1 teaspoon rosemary, well crushed
1 teaspoon marjoram
1/4 teaspoon thyme
1 tablespoon lemon juice
1 teaspoon salt
1/2 teaspoon freshly ground black pepper
1 large onion, thinly sliced
2 cups chopped celery stalks
1/2 cup water
1 cup port wine
1 cup dry white wine or dry vermouth

For the glaze:
3 tablespoons Chinese plum sauce
6 tablespoons mirin (Japanese rice wine)
1 1/2 tablespoons soy sauce
1 1/2 teaspoons Dijon mustard
2 cloves garlic, crushed through a garlic press
1 1/2 tablespoons paprika

1 1/2 tablespoons flour
1 cup chicken broth

1. Ask your butcher to trim one third of the skin off the butt end of the ham and remove most of the fat beneath it, leaving only a 1/3-inch layer.

2. With a sharp knife score a diamond pattern in the remaining skin and fat. Have ham at room temperature before starting to cook. Blend the oil, grated onion, 1 clove garlic, caraway, rosemary, marjoram, thyme, lemon juice, salt, and pepper. Rub the mixture into the ham and let stand for half an hour.

3. Cover the bottom of a roasting pan with onion rings and chopped celery. Add water, put ham on top. Place pan in a preheated 375 degree oven. Roast for 30 minutes. Reduce heat to 350 degrees. Mix port and white wine and baste ham with 3/4 cup of the wine mixture. Baste with wine and pan juices every half hour. Roasting time is 25 minutes per pound of ham.

4. Blend plum sauce, mirin, soy sauce, mustard, garlic, and paprika for the glaze. An hour before the ham is cooked, spread the glaze over the top of the ham. When ham is done, remove to a serving platter or carving board and let rest for 15 minutes.

5. Skim fat off the pan juices in the roaster, stir in the flour, gradually add the chicken broth and cook, while stirring, over low heat until gravy is smooth and thickened.

Makes 10 to 12 servings.

NOTE: Mirin, sweet Japanese rice wine for cooking, is carried in most markets and most specialty food stores. A medium sweet sherry could be substituted.

James Brigham's Hickory Smoked Pork Butt

Slow cooking of 8 to 10 hours is crucial to develop the sweet-smoky flavors of this barbeque.

For basting sauce:
1 quart apple cider vinegar
1/4 cup brown sugar
8 tablespoons butter
4 tablespoons Worcestershire sauce
2 tablespoons Tabasco sauce
3 tablespoons ground black pepper
2 tablespoons salt
1/2 teaspoon cayenne pepper
2 cloves garlic, minced
1 boned pork butt, about 6 pounds

For barbeque sauce:
2 cups apple cider vinegar
1/4 cup tomato juice
1/4 cup soybean or other vegetable oil, or butter
1/4 cup brown sugar
Juice of 1 orange
3 tablespoons Worcestershire sauce

2 tablespoons cornstarch dissolved in a small
   amount of water
2 teaspoons chili powder
1/2 teaspoon paprika
1 teaspoon cumin
1/2 teaspoon cayenne pepper
1 teaspoon ground black pepper
Salt to taste

1. Combine the ingredients for the basting sauce in a saucepan. Bring to the boil, stirring occasionally. Remove from heat.

2. The pork butt should be smoked 8 to 10 hours. A covered barbeque, such as a Weber, is required. Start the fire with about 12 to 15 charcoal briquets. When the briquets are ready, add a handful of hickory chips which have been soaked in water. The pork butt is cooked by indirect heat and should not be placed directly over the coals. Baste the pork about every half hour. Add two to four briquets to the fire about every hour as required. Add soaked hickory chips to the fire about every half hour.

3. To make the barbeque sauce, combine the ingredients—vinegar, tomato juice, oil, sugar, orange juice, Worcestershire, cornstarch dissolved in water, chili powder, paprika, cumin, cayenne, pepper and salt—in a saucepan, stirring with a wire whisk. Simmer for 20 minutes. Stir occasionally. The finished port butt is best served sliced as barbeque sandwiches. These should be made on hamburger buns and served with the barbeque sauce.

Makes enough to serve at least 10 people.

Pork-Cabbage Casserole with Apples

1 tablespoon vegetable oil
2 pounds pork shoulder, cut into 1-inch cubes
3/4 cup chopped onion
1/4 cup chopped fresh parsley
3/4 cup beer
1/2 teaspoon caraway seeds
1 teaspoon salt

1/8 teaspoon pepper
1/8 teaspoon ground allspice
4 cups shredded cabbage
2 apples, cored and cut into thin slivers

1. In a large skillet or Dutch oven heat oil and brown pork on all sides. Add onion and parsley and cook 5 minutes, stirring occasionally.

2. Add beer, caraway seeds, salt, pepper, and allspice. Cover tightly and simmer for 45 minutes. Add cabbage, cover, and simmer 15 minutes. Add apple to pan and cook 15 minutes longer.

Makes 6 servings.

Pork Scaloppine with Parsley Walnut Sauce

Pork cut for scaloppine can be as delicious as veal.

1 1 1/2- pound boneless pork scaloppine
4 tablespoons olive oil, divided
1 clove garlic, minced
2 bunches parsley, chopped fine
1 tablespoon chopped fresh basil or
   1 teaspoon dried
1/2 cup coarsely chopped walnuts
Salt, freshly ground pepper, to taste

1. Brown pork on both sides in 2 tablespoons of olive oil, over fairly high heat. Remove from skillet and keep in a warm place, but not in the oven.

2. Add remaining oil to skillet. Add garlic, toss in oil, and add the parsley, basil, walnuts, and a little salt and a few grindings of pepper. Sauté for about 3 minutes and serve over pork.

Makes 4 servings.

Jeffrey Spiro's Sun-Dried Tomato Sauce

In *Newsday*'s contest for the best pasta sauce, the following three recipes are among the best we found.

2 to 3 leeks
2 cups chicken stock (see page 47)
1 cup cream
¼ pound prosciutto, cut in 2 slices
¼ pound sun-dried tomatoes
    (see recipe below)
2 tablespoons oil
Cayenne pepper
2 tablespoons grated Parmesan cheese
1 pound fresh linguine

1. Clean leeks and parboil in chicken stock for 4 minutes, or until just softened. Remove leeks, slice in ¼-inch rounds. Boil stock until reduced by half, about 1 cup. Reserve.

2. Reduce cream by boiling to approximately ½ cup. Add to stock and reserve.

3. Cut prosciutto first into long, ½-inch-wide strips. Next, cut strips into 1½-inch-long pieces.

4. Cut sun-dried tomatoes lengthwise into thin strips and then horizontally to form small pieces.

5. Sauté leeks in oil over medium heat for 2 minutes. Add tomatoes and continue to sauté for 2 minutes. Add prosciutto and cook for 1 minute. Season with pepper to taste. Add creamy stock mixture and the cheese.

6. While ingredients sauté, cook fresh pasta. This takes only 2 minutes. Drain quickly, allowing pasta to remain moist. Transfer pasta to large, heated, buttered bowl. Add the sauce. Mix well.

Makes 6 servings as a first course, 4 as a main course.

"Sun-Dried" Tomatoes

It is possible to sun-dry tomatoes on Long Island. But the procedure is fraught with problems; rain, bugs, clouds all spell doom for a quality sun-dried product. However, it is quite easy and very acceptable to make "sun-dried" tomatoes in your oven. In doing so you will likely save a lot of money since the imported delicacy is quite costly. Here, then, is the method.

6 pounds plum tomatoes
Salt
Fresh basil or dried oregano
Black peppercorns
Garlic
Olive oil

1. Wash tomatoes and cut in half vertically. Sprinkle cut sides with salt. Cover cookie sheets with aluminum foil. Place halves, cut side up, in a single layer on racks and place racks on cookie sheets.

2. Set the trays of tomatoes on a counter for 8 hours or overnight. The salt will draw liquid out of the tomatoes. Pat the tomatoes dry with paper towels.

3. Place the trays of tomatoes in a preheated 200 degree oven and cook for about 8 hours, turning them over once or twice. Begin testing for doneness after 6 hours; remove any that appear dry. The tomatoes are ready when you press them with your finger and no liquid oozes out. If they are cooked too long, they will become leathery.

4. Layer the dried tomatoes into sterilized jars, alternating with basil or oregano, a few peppercorns and chopped garlic to taste; do not pack them down. Add olive oil to cover by ½ inch. Screw on lid. Set the tomatoes aside for a minimum of 2 weeks to allow the tomatoes to develop flavor. They do not need to be refrigerated.

Connie Savarese's Broccoli Sauce

1 cup olive oil
6 cloves garlic (chopped then mash
    with a fork)
1 cup chopped prosciutto
½ cup white wine
2 heads broccoli, stems cut off or 4½ cups
    broccoli flowerettes, washed and stems cut off
Salt and pepper
1 14-ounce can chicken broth
1½ cups homemade Italian Tomato Sauce
    (see recipe below)
1½ cups chopped olives (half black and half
    green with pimientos)

1 cup fresh Italian parsley and basil, mixed about
    half and half
4 tablespoons butter

1. In a large saucepan heat the oil and add the garlic and prosciutto. Let brown for approximately 10 minutes but do not let garlic burn. Add white wine; simmer for 5 minutes.

2. Add the broccoli and salt and pepper to taste; let cook just until the broccoli is fork-tender, approximately 10 minutes.

3. Add the chicken broth and tomato sauce and simmer another 5 minutes. Add olives; simmer another 3 minutes. Add basil, parsley, and butter.

Makes 8 servings.

Italian Tomato Sauce

4 Italian sweet sausages
6 tablespoons butter
3 medium onions, chopped
5 cloves garlic, crushed
1/2 cup white wine
1 28-ounce can crushed tomatoes
1 28-ounce can whole plum tomatoes
Pinch oregano
Salt to taste
1 teaspoon sugar
1/4 cup chopped fresh basil

1. Brown sausages in the butter. Add the onions and brown slowly until onions and sausages are golden brown. Add crushed garlic and simmer until golden brown, being careful not to burn. Add wine and simmer for about 5 minutes.

2. Add crushed tomatoes and plum tomatoes, which have been slightly mashed with a fork. Add oregano, salt, sugar, and basil. Let come to a boil. Simmer on low heat for approximately 1 1/2 hours, stirring occasionally.

Makes about 2 quarts.

Patricia Gangi's Macaroni with Escarole and Sausage

1 large head escarole or 2 small heads
1 pound sweet Italian sausage, partially frozen
    for ease of slicing
5 large cloves garlic, minced
1 medium-large onion, chopped
1/2 cup raisins
1/4 cup olive oil
1 pound short fusilli macaroni
Grated Parmesan cheese
Plain bread crumbs
Freshly ground pepper

1. Wash escarole leaves thoroughly. Break into bite-size pieces.

2. With sharp serrated knife, cut sausage into slices approximately 1/4 inch to 1/2 inch thick. In a large 12-inch frying pan or Dutch oven, combine sausage, garlic, onion, and raisins. Add olive oil; place escarole on top. Cover and cook over low flame until sausage is cooked, about 15 minutes.

3. In 6 quarts boiling water cook the pasta until just tender. Drain.

4. In individual dishes serve the fusilli, topped with the sausage-escarole mix, mixed together slightly. Sprinkle equal amounts of grated cheese and bread crumbs liberally over macaroni. Add a healthy dose of freshly ground black pepper.

Makes 4 servings.

DESSERTS

Zanghi's New York State Apple Tart

1½ cups all-purpose flour
8 tablespoons butter, chilled and diced
4 tablespoons granulated sugar
1 egg, chilled
Drop of vanilla extract
Pinch salt
6 tablespoons melted butter
2 tablespoons granulated sugar
4 Golden Delicious apples
1 tablespoon cinnamon
1 tablespoon brown sugar
2 tablespoons confectioners' sugar

1. Combine the flour, butter, 2 tablespoons sugar, egg, vanilla extract, and salt. Work it into a dough only long enough to bind the ingredients. If a food processor is used, do not overblend. Refrigerate for at least 4 hours. It may be refrigerated for 1 week or frozen.

2. Roll out the dough on a well-floured surface to a 12-inch diameter about ⅛ inch thick. Transfer to a flat, round tray, pizza tray or metal baking round. Trim any excess dough, leaving the dough flat. Brush off excess flour and refrigerate for 1 hour.

3. Preheat oven to 450 degrees 30 minutes before baking. Prick the pastry with a fork and brush with 2 tablespoons of the melted butter; sprinkle with 2 tablespoons sugar.

4. Place on a cookie sheet and bake in upper half of the oven for 12 minutes. Rotate pan once to ensure uniform browning.

5. When golden, remove from oven and set aside; do not turn off oven.

6. Peel apples, cut into halves and core with spoon or melon scoop. Slice each half into ⅛-inch slices and arrange in an overlapping layer on the pastry. Paint apples with remaining melted butter and sprinkle with cinnamon and brown and granulated sugars.

7. Bake on the middle rack for 12 minutes, rotating once. Remove from oven, cover lightly with foil and bake again for an additional 12 minutes. Before serving, dust with confectioners' sugar.

Makes 6 to 8 servings.

Apple Pecan Bake

4 to 5 apples, to make 4 cups minced
2 eggs, separated
1 cup chopped pecans
2 teaspoons lemon juice
½ teaspoon cinnamon
½ cup brown sugar
2 tablespoons butter
Heavy cream

1. Core and mince apples, leaving the peels on. Turn into a mixing bowl.

2. Beat egg yolks. Add to apples along with the pecans, lemon juice, cinnamon, and sugar and mix well.

3. Beat egg whites until stiff. Fold into the apples. Pour the mixture into a flat, buttered baking dish and set the dish in a pan filled 1 inch deep with hot water.

4. Bake in preheated 350 degree oven for about 45 minutes or until a tester comes out clean. Serve hot or at room temperature with heavy cream or whipped cream.

Makes 6 to 8 servings.

Apple Pie

For fall, a classic apple pie.

For pastry:
2 cups all-purpose flour
1 tablespoon granulated sugar
1/2 teaspoon baking powder
1/4 teaspoon salt
1/3 cup shortening
1/3 cup butter
1 egg, lightly beaten
2 tablespoons cream

For filling:
8 cups pared, sliced apples
2 teaspoons fresh lemon juice
3/4 cup brown sugar
1 tablespoon flour
1/2 teaspoon cinnamon
1/4 teaspoon allspice
1/4 teaspoon salt
2 tablespoons butter
Lightly beaten egg white

1. In a medium bowl, combine the flour, sugar, baking powder, and salt. Cut in shortenings until mixture is the size of peas. Combine egg and cream and add to dry mixture, one tablespoon at a time. If mixture is too dry, add a teaspoon more of cream. Gather dough together in a ball, wrap in waxed paper, and chill for 2 hours.

2. Remove dough from refrigerator and cut in half. Roll one half out on a lightly floured pastry cloth. Fit pastry into 10-inch pie pan and trim edge, leaving 1/2 inch of dough hanging over the rim. If kitchen is warm, place in refrigerator while preparing filling.

3. Sprinkle the apple slices with lemon juice. In a separate bowl combine the brown sugar, flour, cinnamon, allspice, and salt. Mix well and spoon half the mixture on the bottom of the pie shell. Toss the rest with the apple slices. If the apples are very juicy, add an additional tablespoon of flour. Spoon apple slices into pan, mounding them high in the center. Dot with butter.

4. Roll out upper crust to an 11-inch circle and arrange over filling; trim to 1 inch around edge. Fold upper crust under lower crust and pinch together. Flute dough around rim of pie plate.

5. Cut three slits in top crust. Brush with egg white.

6. Bake in a preheated 425 degree oven for 15 minutes. Lower heat to 350 degrees and bake an additional 45 minutes.

Makes 8 servings.

Baked Apples à la Mirabelle

4 Golden Delicious apples
1/4 cup (1/2 stick) sweet butter, softened
1/4 cup sugar

1. Peel and core the apples, halve them lengthwise, and cut a crosshatch pattern over each half. Butter a baking dish well with some of the butter and arrange the apples in it. Place some of the butter on the top of each apple half and sprinkle each half with some of the sugar.

2. Bake the apples in a preheated 350 degree oven for 20 to 30 minutes

Makes 8 servings.

Marie's Apple Wheat Loaf

1 1/2 cups peeled, grated apples
1 cup brown sugar
1 teaspoon baking soda
1 tablespoon oil
1 cup boiling water
2 eggs, slightly beaten
1 1/2 cups all-purpose flour
2 1/2 teaspoons baking powder
1 teaspoon salt
1/2 teaspoon cinnamon
1 cup whole wheat flour
1 cup chopped nuts (walnuts or pecans)

1. In a large bowl combine the apples, brown sugar, baking soda, and oil. Add boiling water and mix well. Allow to cool. Add eggs.

2. In a medium bowl, combine the flour, baking powder, salt, and cinnamon. Toss lightly with a fork. Stir in the whole wheat flour. Add to apple mixture and mix well. Fold in nuts.

3. Spoon into a buttered 9-by-5-inch loaf pan and bake in a preheated 350 degree oven for 1 hour or until bread tests done.

Makes about 16 servings.

Cantaloupe Ice

In the past couple of years, fruit ices have come into vogue. Considering how easy they are to make and refreshing, their popularity is understandable. You can, of course, vary the fruit as you desire.

> 1 medium ripe cantaloupe
> 1/3 cup granulated sugar
> 1/3 cup water
> 1 envelope unflavored gelatin
> 2 tablespoons cold water
> 1 tablespoon lime juice
> 2 tablespoons rum

1. Peel and seed melon. Cut into cubes and purée in food processor or blender. Measure out 2 cups and return this to processor.

2. In a small saucepan, boil together the sugar and water for 5 minutes. Cool slightly. Sprinkle gelatin over cold water. Stir over low heat until dissolved. Add lime juice. Cool.

3. With processor on, add sugar syrup through opening and process until just blended. Add gelatin mixture and the rum.

4. Pour into a non-glass container and freeze until firm. Remove from freezer and break up into chunks. Purée again in food processor or blender. Refreeze.

Makes 1 pint.

24 Carat Cake

For carrot cake lovers, this is Marie Bianco's interpretation of a classic.

> 8 medium carrots (for cake and frosting)
> 2 cups all-purpose flour
> 2 teaspoons baking powder
> 1/2 teaspoon baking soda
> 1/4 teaspoon salt
> 1 teaspoon cinnamon
> 1/2 teaspoon mace
> 1/2 teaspoon ground cloves
> 1 cup (2 sticks) butter or margarine,
>   at room temperature
> 1 cup granulated sugar
> 1 cup brown sugar
> 4 eggs, separated
> 1 cup chopped walnuts
> Golden Carrot Frosting (recipe below)

1. Peel and slice carrots. Cook, covered, until tender in 1 cup water. Drain, reserving 1/3 cup of the cooking liquid. Purée the carrots in a ricer, blender or food processor. There should be 1 cup of purée. Use 3/4 cup for cake and reserve 1/4 cup for the frosting.

2. Sift together the flour, baking powder, baking soda, salt, cinnamon, mace, and cloves. Cream butter and both sugars together until light and fluffy. Beat in the egg yolks one at a time.

3. Blend in the dry ingredients, a third at a time, alternating with the carrot purée and carrot liquid. Stir in the nuts.

4. Beat egg whites until stiff and gently fold into batter. Spread in a greased and floured 9-by-13-inch baking pan.

5. Bake in a preheated 350 degree oven for 45 minutes. Cool for 10 minutes and turn out onto wire rack to cool. Frost with Golden Carrot Frosting.

Makes 12 servings.

Golden Carrot Frosting

¼ cup butter, at room temperature
3 cups confectioners' sugar, sifted
¼ cup reserved cooked carrot
2 tablespoons orange juice
1½ teaspoons grated fresh orange peel

1. Cream butter until soft and gradually beat in confectioners' sugar, alternating with cooked carrot and orange juice.
2. When smooth and fluffy, stir in grated orange peel.

Summery Peach Tart

When peaches are in season, look for the ripest you can find. Other fruits, plums, cherries, apples, or dried fruits, could be substituted.

For crust:
1 cup all-purpose flour
⅛ teaspoon salt
6 tablespoons unsalted butter
   (cold but pliable)
2 tablespoons granulated sugar
1 egg yolk

For filling:
4 medium ripe peaches
2 tablespoons fresh lemon juice
2 tablespoons light brown sugar
1 cup sour cream
2 eggs

Summery Peach Tart (recipe above), and Peach and Raspberry Cup (recipe, page 162)

¹/₃ cup granulated sugar
¹/₂ teaspoon vanilla extract

For topping:
3 tablespoons light brown sugar
3 tablespoons bread crumbs
1 tablespoon butter

1. For crust, place flour and salt in a bowl. Make a well and break the butter into it along with the sugar and egg yolk. Gradually incorporate the flour until it is completely blended and bowl is clean. Press the soft dough into an 8-inch pie pan, quiche pan, or ceramic dish. Refrigerate. Preheat oven to 400 degrees.

2. Blanch peaches by immersing them in boiling water for 1 or 2 minutes. Immediately plunge into cold water.

3. Prepare a bowl with lemon juice in it. Skin peaches. If peaches are ripe, skins will slip off. Roll peaches in the lemon juice. Pit peaches and slice into ¹/₄-inch slices. Turn them in the lemon juice.

4. Sprinkle brown sugar over the bottom of the pie crust. Place peach slices in one layer over the bottom, making concentric circles.

5. Beat the sour cream, eggs, sugar, and vanilla. Pour evenly onto peaches. Combine the brown sugar, bread crumbs, and butter and sprinkle over top. Bake for 40 minutes.

Makes 8 servings.

NOTE: Pie shell may be baked "blind." Place aluminum foil over dough and press down. Fill foil shell with dried beans or baking aluminum nuggets. Bake in 400 degree oven for 10 minutes. Remove beans and foil, prick with a fork and bake another 5 minutes, uncovered. Then, proceed with recipe. To keep shell from shrinking, place dough in pie pan and refrigerate for a minimum of 1 hour.

Pumpkin Chiffon Pie (recipe, page 163), Pumpkin-Date Torte (recipe, page 166), and Pumpkin Cheesecake (recipe, page 175)

Stuffed Peaches

1 1/2 cups water
1/2 cup dry vermouth
2 tablespoons lemon juice
1/2 cup sugar
4 ripe peaches
1/4 cup ground blanched almonds
1 tablespoon sour cream
1 teaspoon minced candied ginger
2 tablespoons sugar
1/4 teaspoon vanilla extract

1. Place water, vermouth, lemon juice, and sugar in a saucepan, bring to a simmer and cook gently for 10 minutes.

2. Blanch peaches by placing in boiling water for 1 or 2 minutes, slip off skins, cut in half and remove pits. Place halves immediately into the simmering syrup to prevent browning. Simmer for a few minutes until fruit is tender but still firm.

3. Remove peaches, place in a bowl, and chill. Reduce syrup to about 3/4 cup, cool and chill. Blend the almonds, sour cream, ginger, sugar, and vanilla. To serve place peach halves in individual bowls, stuff the centers with the almond mixture, and spoon syrup over the peaches.

Makes 4 servings.

Peach and Raspberry Cup

6 large ripe peaches
1 cup sugar
1/2 cup dry white wine or water
1 thin slice of lemon
1 pint raspberries
3 tablespoons Grand Marnier
  or Curacao liqueur
1 tablespoon kirsch brandy, optional

1. Blanch peaches in boiling water for about 1 minute and cool under cold running water. Slip off skin and halve the peaches. Combine sugar, wine, and lemon in a saucepan and boil for about 10 minutes until the syrup has thickened somewhat.

2. Add peach halves and simmer them gently for about 10 minutes until tender but not mushy. Remove them with a slotted spoon and cool. Boil the syrup down until quite thick and pour half of it over the peaches; cool and chill the peaches along with the remaining syrup.

3. Rub berries through a sieve, combine the purée with the liqueurs and the remaining syrup. Chill well. To serve, place peach halves in a serving bowl, spoon the raspberry purée over them. Garnish with a little whipped cream if desired.

Makes 6 servings.

Pears in Cream Sauce

Pears cooked in wine are one of my favorite desserts; this version is especially elegant.

8 pears
1 bottle dry white wine or champagne,
  about 3 1/3 cups
2 cinnamon sticks
1 generous cup sugar
1/4 cup pear-flavored brandy or Cognac,
  optional
1 cup heavy cream

1. Peel pears and slice off enough of the bottom so that pears will stand upright. Combine the wine, cinnamon, sugar, and brandy in a saucepan and bring to a boil. Add pears, reduce heat, cover and simmer until pears are tender, turning occasionally. Depending upon ripeness, pears may take as long as 1 hour. They should be very tender.

2. When pears are done, remove and set aside. Reduce remaining cooking liquid until thick and amber in color. Be careful not to reduce too much or liquid will burn. Let cool. Whip cream until stiff. Stir in a small amount of whipped cream into reduced cooking liquid, stir completely, then add remaining cream. To serve, spoon cream on bottom of plate. Top with pear.

Makes 8 servings.

Fresh Pear Upside Down Cake

3/4 cup butter or margarine, melted
1/4 cup packed light brown sugar
3 fresh pears, pared, cored, and halved
1 cup granulated sugar
1 egg
1 teaspoon grated orange rind
1 teaspoon vanilla extract
1 2/3 cups all-purpose flour
2 teaspoons baking powder
1/2 teaspoon salt
1/2 cup milk

1. Preheat oven to 325 degrees.
2. Pour 1/4 cup of the butter in a 10-by-6 1/2-inch baking dish. Tilt to coat evenly. Sprinkle brown sugar over butter. Arrange pears, cut side down, over brown sugar.
3. Beat granulated sugar, remaining 1/2 cup butter, egg, orange rind, and vanilla in a large mixing bowl until light and fluffy. Add the flour, baking powder, salt, and milk; beat until well blended. Pour batter evenly over pears.
4. Bake in preheated oven until wooden pick inserted in center of cake comes out clean, 50 to 60 minutes. Remove cake from oven and immediately invert onto serving plate. Cool. Cut cake into squares and serve warm.

Makes 6 servings.

Basic Pie Crust

2 1/4 cups flour
Pinch salt
12 tablespoons butter (1 1/2 sticks), placed in freezer for 30 minutes
6 to 7 tablespoons very cold water

1. *If using a food processor,* place flour and salt in the bowl of food processor. Cut butter in chunks and add. Blend briefly, just until flour has consistency of coarse meal. Be careful not to overprocess.
2. With machine running, slowly pour in water until a ball of dough is formed. You may not need all

of the water. Chill for 30 minutes before using.
3. *If preparing by hand,* combine flour, salt, and butter with pastry blender until flour has consistency of coarse meal. Add water and shape into a ball.

Makes enough dough for 2 pie shells (9 or 10 inches).

NOTE: For a sweet pastry, see page 171.

Pumpkin Chiffon Pie

This is a sure-fire light-weight pumpkin pie.

1 1/4 cups cooked, puréed pumpkin
2 eggs, separated
1 cup evaporated milk
1 1/2 cups dark brown sugar
1/2 teaspoon salt
1/2 teaspoon nutmeg
1/2 teaspoon cinnamon
1/4 teaspoon ginger
1 envelope unflavored gelatin
1/2 cup cold water
1/4 cup dark brown sugar
1 tablespoon bourbon, optional
1 9-inch baked pie shell (see recipe above)
Whipped cream or ice cream

1. Mix together the pumpkin, egg yolks, milk, brown sugar, salt, nutmeg, cinnamon, and ginger in a heavy saucepan. Cook over low heat, stirring constantly, about 10 minutes for mixture to barely simmer. It will be smooth—somewhat like custard. Remove from heat.
2. Stir gelatin and water together. Add gelatin mixture to hot pumpkin. Transfer to a bowl and cool over ice or refrigerate. When pumpkin becomes thick and sticks to sides of bowl, beat egg whites, adding sugar gradually. Fold egg whites into pumpkin; add bourbon.
3. Spoon into pie shell; refrigerate. Can be prepared 24 hours in advance. Decorate with whipped cream or serve with ice cream.

Makes 8 servings.

Fruit Growers & Fruit

Apples you might expect on Long Island, the Northeast being well known for its crop. But peaches? Apricots? Strawberries we know. Pick-your-own signs for strawberries crop up all over the Island where farmers devote as much as 300 acres to the intensely sweet berries. Later, raspberries ripen, which are cheaper than the imports but still a precious commodity.

Yet the favorable climate that nurtures cauliflower and ducks is equally beneficent to fruit.

"This is really one of the choicest places in the East to grow fruit," says John Wickham who owns a 350-acre farm in Cutchogue. "Being an island, we are completely surrounded by water, and particularly this North Fork with the bay on the south, the Sound on the north. There's no place in the Town of Southold where you can get more than a mile and a half from water."

"In reality, we have an oceanic climate, whereas Connecticut right across the Sound has a continental climate," says Wickham. "On a real cold night, it would be 10 degrees lower or more over there."

Wickham gradually abandoned the potatoes that were starting to become less profitable and more of a bother after a trip in the late 1930s to Argentina. On assignment to inspect potato growing, Wickham fell in love instead with the nectarine trees. "We started with ten trees here and they did so well that we said let's go into fruit," he says. By 1968, potatoes were a crop of the past, and now nearly 6,000 apple, 5,000 peach, and 400 apricot trees cover the graceful land, hugging the shore of Peconic Bay, lining the dirt road to the farmhouse built in the middle 1700s.

On the Sound, Briermere Farms had a long heritage of fruit trees started in 1902, but the original owners let the orchards deteriorate. When Gertrude and Leonard McCombe bought the property in 1961, she set about rectifying that situation. "The first decision we made was to cut out potatoes and concentrate on fruit trees. So I planted quite a few apple trees." The original 60 acres grew to 300, with most of the hills planted in apples, peaches, pears, almost down to the Sound.

It's necessary to plant a wide variety so that there will be a supply for months, the early July red

apples through the last of the season—Newtown Pippins, Rome, and Winesap. And such planting represents a great faith in the future, with apple trees taking five years before full maturity, and peaches as long as three or four.

There are about fifteen orchards in Suffolk County, on both Forks. Peaches are the biggest crop, followed by apples—including a few older varieties that are losing ground, literally, to the fast-growing, hardier, but, alas, less tasty strains. "Beginning the first of August, we have the Gravenstein, an old-fashioned apple," says Gertrude McCombe. "But once people get to know it, they love it. It makes the most wonderful apple pie and applesauce. They're good for eating too." Listen seriously to Gertrude McCombe on the matter of pies. What started as a way to use up leftover or damaged fruit has turned into a full-time, commercial operation, supplying fresh fruit pies to many Long Island farm stands.

Pears rank third in production, and in good years it's possible to buy a ripe, juicy, tender, tasty pear at a farm stand, instead of settling for the rock-hard fruit picked before it's ripe and shipped to supermarkets.

Many farmers love the challenge of introducing new crops, and love the income from being the first with a new product. Wickham is probably the only Northeastern farmer with apricot trees, two acres worth. He is also experimenting with Asian persimmons and, on reclaimed swampland, blueberries. "This land, presumably, will not grow tree fruit but it is simply ideal for blueberries and cranberries," says Wickham. Fifty years ago there were over 200 acres of cultivated cranberries on eastern Long Island; today there are none, due to a declining market coupled with competition from Massachusetts and the West Coast.

On the South Fork, Ray Halsey is experimenting with commercial blackberries. "The trouble with blackberries is that the older varieties have thorns on them," says Halsey. "You shove your whole arm and leg in to pick three berries. I just set some new ones out about a year ago which are a new type, thornless. They're not quite as flavorful, but at least you can pick them."

While Long Island farmers don't have to fret too much about damage from icy winters, they do battle against mold and assorted bugs as well as the overproduction that such a good climate can foster. "Because we have a heavy bloom almost every year, we have to use a thinning spray," says Wickham. Otherwise, there is too much fruit for each piece to develop properly. "It saps the tree's strength to make each one perfect. Peaches, in particular, will set like beads on a string. There'll be 20 peaches on a branch 12 inches long. They couldn't possibly all turn out to be 2½ to 3 inches, there wouldn't be room for them." Naturally, the tree decides in mid June that it can't possibly carry all of the fruit and drops half to three quarters of it; the farmers just help along that decision with a spray to "shock" the tree and make it shed excess fruit.

Seedless grapes—one of the crops Wickham pioneered growing on Long Island in cooperation with Cornell University—also need a nudge from the farmer. Because they have no seeds, they are deficient in a growth hormone that the farmers add artificially.

In bad years, when the weather doesn't cooperate and rain pummels the crops at crucial times, when a huge wind blows blossoms off and reduces the set, when the sun refuses to shine on schedule, then Long Island fruit doesn't look much better than off-Island competitors. Too much rain, particularly, seems to get in the way of flavorful fruit, swelling peaches to market size before their natural flavor develops. Not only that, but a few days of rain can wipe out a whole crop, leaving little moldy spots on the fruit. Melons, strawberries, and raspberries all fall victim to this and other unknown factors that make for average fruit some years.

Yet, when everything clicks, in those perfect growing seasons, nothing, no sweet Georgia peach, no Washington State apple can touch the local fruit.

John Wickham

Pumpkin-Date Torte

1/2 cup chopped dates
1/2 cup chopped walnuts
2 tablespoons all-purpose flour
1/4 cup butter, melted
1 cup firmly packed brown sugar
2/3 cup cooked, puréed pumpkin
1 teaspoon vanilla extract
2 eggs
1/2 cup all-purpose flour
1/2 teaspoon baking powder
1/4 teaspoon baking soda
1/2 teaspoon cinnamon
1/2 teaspoon nutmeg
1/4 teaspoon ground ginger
1 cup heavy cream, whipped to soft peaks

1. In a small mixing bowl, mix together the dates, nuts, and 2 tablespoons flour. Set aside.

2. In a large mixing bowl, mix together the butter, brown sugar, pumpkin, vanilla, and eggs.

3. Sift together 1/2 cup flour, baking powder, baking soda, cinnamon, nutmeg, and ginger. Stir into the pumpkin mixture. Stir in the floured dates and nuts, then turn into a greased 9-inch cake pan.

4. Bake in a preheated 350 degree oven for 20 to 25 minutes or until cake tester comes out clean. Serve warm with a topping of whipped cream.

Makes 8 servings.

Raspberry Mousseline

If you can keep from eating the raspberries just as is, save them for this dessert.

1 quart fresh raspberries reserving a few for a
    garnish
3/4 cup sugar
1 tablespoon lemon juice
2 tablespoons unflavored gelatin
1/4 cup cold water
1/4 cup dry white wine
1/2 teaspoon vanilla extract
4 tablespoons kirsch brandy, optional

1 1/2 cups heavy cream, whipped
Ladyfingers

1. Rub raspberries through a sieve into a bowl to remove the seeds. In a medium bowl combine the purée with the sugar and lemon juice, stir until sugar has dissolved. Sprinkle gelatin with cold water to soften, place it in a small pan, add wine and heat while stirring until gelatin has dissolved.

2. Add the wine mixture, vanilla, and kirsch to the raspberry purée, blend, and place the bowl into a large bowl of crushed ice. Stir until the purée starts to thicken. Fold in the whipped cream.

3. Rinse a 1 1/4-quart mold with cold water, pat dry, and line sides with ladyfingers. Spoon the purée into the mold and chill several hours until well set. Unmold on a chilled serving plate, garnish with a few whole berries and a little more whipped cream if desired.

Makes 6 servings.

Deep Dish Rhubarb Pie

6 cups fresh rhubarb, cut into 1-inch pieces,
    about 2 pounds
3/4 to 1 cup sugar
1/3 cup cornstarch
1/3 cup light corn syrup
1 tablespoon butter
Pastry for single crust pie (see page 163)

1. Toss rhubarb with sugar and cornstarch. Mix with corn syrup. Place mixture in a buttered 8-inch square baking pan and dot with butter.

2. Roll pastry to a 9-inch square. Cover rhubarb mixture with pastry and tuck edge between rhubarb and side of pan. Flute crust. Cut several slits in top. Bake in a preheated 425 degree oven for 55 minutes or until rhubarb is tender and crust is browned.

Makes 6 servings.

Oatmeal-Rhubarb Crunch

1 cup sifted flour
3/4 cup uncooked oatmeal
1 cup brown sugar, firmly packed
1/2 cup melted butter
1 teaspoon cinnamon
4 cups diced rhubarb
1 cup granulated sugar
2 tablespoons cornstarch
1 cup water
1 teaspoon pure vanilla extract
Heavy cream or whipped cream

1. In a bowl, mix together with a fork the flour, oatmeal, brown sugar, melted butter, and cinnamon until crumbly.

2. Press half the mixture into a greased 9-inch square or round baking pan. Cover crumb mixture with diced rhubarb.

3. In a saucepan, combine the sugar, cornstarch, water, and vanilla. Cook until a thick syrup forms. Pour sauce over rhubarb. Top with remaining half of crumb mixture. Bake in a preheated 350 degree oven for 1 hour. Serve warm, in bowls, topped with heavy cream or whipped cream.

Makes 8 servings.

Spiced Rhubarb and Strawberry Shortcake

Rhubarb and strawberries are a natural pairing, particularly at shortcake time.

For spiced fruit:
1 pound rhubarb
2/3 cup sugar
1 1/2 tablespoons cornstarch
1 1/2 teaspoons cinnamon
1/8 teaspoon salt
2 cups strawberries, hulled and halved

For shortcake:
2 cups all-purpose flour
1/4 cup sugar

1 tablespoon baking powder
1/4 teaspoon salt
1/4 teaspoon nutmeg
1/2 cup butter or margarine
2 eggs, beaten lightly
1/2 cup milk
1 cup heavy cream whipped

1. Trim base and leaves from rhubarb, then cut stalks into 1-inch chunks, making about 2 1/4 cups. Make a layer of the rhubarb in a buttered 2-quart casserole.

2. In a small bowl, combine the sugar, cornstarch, cinnamon, and salt. Sprinkle half of this mixture over the rhubarb. Add another layer of rhubarb, then remaining sugar mixture. Mix well. Cover and bake in a preheated 375 degree oven until rhubarb is soft, about 30 minutes. Stir in the strawberries, cover, and bake 5 minutes longer. Cool and eat as a sauce or use over shortcake.

3. Prepare the cake. In a large bowl, combine the flour, sugar, baking powder, salt, and nutmeg. Cut in butter with a pastry blender or two knives, until mixture resembles coarse crumbs. Add eggs and milk, stir with a fork just until blended.

4. Spoon into an 8-inch cake pan that is greased and lined with waxed paper. Bake in a preheated 425 degree oven until brown, and a cake tester tests clean. Turn out onto a rack, cook, and cut in half crosswise. Fill with half the spiced fruit mixture, then top with cake and the remaining fruit. Serve with whipped cream, if desired.

Makes 8 servings.

Double Strawberry Sorbet

1 quart ripe strawberries, washed and hulled
1 1/2 cups strawberry preserves
2 teaspoons lemon juice

1. In a blender or food processor, purée the fresh berries. If using a blender, it may be necessary to do this in several batches. Remove purée and set aside.

2. Without cleaning the machine's container, purée the strawberry preserves with the lemon juice.

3. Combine the two purées in the canister of an

ice cream machine and stir well. Process according to manufacturer's directions, using the maximum amount of salt recommended. When fairly firm, pack down in the canister and place in freezer to ripen for several hours.

Makes about 1¹/₂ quarts.

NOTE: Purée can be placed in a freezer container and frozen overnight. It will not have as nice a texture, but will still be delicious.

Strawberries with Zabaglione

The Italian favorite, zabaglione, calls for marsala; here Marie Bianco has substituted white wine for a lighter effect.

4 egg yolks
²/₃ cup sugar
²/₃ cup white wine
1 cup heavy cream, whipped
2 pints perfect strawberries

1. In the top of a double boiler, beat egg yolks with whisk until thick. Gradually add sugar, beating constantly. Stir in wine. Place over hot, not boiling, water and cook until mixture thickens, stirring constantly—about 15 to 20 minutes. Remove from heat. Cool slightly. Stir in whipped cream.

2. Wash berries carefully and pat dry. Spoon into dessert glasses and top with zabaglione.

Makes 6 to 8 servings.

FROM THE TOP, CLOCKWISE *Fruit Tarts (recipe, page 171),*
Double Strawberry Sorbet (recipe, page 167), and
Strawberries with Zabaglione (recipe opposite)

Chilled Strawberry Mousse Cake

At the height of the strawberry season, serve this light, airy creation.

 1/2 cup cold water
 1/4 cup orange juice
 3 envelopes unflavored gelatin
 3 pints strawberries, cleaned and hulled
 1 1/2 tablespoons fresh lime juice
 2 tablespoons kirsch brandy, optional
 3 eggs
 1 cup sugar
 1 pint heavy cream, whipped
 Pound cake
 Whole strawberries for garnish

1. Put water and orange juice in top of a double boiler, and sprinkle gelatin over to soften. Stir over boiling water until gelatin has dissolved; remove from heat and cool.

2. Purée the berries in a blender or food processor; stir in lime juice and kirsch. Combine and mix with dissolved gelatin.

3. Beat eggs until frothy, add sugar and continue beating until mixture is very light and lemon colored. Add the strawberry mixture and fold in the whipped cream, blend gently.

4. Line the sides of a 9- or 10-inch springform pan with 1/2-inch-thick slices of pound cake. Pour the strawberry mixture into the pan, smooth the top and refrigerate for 8 hours. There will be extra mixture; pour it into individual custard cups and refrigerate.

5. To serve: remove the sides of the pan, place cake on a serving dish and garnish with a few whole berries and additional whipped cream, if desired.

Makes 8 servings.

Strawberry Cake with Strawberry Glaze

For cake:
 3 cups sifted cake flour
 2 teaspoons baking powder
 1 1/2 cups granulated sugar

 1 teaspoon salt
 1 cup butter, at room temperature
 4 eggs
 1/3 cup milk
 2 teaspoons vanilla extract
 1 cup fresh strawberries, chopped,
   about 2/3 pint
 1/2 cup chopped nuts

For glaze:
 1 egg yolk
 1 tablespoon butter, at room temperature
 1 1/2 cups sifted confectioners' sugar
 1/2 cup crushed strawberries

1. In a mixer bowl, place flour, baking powder, sugar, and salt. Toss lightly with a fork to combine.

2. Add the butter, eggs, milk, and vanilla. Beat until blended. Fold in strawberries and nuts.

3. Spoon batter into buttered and floured 9-inch tube pan. Bake in a preheated 375 degree oven for 1 hour and 15 minutes or until cake tests done. When cool, cover with glaze.

4. To prepare glaze, beat egg yolk well with fork or whisk. Add the butter and half the confectioners' sugar. Blend well. Gradually add the remaining sugar and beat until smooth. Fold in strawberries.

Makes 16 servings.

Chocolate Dipped Strawberries

The secret to perfect dipped strawberries is to take the chocolate off the heat as it starts to melt; otherwise it turns grainy.

 3 pints strawberries
 1 pound semisweet chocolate morsels

1. Use only perfect strawberries. Wash and carefully pat dry.

2. Place chocolate in top of double boiler and heat over simmering water. Do not allow water to touch bottom of pan. Remove from heat when thermometer reads 120 degrees or when chocolate just begins to melt. Continue to stir until temperature drops to 70 degrees. Or place chocolate in a plastic

bowl and melt in a microwave oven using 50 percent power. Be sure to remove chocolate from heat as soon as it melts or it will become gritty.

3. To dip berries, hold them by the stem and dip into warm chocolate, up to but not including green stem leaves. Allow excess chocolate to drip off. Rest berries on waxed paper until chocolate hardens and place in refrigerator if room temperature is above 70 degrees. Since chocolate-dipped strawberries do not keep well, plan on eating them within a few hours.

Makes about 40 strawberries

Fruit Tart in a Caramel Cage

For extra panache, you can make a "cage" out of caramel to cover the tart; however, the dessert, from Karen Frame Pancake at Peche Mignon, will be just as delicious without it. The amount of water in the pastry will vary with the season; start with ¼ cup and add more as needed.

For the pâte sucrée:
1½ cups flour
¼ cup sugar
7 tablespoons sweet butter, chilled
1 egg yolk beaten with about ¼ cup water

For crème pâtissière:
5 egg yolks
½ cup sugar
Generous ½ cup flour
1¾ cups scalded milk
1 tablespoon sweet butter
1 teaspoon real vanilla extract
½ cup whipped cream

For glaze:
¼ cup currant jelly
1 tablespoon water
Strawberries, raspberries, or other desired fruit

For caramel cage:
1½ cups sugar
¼ cup water

1. For pâte sucrée, blend flour and sugar together in a bowl. Cut butter into small pieces and toss with the flour mixture. With the tips of your fingers, work the butter into the flour until the butter resembles pieces of oatmeal. Make a well in the center and add the egg-water mixture. With a fork, quickly mix this into the flour until moist enough to form a ball, adding a bit more water if necessary. Wrap in plastic and refrigerate until just firm enough to roll out. Roll out on a floured surface (preferably marble) to ⅛-inch thickness. This dough will make 8 to 10 4-inch tarts or 1 larger tart, about 10 inches in diameter. Turn the tart pans upside down on the dough, cut around them and place the rounds of dough in the pans. Put aluminum foil in each tart and fill with dried beans or rice to keep dough from shrinking during baking. Bake in a preheated 375 degree oven for 10 minutes, remove foil and return tarts to oven for 5 minutes or until lightly browned.

2. For the crème pâtissière: beat the egg yolks, gradually adding sugar, until pale and fluffy. Slowly beat in the flour and add the hot milk in a stream. Mix until completely incorporated. Transfer pastry cream to a heavy, nonaluminum saucepan and, over medium-high heat, whisk constantly until the mixture becomes very thick. Continue to whisk while boiling for about a minute. Remove from heat and whisk in the butter and vanilla. Put in the food processor for several seconds to make completely smooth. Cool in a bowl, rubbing butter on top to prevent a skin from forming. Refrigerate until ready to use, then fold in the whipped cream.

3. To assemble: heat the jelly and water until liquid. Place a layer of pastry cream in the bottom of the cooked shells, then top with an attractive array of strawberries, raspberries, or other fruit. Brush on glaze so that the fruit glistens.

4. The tarts are delicious as is, but for a more elegant presentation, make the caramel cage. Melt the sugar and water over medium heat. Stir initially to mix, then swirl occasionally as it melts and turns a light nut brown. Remove from the heat and let cool until the consistency of honey. Butter the outside of a glass bowl large enough to cover tart. Dip a soup spoon into the caramel. In a continuous motion, swirl the dripping caramel over the bowl in loops. Let cool. Carefully remove the cage by gently pushing from the bottom.

5. To serve: remove the sides of the pan, place cake on a serving dish and garnish with a few whole berries and additional whipped cream, if desired.

Makes 8 to 10 4-inch tarts or 1 10-inch tart.

Berries over Ice Cream

As one of the easiest desserts you'll make, this is also one of the best. If you have a lot of raspberries, you could purée half of them instead of the blueberries, flavoring them with Grand Marnier.

> 1 pint blueberries
> Pinch sugar
> 1 to 2 tablespoons crème de cassis
> 1 quart vanilla ice cream
> 1/2 pint fresh raspberries

Purée half of the blueberries in a food processor or blender. Add sugar and crème de cassis to taste. If desired, press puréed mixture through a fine sieve. To serve, spoon ice cream into dishes and top with blueberry purée and then scatter remaining blueberries and all of the raspberries on top.

Makes 6 servings.

Old-fashioned French Vanilla Ice Cream

> 6 egg yolks
> 2 cups milk
> 1 cup sugar
> 1/4 teaspoon salt
> 2 cups heavy cream
> 2 tablespoons vanilla extract

1. In the top of a double boiler, beat egg yolks and milk until well blended. Stir in sugar and salt.

2. Cook, stirring constantly, over hot (not boiling) water until mixture is thick and coats a metal spoon. Cool, then cover and refrigerate until chilled.

3. Stir in cream and vanilla extract. Pour into ice cream freezer and churn according to manufacturer's directions.

Makes 2 quarts.

PRECEDING PAGE *Berries over Ice Cream, Sour Cream Chocolate Ice Cream (recipes, page 174), and Wholesome Chocolate Chip Cookies (recipe, page 178)*

Sour Cream Chocolate Ice Cream

A true summertime delight—homemade ice cream, made richer still with chocolate and sour cream.

> 1 cup sugar
> 1 tablespoon flour
> 2 eggs, beaten
> 1 quart sweet milk
> 2 squares bitter chocolate, melted
> 1 teaspoon vanilla extract
> 1 pint sweet milk
> 3/4 cup sugar
> 1 pint sour cream, preferably
>   naturally soured

1. Place sugar and flour in a large saucepan. Make a paste by adding the eggs, then the quart of milk, a little at a time. Cook over medium heat, stirring with a wooden spoon, until custard coats the spoon. Add melted chocolate. Let cool.

2. Add the vanilla, pint of milk, 3/4 cup sugar, and sour cream. Beat thoroughly, and freeze in a churn-type freezer, according to manufacturer's directions.

Makes about 1 gallon.

Creamy Cheesecake

Marie Bianco is the resident cheesecake expert. This is her favorite plain cheesecake, adapted from an A&S cheesecake contest winner. She perfected the chocolate cheesecake and pumpkin, too.

> 32 ounces (2 pounds) whipped cream cheese
> 6 tablespoons sweet butter
> 12 ounces sour cream
> 2 tablespoons cornstarch
> 1 teaspoon vanilla extract
> 1 teaspoon grated lemon rind
> 1 cup sugar
> 6 eggs
> Butter
> Cookie or graham cracker crumbs

1. Have all ingredients at room temperature. In the large bowl of an electric mixer, blend together the

whipped cream cheese, butter, sour cream, cornstarch, vanilla, lemon rind, and sugar.

2. Beat eggs into mixture one at a time, mixing well after each addition.

3. Liberally grease a 10-inch springform pan with butter. Sprinkle lightly with crumbs and shake out excess. Wrap outside with aluminum foil to contain any leaks. Pour mixture into prepared pan. Place pan on shelf in middle of oven; place a roasting pan with 1 inch of water on the lower shelf.

4. Bake in a preheated 350 degree oven for 1 hour. The center of the cheesecake will not be completely set; it may still "jiggle." Remove and cool away from drafts. Refrigerate for 24 hours before serving. Remove 1 hour before serving.

Makes 16 servings.

gree oven for 5 minutes. Remove from oven; set aside to cool. Do not turn off oven.

2. In the large bowl of an electric mixer, beat the eggs with sugar until light and creamy. Beat in softened cream cheese. Add melted chocolate, vanilla and almond extracts, salt, and sour cream. Beat until smooth and creamy. Pour into prepared crust and bake at 350 degrees for 1 hour or until firm.

3. Cool cheesecake completely, preferably overnight. Remove side of springform pan. Just before serving, beat cream until almost stiff; add confectioners' sugar and almond extract. Continue beating cream until stiff. Place in a pastry bag and pipe out around edge of cake. Sprinkle with slivered almonds.

Makes 16 servings.

Chocolate Cheesecake

For crust:
1 8 1/2-ounce package chocolate wafers
6 tablespoons melted butter
1 tablespoon granulated sugar

For filling:
3 eggs
3/4 cup granulated sugar
24 ounces (1 1/2 pounds) cream cheese, at room
    temperature
2 cups (12 ounces) semisweet chocolate
    morsels, melted
1/2 teaspoon vanilla extract
1/2 teaspoon almond extract
Pinch salt
1 cup sour cream

For garnish:
1 cup heavy cream
1 tablespoon confectioners' sugar
1/4 teaspoon almond extract
Slivered almonds

1. To prepare crust, crush chocolate wafers in a blender or food processor. In a medium bowl, combine crushed wafers, melted butter, and sugar. Press around sides and bottom of a lightly buttered 9-inch springform pan. Bake crust in a preheated 350 de-

Pumpkin Cheesecake

For crust:
1 1/2 cups zwieback crumbs
3 tablespoons sugar
3 tablespoons melted butter

For filling:
16 ounces cream cheese, at room
    temperature
1 cup light cream
1 cup mashed cooked pumpkin
3/4 cup sugar
4 eggs, separated
3 tablespoons flour
1 teaspoon vanilla extract
1 teaspoon cinnamon
1/2 teaspoon ginger
1/2 teaspoon nutmeg
1/4 teaspoon salt

For topping:
1 cup sour cream
2 tablespoons sugar
1/2 teaspoon vanilla extract

1. Combine zwieback crumbs, sugar, and melted butter. Press onto bottom and sides of a buttered 9-inch springform pan. Bake in a preheated 350 degree oven for 5 minutes. Cool slightly. Do not turn off oven, but reduce heat to 325 degrees.

Pick-your-own pumpkins, Stakey Farm in Aquebogue

2. In the large bowl of an electric mixer, combine cream cheese, cream, pumpkin, sugar, egg yolks, flour, vanilla, cinnamon, ginger, nutmeg, and salt. Beat until smooth.

3. Beat egg whites until stiff, fold into pumpkin mixture. Pour into crust. Bake at 325 degrees for 40 minutes. Remove from oven.

4. Combine sour cream, sugar, and vanilla. Spread over cake. Return to oven 5 minutes longer. Turn oven off; allow cake to cool in oven for about 2 hours.

Makes about 16 servings.

The Alternate Ultimate Chocolate Cake from Bernie Leibman

Bernie Leibman is always searching for the ultimate chocolate cake, and has been through at least three "ultimate" cakes, with variations. This is the reigning favorite.

4 ounces sweet chocolate
$1/2$ cup water
1 cup (2 sticks) butter or margarine, at room temperature
2 cups sugar
4 eggs, separated
2 teaspoons vanilla extract
$2^1/4$ cups flour
1 teaspoon baking soda
$1/2$ teaspoon salt
1 cup plain yogurt
Cocoa
Chocolate Frosting (see recipe below)

1. Bring the water to a boil. Remove from heat, add the chocolate, and stir to melt. Let cool.

2. Cream the butter or margarine and sugar until fluffy. Add the egg yolks one at a time, beating well after each addition. Blend in the vanilla and the chocolate.

3. Sift the flour, baking soda, and salt. Add this with the yogurt to the chocolate mixture, beating after each addition until smooth.

4. Beat the egg whites and fold into the batter.

5. Line three 9-inch layer pans with waxed paper and dust with cocoa. Pour batter into pans. Bake in a preheated 350 degree oven for 30 to 35 minutes. Cool before frosting.

Makes about 12 servings.

Chocolate Frosting

12 ounces Tobler bittersweet chocolate bits
4 tablespoons butter
4 tablespoons light corn syrup
6 tablespoons milk or half and half

Combine chocolate pieces and butter in top of a double boiler. Melt, stirring frequently over hot, not boiling, water. Stir in the corn syrup and milk. Heat until smooth. Spread the glaze while still warm over the cake.

German Chocolate-Cheese Brownies

2 4-ounce packages German sweet chocolate
10 tablespoons butter, at room temperature
2 3-ounce packages cream cheese, at room temperature
2 cups sugar
6 eggs
1 cup plus 2 tablespoons all-purpose flour
2 teaspoons vanilla extract
1 teaspoon baking powder
$1/2$ teaspoon salt
$1/2$ teaspoon almond extract
1 cup chopped toasted almonds

1. Combine chocolate and 6 tablespoons of the butter in a 2-quart saucepan. Place over low heat, stirring occasionally, until melted. Remove from heat; cool to room temperature.

2. Cream together the cream cheese and 4 tablespoons butter in a bowl, using electric mixer on me-

dium speed. Add ½ cup of the sugar, beating until light and fluffy. Blend in 2 eggs, 2 tablespoons flour, and 1 teaspoon vanilla. Set aside.

3. Beat remaining 4 eggs in another mixing bowl until foamy, with electric mixer on high speed. Gradually add the rest of the sugar, beating until thick and lemon-colored.

4. Sift together the 1 cup flour, baking powder, and salt. Add to egg mixture, mixing well. Blend in cooled chocolate mixture, vanilla and almond extracts. Stir in almonds. Reserve 2 cups of chocolate batter. Spread remaining chocolate batter in a greased 9-by-13-inch baking pan. Spread cream cheese mixture over first layer. Spoon remaining 2 cups chocolate batter over all. Use a metal spatula to swirl layers to give a marbled effect.

5. Bake in a preheated 350 degree oven for 50 minutes or until done. Cool on rack. Cut into 2-inch squares.

Makes 24 brownies.

Wholesome Chocolate Chip Cookies

½ cup unsalted butter, at room temperature
½ cup shortening
1 cup packed brown sugar
⅓ cup molasses
2 eggs
1 teaspoon vanilla extract
2 cups whole wheat flour
¼ cup wheat germ
¼ cup instant nonfat dry milk
1 teaspoon salt
1 teaspoon baking soda
1 12-ounce package semisweet chocolate chip morsels or 2 cups chips

1. Preheat oven to 375 degrees.
2. In mixing bowl, blend together the butter, shortening, brown sugar, molasses, eggs, and vanilla.
3. On a piece of waxed paper or in a bowl, mix together the flour, wheat germ, dry milk, salt, and baking soda. Add to the first mixture, a little at a time, until blended.

4. Add the chocolate chips and beat in with a wooden spoon.

5. Drop by teaspoonfuls onto greased cookie sheets. Bake at 375 degrees for 10 to 12 minutes or until light brown. Remove immediately and cool thoroughly on wire racks.

Makes about 90 2½-inch cookies.

Bernie's Triple Chocolate Cookies

2 ounces unsweetened chocolate
6 ounces semisweet chocolate
2 tablespoons butter
2 large eggs
¾ cup sugar
2 teaspoons instant espresso or regular coffee
⅛ teaspoon salt
1 teaspoon vanilla extract
¼ cup sifted all-purpose flour
¼ teaspoon baking powder
1 cup broken-up walnuts
1¼ cups semisweet chocolate bits, about 12 ounces

1. Preheat oven to 350 degrees. Melt chocolate squares and butter in top of double boiler.

2. Combine the eggs, sugar, coffee, salt, and vanilla and beat with mixer on high speed until smooth. Add melted chocolate.

3. Add flour and baking powder and mix on low speed. Do not overbeat. Stir in walnut and chocolate bits.

4. On an unbuttered cookie sheet or foil, place 2 heaping teaspoons of dough for each cookie—mixture does not spread. Bake 10 to 12 minutes. Remove quickly when cookie "cracks" on top. Cookies may be reheated before serving.

Makes about 4 dozen.

Sheila Sarrett's Meringue Cookies

These meringue cookies may be baked either after the oven has been used and is still hot or by themselves in a 225 degree oven.

  2 egg whites
  ½ cup sugar
  Scant ¼ teaspoon salt
  ¼ teaspoon cream of tartar
  1 teaspoon vanilla extract
  1 6-ounce package semisweet chocolate
    morsels

1. Preheat oven to 225 degrees or bake cookies after using oven for other cooking. Line a large cookie sheet with lightly greased aluminum foil.

2. Whip egg whites until frothy.

3. Add sugar and continue to whip while adding salt, cream of tartar, and vanilla.

4. Whip on high speed until egg white mixture is very stiff. The consistency should be like marshmallow topping. It should take about a total of 15 minutes for it to reach this consistency, starting from the time you begin Step 2.

5. Fold in the chocolate morsels.

6. Using a tablespoon, drop generous-sized mounds of mixture onto the greased cookie sheet.

7. Immediately place cookie sheet into the hot oven and shut oven door. Bake cookies for 1 hour or until dry. Or turn oven off and keep them in the oven with door shut for about 7 hours or overnight.

Makes about 24 cookies.

Linzer Tarts

These cookies are elegant and delicious.

  1 cup (2 sticks) sweet butter, at room
    temperature
  1 cup granulated sugar
  2 eggs
  ½ teaspoon almond extract
  2½ cups all-purpose flour
  2 teaspoons baking powder
  Raspberry preserves
  Confectioners' sugar

1. Cream butter and sugar together until light and creamy. Beat in eggs one at a time, then add almond flavoring.

2. Sift together the flour and baking powder and stir into creamed mixture. Wrap dough in wax paper and chill overnight.

3. Roll out a small portion of the dough on a lightly floured board to ¼-inch thickness. Keep remaining dough refrigerated. Cut into 3-inch rounds. Cut out the centers of half the rounds using a small canapé cutter or a round plastic pill container, about 1 inch in diameter. Or a doughnut cutter can be used to cut out the top cookie. Repeat with remaining dough.

4. Bake on an ungreased baking sheet in a preheated 375 degree oven about 8 to 10 minutes. Do not allow the cookies to brown. Remove from pan and cool on a rack.

5. To assemble tarts, spread 1 teaspoon of jam on a plain cookie and top with one with a hole. Dust with confectioners' sugar. Store in an airtight container.

Makes 24 tarts.

A List of Long Island Farm Stands

Farm stands come and go. Please use this list as a guide only. The farm stands listed below are arranged geographically, from east to west.

1. KLEIN'S FARM STAND, 194-15 73rd Ave., Flushing. Vegetables sold: cabbage, lettuce, scallions, radishes, carrots, beets, rhubarb, corn, tomatoes, green beans, cucumbers, zucchini, potatoes, onions, eggplant, butternut squash, basil, dill, parsley, broccoli, cauliflower, and turnips. Also melons, apples, and pears. Open seven days, 9 A.M.-6 P.M.

2. JAMAICA FARMERS MARKET, Parsons Blvd. and Jamaica Ave., Jamaica. Specialties are Filipino dishes, breads and muffins, apple cider. Apples, strawberries, peaches, pears, cauliflower, broccoli, squash, melons, tomatoes, cucumbers, onions, peppers, cabbage, peas, beets, corn, potatoes, okra, beans, spinach, escarole, collards, parsley, Brussels sprouts, mustard greens, scallions, and Swiss chard. Also house and garden plants. Open Fridays and Saturdays, 8 A.M.-6 P.M., April to December.

3. ROTTKAMP'S FARM STAND, 554 Hempstead Tpke., Elmont. Homegrown corn, tomatoes, Swiss chard, cucumbers, beets, carrots, cantaloupes, lima beans, kohlrabi, collards, and mustard greens. Open Tuesdays, Fridays, Saturdays, and Sundays, 9:30 A.M.-6 P.M. until Sept. 30.

4. GROSSMANN'S FARMS, 488 Hempstead Ave., Malverne. Locally grown corn, carrots, beets, radishes, scallions, broccoli, many varieties of lettuce, squash, tomatoes, basil, beans, and local muskmelons. Homemade jams and jellies. Cut flowers and floral arrangements. Open seven days, 9 A.M.-5 P.M. until Dec. 1.

5. SWEET PEA FRUIT EXCHANGE INC., 3370 Hillside Ave., New Hyde Park. Enormous variety of all fruits and vegetables from all over the world. Complete line of Japanese and Chinese vegetables, 700 varieties of cheeses from France, Switzerland, Austria, and Holland. Melons and tomatoes from Israel in season, strawberries and raspberries from New Zealand, gourmet fish market, gourmet deli, and yogurt parlor. Open 24 hours daily, year-round.

6. PARKER'S FARMS, Newbridge Road, north of Sunrise Hwy., Bellmore. All homegrown vegetables in season; homegrown corn a specialty. Second stand on Pulaski Road, west of Oakwood Road, Cold Spring Harbor. Open seven days, 9 A.M.-6 P.M.

7. YOUNGS' FARM, Hegeman's Lane (north of Route 25A), Old Brookville. Homegrown corn, berries, melons, squash, and tomatoes. Homemade pies and breads. Homemade jams. Greenhouse tomatoes and geraniums in spring. Open Tuesdays-Saturdays, 10 A.M.-5 P.M. and Sundays, 10 A.M.-3 P.M. (closed Mondays). Closed January.

8. VAN SISE FARMS, 8047 Jericho Tpke., Woodbury. Local fruits and vegetables, Chinese vegetables including bok choy, nappa, snow peas, bean sprouts. Several varieties of lettuce, hybrid European ("burpless") cucumbers, kohlrabi, nuts, large variety of melons, Jerusalem artichokes, exotic fruits including kiwi, mango, and papaya. Fresh homemade cider in fall. Open seven days, 9 A.M.-6 P.M. year-round.

9. MEYER'S FARM, Woodbury Road, Woodbury. Homegrown summer and winter squash, corn, tomatoes, peppers, white and purple cauliflower, cucumbers, kirby's (small cucumbers often used for pickling), Brussels sprouts, eggplant, broccoli, pumpkins, cantaloupes, watermelons, and Crenshaw melons. Fresh apple cider made on premises in fall. Open seven days, 9 A.M.-6 P.M. until Thanksgiving.

10. MEDIAVILLA FRUIT FARM, 1501 E. Jericho Tpke., Huntington. Homegrown tomatoes, eggplant, corn. Freshly pressed apple cider in fall. Twelve varieties of apples from Labor Day to Thanksgiving. Also dwarf fruit trees available for spring planting. Open seven days, 10 A.M.-6 P.M.

11. SUNNY POND FARM, 478 Park Ave., Huntington. Organic homegrown vegetables, dried fruits, fresh home-baked breads, dried herbs and teas. How-to recipes available on blackboard. Open daily except Mondays, 9:30 A.M.-5:45 P.M., April to Thanksgiving.

12. ARTHUR SILBERSTEIN'S FARM STAND, Pulaski and Oakwood Roads, Huntington. All homegrown vegetables including six varieties of bicolor corn, eight varieties of squash, six varieties of tomatoes, broccoli, cucumbers, peppers, eggplant, cantaloupes, burpless cucumbers, watermelons, and green beans. Open seven days, 9 A.M.-6 P.M., until Oct. 31.

13. MEYER'S FARM, Old Country Road, Melville, (a quarter-mile north of Long Island Expressway exit 48). A complete selection of locally grown produce. Pick-your-own tomatoes, plum tomatoes, peppers, and eggplant starting in August. Also, house plants and homemade zucchini bread. Open seven days, 10 A.M.-6 P.M.

14. MEGLIO FARM STAND, Ruland Road, west of Pinelawn Road, Melville. Homegrown vegetables include herbs, squash, cabbage, beets, corn, tomatoes, and green beans. Open seven days a week, 10 A.M.-5 P.M. until mid-November.

15. SCHMITT'S FARM STAND, 26 Pinelawn Road, Melville. Homegrown vegetables in season include iceberg, romaine, Boston, red leaf and salad-bowl lettuces, beans, beets, peppers, radishes, spinach, squash, tomatoes, and corn. Pick-your-own pumpkins for nursery school, kindergarten, first and second-grade children on weekdays; family picking on weekends only. Open seven days, 8:30 A.M.-5:30 P.M., until Oct. 31.

16. WHITE POST FARM MARKET AND GREENHOUSE, 250 Old Country Road, Melville. Homegrown vegetables: six varieties of lettuce, tomatoes, sweet corn, peppers, zucchini, cucumbers, eggplant, beets, celery, radishes, scallions, broccoli, spinach, and more. Specialties: hard-to-find vegetables such as arugula, Swiss chard, dandelion, watercress, basil, dill, and a full line of Oriental vegetables. Greenhouse is filled with annuals, perennials, hanging baskets, and holiday plants. Open six days, 9:30 A.M.-5:30 P.M. (closed Wednesdays), year-round.

17. REDWOOD FARM STAND, Route 110, Farmingdale. Homegrown tomatoes, cucumbers, squash, peppers, eggplant,

bicolor corn, and other top-quality fruits and vegetables. Open seven days, 10 A.M.-6 P.M., year-round.

18. KALER'S FARMS, 580 W. Montauk Hwy., Lindenhurst. Summer squash, peppers, eggplant, tomatoes, peas, cantaloupes, cauliflower, broccoli, cucumbers, radishes, and cabbage. Open seven days, 10 A.M.-6 P.M.

19. KAUFOLD FARMS, 1748 Straight Path, Wheatley Heights. Full line of fresh vegetables and fruits. Garden mums in fall. Pick-your-own strawberries, plum tomatoes, beefsteak tomatoes, peppers, frying peppers, green beans, eggplant, pumpkins, cucumbers, and squash. Pick-your-own pumpkin in October. Call for season dates and hours, which may vary according to weather conditions. Open August 1 to Oct. 31, seven days, 9 A.M.-5 P.M.

20. DAVIS FARM STAND, 624 Deer Park Ave., Dix Hills. Homegrown produce includes sweet corn, tomatoes, cucumbers, peppers, melons, squash, green beans, eggplant, herbs, bedding plants, and pick-your-own pumpkins. In fall, forty varieties of apples, six varieties of pears, cider without preservatives. Open seven days, 10 A.M.-6 P.M., year-round.

21. RED BARN FARM, Bagatelle and Half Hollow Roads, (take LIE exit 50), Dix Hills. Homegrown tomatoes, corn, peppers, cucumbers, squash, lettuce. Greenhouse with hanging baskets. Open seven days, 9:30 A.M.-6:30 P.M., until Dec. 20.

22. DeROSA'S FARM STAND, 800 Deer Park Ave., Dix Hills. Local vegetables in season for both wholesale and retail. Open Sundays and Mondays, 10 A.M.-5 P.M.; Tuesdays to Saturdays, 9 A.M.-7 P.M., year-round.

23. RICHTER'S ORCHARD, Pulaski Road, East Northport. Wide variety of apples and peaches for eating, cooking, and canning. Fresh-pressed cider made on premises. Open seven days, 9 A.M.-5 P.M., from Aug. 10 to April 1.

24. ACKERLY'S FARM STAND, Stoothoff Road, Northport. Homegrown corn, squash, tomatoes, peppers, eggplant, beans, and peas. Open seven days, 10 A.M.-5:30 P.M. until Oct. 31; closed Mondays after Labor Day.

25. JOHNSON FARM STAND, 123 Cedar Rd., East Northport. Homegrown sweet corn (yellow, white, and bicolor), tomatoes, peppers, green beans, cucumbers, eggplant, and pumpkins. Open seven days, 9 A.M.-6 P.M., until Oct. 31.

26. ARTHUR SILBERSTEIN'S FARM STAND, 319 Cuba Hill Road, East Northport. All homegrown vegetables including six varieties of bicolor corn, eight varieties of squash, six varieties of tomatoes, plus broccoli, cucumbers, peppers, eggplant, cantaloupes, burpless cucumbers, yellow baby watermelon, and green beans. Open seven days, 9 A.M.-6 P.M., until Oct. 31.

27. DAVID F. WICKS FARM AND GARDEN, 445 N. Country Road, St. James. Lettuce, corn, tomatoes, and pumpkins. Homemade jams, jellies, and pickles. Cut flowers; annuals, perennials, hanging baskets, holiday plants. Open seven days, 9:30 A.M.-5:30 P.M.

28. FILASKY'S FARMS, Smithtown Bypass (Route 347), Nesconset. Specialties: honey and cream corn, tomatoes, vegetables in season. Pumpkins, gourds, and cauliflower in fall. Apple cider made on premises after Sept. 1. "Johnny Appleseed" story in greenhouse. Also, fresh home-baked pies. Open seven days, 8:30 A.M.-7:30 P.M., year-round.

29. BRIGHTWATERS FARMS, 1624 Manatuck Blvd., Bay Shore. Organically grown fruits and vegetables in season. Organic California produce during winter. Open Thursdays, Fridays, and Saturdays, 12:30-4:30 P.M., year-round.

30. OAKDALE FARMSTAND, 1380 Montauk Hwy., Oakdale. Long Island fruits and vegetables in season. Famous for sweet corn and tomatoes. Open seven days, 10 A.M.-6 P.M. (Sunday open until 2 P.M.), mid-March through Christmas.

31. KALER'S FARM, Montauk Hwy., West Sayville. Summer squash, peppers, eggplant, tomatoes, peas, cantaloupe, cauliflower, broccoli, cucumbers, radishes, and cabbage. Open seven days, 10 A.M.-6 P.M.

32. KALER'S FARM, Sunrise Hwy., Bohemia. Summer squash, peppers, eggplant, tomatoes, peas, cantaloupe, cauliflower, broccoli, cucumbers, radishes, and cabbage. Open seven days, 10 A.M.-6 P.M.

33. BLUE POINT FARMS, 171 Montauk Hwy., Blue Point. Local vegetables and fruit in season. Homemade pies, honey, nuts, dried fruit, fruit baskets, Vermont syrups and preserves. Open April 1 to Jan. 1, daily except Mondays, 9:30 A.M.-6 P.M.

34. BORELLA'S AGWAY STAND, Route 25A, Mount Sinai. Local vegetables, including white, yellow-and-white, and yellow corn, kohlrabi, beets, peppers, pumpkins, broccoli, tomatoes, fruit. Vegetables available in quantity for home freezing. Open seven days, 9 A.M.-6 P.M., until Thanksgiving.

35. DAVIS PEACH FARM, Route 25A, east of County Road 83, Mount Sinai. Ninety varieties of peaches (white, yellow, freestone, and cling), plus five varieties of nectarines. Upstate apples, plums, and pears in season. Fresh cider. Open seven days, 8 A.M.-8 P.M., during the peach season; shorter hours during late fall and winter.

36. SCAPPY'S FARM, 284 Boyle Road, Port Jefferson Station. Tomatoes, peppers, eggplant, dandelions, Swiss chard, beets, kohlrabi, lettuce, green beans, carrots, cucumbers, scallions, radishes, spinach, and broccoli. Open Mondays-Saturdays from 9 A.M.-6 P.M., and Sundays from 9 A.M.-5 P.M., March through November.

37. VALLEY FARM, Echo Ave., Miller Place. Homegrown produce includes green beans, cabbage, fennel, and spinach. Open seven days, 8 A.M.-6 P.M; March-November.

38. KENNEDY BROS. FARMSTAND, 530 Horseblock Road, (east of Waverly Ave.), Farmingville. Homegrown yellow and white peaches (cling and freestone), bartlett and bosc pears, sweet bicolor corn, beefsteak and plum tomatoes, broccoli, beets, lettuce, cauliflower, Brussels sprouts, eggplant, squash, green beans, melons, peppers, cucumbers, pumpkins, apples, basil, and cider. Open seven days, 7 A.M.-7 P.M. to November.

39. CIRCLE M AND GOUZ OF SUFFOLK, Route 112, Medford. Local broccoli, scallions, potatoes, lettuce, tomatoes, and corn in season. Special discounts on case lots for freezing. Open Sunday, 8 A.M.-6 P.M., Monday, Tuesday, Wednesday, and Saturday, 8 A.M.-8 P.M., Thursday and Friday, 8 A.M.-9 P.M.

40. LOHMANN'S FARMSTAND, South Country Road, Brookhaven (east of Bellport). Large selection of homegrown vegetables. Vegetable gift baskets made. Open Mondays through Saturdays, 10 A.M.-5:30 P.M.; Sundays, 10 A.M.-3 P.M., until Labor Day. Then Mondays, Wednesdays and Saturdays, 10 A.M.-5:30 P.M. through October.

41. BORELLA'S FARM, Old Town Road, East Setauket. Local vegetables, including white, yellow-and-white, and yellow corn, kohlrabi, beets, peppers, pumpkins, broccoli, tomatoes, fruit. Vegetables available in quantity for home freezing. Open seven days, 9 A.M.-7 P.M., until Nov. 31.

42. DAVIS YANKEE FARM, Route 25 (Jericho Tpke.), Coram. Homegrown corn, beans, peas, pumpkins, cucumbers, onions, and squash. Local peaches and apples in fall. Pick-your-own. Open seven days, 10 A.M.-6 P.M., until Oct. 31.

43. SOUTH MANOR FARMS, 184A Wading River Road, Manorville. Fresh produce and strawberries in season. Homemade jellies and jams. Fresh duck and chicken eggs year-round. Hanging baskets. Rabbits, chickens, goats, calves, and piglets; also hay and feed. Fresh chicken, duck, and turkey. Open seven days, 10 A.M.-6 P.M.

44. CONDZELLA FARM, Route 25A, Wading River. Tomatoes (including pick-your-own plum tomatoes), eggplant, bell peppers, hot peppers, cranberry beans, green beans, lima beans, blackeye peas, kirby pickles, pumpkins, vegetables to purchase off stands. Homegrown cantaloupes, cucumbers, zucchini, broccoli, cauliflower, red and white cabbage, Brussels sprouts. Open seven days, 8 A.M.-5 P.M. until Thanksgiving.

45. MAY'S FARM, Route 25A, Wading River. Homegrown vegetables including broccoli, corn, cauliflower, Brussels sprouts, cucumbers, purple cauliflower, tomatoes, peppers, eggplant, squash, zucchini, acorn and butternut squash, gourds, and pumpkins. Pick-your-own tomatoes, peppers, eggplant, strawberries, and pumpkins in season. Open Tuesdays through Sundays, 9:30 A.M.-6 P.M. through Nov. 1.

46. LEWIN FARMS, Sound Ave., Wading River. Local produce in season, including corn, potatoes, Indian corn, broccoli, kohlrabi, cabbage, cauliflower, melons, green beans, onions, gourds, tomatoes, eggplant, peppers, squash, pumpkins, and apples. Pick-your-own peaches, tomatoes, plum tomatoes, eggplant, cucumbers, peppers, squash, pumpkins, apples in season. Fresh cider during apple season. Open daily except Tuesdays, 8 A.M.-6 P.M., until Dec. 1.

47. OLISH'S FARM, Eastport-Manorville Road, Eastport. Homegrown tomatoes, corn, pumpkins, cheese pumpkins, and a variety of vegetables. Open 8:30 A.M.-6 P.M., from May to November.

48. FOX HOLLOW FARM STAND, Sound Ave., Calverton. Specializing in bicolor corn. Homegrown muskmelons, shallots, tomatoes, yellow baby watermelons, beans, squash, pumpkins, rhubarb, cabbage, cucumbers, purple and white cauliflower, lettuce, and broccoli; strawberries in season. Also pick-your-own pumpkins. Open daily 9 A.M.-5:30 P.M. except Wednesdays, until Oct. 31.

49. SPRUCE ACRES FARM, Main Road, Calverton. Locally grown vegetables in season; potatoes, tomatoes, green beans, cucumbers, cauliflower, and cabbage; flowers. Open seven days, 10 A.M.-6 P.M.

50. REEVE FARM, Sound Ave., Riverhead. Cabbage, cauliflower, tomatoes, squash, pumpkins, onions, turnips, Brussels sprouts, ornamental corn, green mountain and russet potatoes. Also statice and hardy mums. Open weekends and holidays only, 10 A.M.-5 P.M., until Thanksgiving.

51. FARMER JOHN STAND, Route 25 and County Road 58, Riverhead. Homegrown vegetables in season, including corn, tomatoes, peppers, broccoli, cauliflower, cabbage, beets, carrots. Open seven days, 9 A.M.-6 P.M., until Thanksgiving.

52. YOUNG'S ORCHARD AND COUNTRY GIFT SHOP, Sound Ave., (east of Roanoke Avenue), Riverhead. Seasonal fruits and vegetables, including eight varieties of apples and two kinds of pears. Dried corn, fresh peanut butter, honey, cheeses, and syrup. Jams, jellies, sweet breads, and apple cider (in fall) made on premises. Open daily except Mondays, 9 A.M.-6 P.M., until December.

53. BRIERMERE FARMS, 79 Sound Ave. (north end of Route 105), Riverhead. Homegrown fruits and vegetables. Wide variety of home-baked fruit pies (fresh peach, blueberry, raspberry cream pies in season) and specialties, including lemon meringue and coconut meringue pies. Large varieties of cakes, including pecan and chocolate, cookies, breads, including datenut, jams, jellies, honey, and cider. Pick-your-own apples, pears, peaches, raspberries, and pumpkins. Hanging baskets. Open seven days, 9 A.M.-6 P.M., until Jan. 1.

54. BENNY GATZ, 119 ½ Sound Ave., Riverhead. Homegrown green mountain and russet potatoes, kale, spaghetti squash, Brussels sprouts, tomatoes, shallots, turnips, cabbage, kohlrabi, cauliflower, onions, and pumpkins. Open seven days, 9 A.M.-6 P.M., until December.

55. MCKAY'S FARMSTAND, Main Road, Aquebogue. Homegrown peas, green beans, tomatoes, squash, berries, corn, pumpkin, cauliflower, and broccoli. Also statice and bedding plants in spring. Open seven days, 9 A.M.-6 P.M., April to December.

56. BINGER'S PICK-YOUR-OWN PUMPKINS, Main Road, Aquebogue. Pick-your-own pumpkins, gourds, turban squash, Indian corn. Open the month of October, seven days, from 11 A.M.-6 P.M.

57. LITTLE CHIEF FARM STAND, Route 25 (north side of road), Jamesport. Local produce in season including lettuce, corn, green beans, cucumbers, pickles, rhubarb, broccoli, cauliflower, cabbage, tomatoes, onions, Brussels sprouts, potatoes, turnips, beets, carrots, apples, peaches, and pumpkins. Freezer specials always available. Open seven days, 9 A.M.-6 P.M.

58. LITTLE CHIEF FARM STAND, Route 25A (a mile east of the village), Aquebogue. Local produce in season including lettuce, corn, green beans, cucumbers, pickles, rhubarb, broccoli, cauliflower, cabbage, tomatoes, onions, Brussels sprouts, potatoes, turnips, beets, carrots, apples, peaches, and pumpkins. Freezer specials always available. Open seven days, 8:30 A.M.-6:30 P.M.

59. RED BARN FARM STAND, Main Road, Aquebogue. Homegrown vegetables in season.

60. SKELLY'S FARM STAND, Main Road, Aquebogue. Large variety of homegrown fruits and vegetables. Cut flowers. Local organic honey. Fresh ducklings; chicken and duck eggs. Open seven days, 9 A.M.-6 P.M., until Christmas.

61. THE CIDER MILL, Main Road, Laurel. Locally grown vegetables including sweet corn, peppers, cauliflower, tomatoes, and lettuce; assorted fruits and homebaked pies, including peach, blueberry, apple, strawberry, and rhubarb. Cider in the fall. Open seven days, 9 A.M.-8 P.M., year-round.

62. MANOR HILL FARM, Main Road, Mattituck. Homegrown corn, tomatoes, peppers, squash, potatoes, cucumbers, beets, broccoli, cauliflower, Brussels sprouts and fresh dill. Open seven days, 9 A.M.-6 P.M., until late November.

63. COOPER FARMS, Breakwater Road, Mattituck. Homegrown tomatoes, cucumbers, and white and yellow corn. Pick-your-own tomatoes. Wholesale tomatoes starting mid-July. Open seven days, 8:30 A.M.-noon, until Sept. 15.

64. GENESIS FARMS, Damascus Road (off of Lewis Road),

East Quogue. Organically grown produce: lettuce, tomatoes, melon, squash, peppers, onions, and seasonings. Open Tuesday, Thursday, and Friday, 9 A.M.-5 P.M., summer and fall.

65. WICKHAM'S FRUIT FARM, Route 25, Cutchogue. Home-grown tomatoes, peaches, apples, pears, and muskmelons. Pick-your-own apples, raspberries, and grapes. Fresh cider in fall. Homemade fruit pies and preserves. Open daily except Sundays, 9 A.M.-5 P.M., until Christmas.

66. FARMER MIKE'S FARMER STAND, Route 25, Cutchogue (a mile east of Mattituck-Cutchogue Elementary School). Homegrown spaghetti squash, corn, tomatoes, potatoes, peppers, beans, beets, squash, gourds, cauliflower, cabbage, and cucumbers. Open seven days, 9 A.M.-6 P.M., until Christmas.

67. HARVEST TIME FARMS, Route 25, Cutchogue. Most vegetables in season: corn, tomatoes, squash, peas. Cut flowers. Open 7 days, 9 A.M.-6 P.M., until Nov. 1.

68. LITTLE CHIEF FARM STAND, corner of Bridgehampton–Sag Harbor Tpke. and Scuttlehole Road. Local produce in season including lettuce, corn, green beans, cucumbers, pickles, rhubarb, broccoli, cauliflower, cabbage, tomatoes, onions, Brussels sprouts, potatoes, turnips, beets, carrots, apples, peaches, and pumpkins. Freezer specials always available. Open seven days, 9 A.M.-6 P.M.

69. LITTLE CHIEF FARM STAND, Montauk Hwy., in Bridge-hampton, Hayground Market (just east of Corrigan's gas station). Local produce in season including lettuce, corn, green beans, cucumbers, pickles, rhubarb, broccoli, cauliflower, cabbage, tomatoes, onions, Brussels sprouts, potatoes, turnips, beets, carrots, apples, peaches, and pumpkins. Freezer specials always available. Open seven days, 9 A.M.-6 P.M.

70. THE GREEN THUMB, Montauk Hwy., Water Mill. Locally grown vegetables in season including 15 varieties of lettuce, a variety of squash, and cucumbers (including lemon cucumbers), yellow-and-white corn, white corn, zucchini, hot peppers, wax peppers, sweet cherry peppers, basil, parsley, mint, thyme, dill, watercress, arugula, chives, and coriander. Pick-your-own pumpkins after Oct. 1. Open seven days, 9 A.M.-5 P.M., until mid-December.

71. THE MILK PAIL, Montauk Hwy., Water Mill. Vermont cheeses, maple syrup, many varieties of apples, doughnuts, fudge, and local peaches. Fresh cider all year. Open Mondays to Saturdays, 10:30 A.M.-5 P.M.; Sunday, 2-5 P.M., year-round.

72. KRASZEWSKI FARM STAND, edge of Woods Road, Water Mill. Homegrown vegetables: sweet corn, tomatoes, peppers, cabbage, cauliflower, broccoli, Brussels sprouts, potatoes, beans, pumpkins, cantaloupe, watermelons, and flowers. Open seven days, 9 A.M.-6 P.M.

73. HANK'S FARM STAND, corner of Noyac Rd. and Stoney Hill Rd, Sag Harbor. Sweet corn, tomatoes, peppers, cabbage, cauliflower, broccoli, Brussels sprouts, potatoes, beans, peas, squash, melons, lettuce, and flowers. Open seven days, 9 A.M.-6 P.M.

74. HANK'S FARM STAND ON THE HIGHWAY, Montauk Hwy., Water Mill, 2 miles east of village. Sweet corn, tomatoes, peppers, cabbage, cauliflower, broccoli, Brussels sprouts, potatoes, beans, squash, melons, lettuce, and flowers. Open July to September, seven days from 9 A.M.-6 P.M.

75. NORTH SEA FARMS, Noyac Road, Southampton. Home-grown corn, squash, cucumbers, tomatoes, beets, carrots, lettuce, beans, and peas. Fresh eggs and poultry year-round. Geese, turkeys, muscovy ducks (year-round) available Thanksgiving to New Year's Day. Baked goods from Kathleen's Cookie. Open seven days, 9 A.M.-6 P.M., year-round.

76. THUNDERBIRD FARMS, Main Road, Peconic. Home-grown corn, tomatoes, green beans, squash, melons, snow peas, Brussels sprouts, lettuce, cauliflower, cabbage, onions, spinach, berries, peaches, nectarines, apples, radishes, cucumbers, broccoli, peas, scallions, shallots, radishes, zucchini, and local honey. Local fresh eggs. Open seven days, 9 A.M.-7:30 P.M., year-round.

77. WESNOFSKE'S FARM STAND, North Road, Peconic. Homegrown vegetables include potatoes, broccoli, white corn, yellow corn, red potatoes, cabbage, onions, squash, peppers, carrots, beets, cauliflower, and beans. Also large quantity of baby's breath. Open seven days, 8 A.M.-5 P.M., until December.

78. KRUPSKI PUMPKIN FARM, Route 25, Peconic. Specializing in early June peas, white sweet corn, rhubarb, acorn squash, white and purple cauliflower, three varieties of cabbage, Brussels sprouts, beans, broccoli, many varieties of pumpkins, gourds, Indian corn. Also U-pick pumpkins. Open seven days a week, 8 A.M.-sunset.

79. COVEY'S FARM STAND, Main Road, Southold. Home-grown tomatoes, corn, potatoes, onions, beans, pumpkins, squash, beets, and cucumbers. Open seven days, 9 A.M.-6 P.M., year-round.

80. BENNY'S FARM STAND, Mitchell Lane, Bridgehampton. Homegrown corn, potatoes, tomatoes, melons, beans, cucumbers, squash, kirbys. Open daily except Sunday, 9 A.M.-5 P.M.

81. SAGG SWAMP FARMS, Montauk Hwy., Sagaponack. Sweet corn, melons, potatoes, cauliflower, squash, pumpkins, and flowers. Pick-your-own tomatoes and raspberries. Open Monday-Saturday, 9 A.M.-6 P.M., and Sunday afternoon through October.

82. DOUG'S VEGETABLE PATCH, Montauk Hgwy. Bridge-hampton. Wide selection of local and imported vegetables; new gourmet shop includes fresh ground coffee beans, fresh and dried herbs, imported wine vinegar, olive oils, pastas, a wide variety of homemade jellies and preserves, and over thirty-five different types of freshly baked pies. Open seven days a week, 9:15 A.M.-6 P.M.

83. CARD FARM STAND, Route 114 (near IGA), Shelter Island. Help-yourself stand. Homegrown vegetables, raspberries, blackberries, fruits. Also dahlias. Open seven days, 10 A.M.-7 P.M., until end of October.

84. LATHAM'S FARM STAND, Main Road, Orient. Home-grown bicolor corn, melons, raspberries, cauliflower, broccoli, tomatoes, green beans, onions, potatoes and lettuce. Open seven days, 9 A.M.-5 P.M., until Thanksgiving.

85. SEP'S FARM STAND, East Marion, Orient. Locally grown vegetables: tomatoes, broccoli, potatoes, lettuce, corn, peppers, eggplant, carrots, beets, onions, cabbage, melons, squash, pumpkins, sprouts, turnips, and shallots. Also cut flowers and hanging baskets. Open seven days, 8 A.M.-5 P.M., through Thanksgiving.

Contributors to the Book

Acknowledgments

To the farmers and fishermen of Long Island who shared their time and expertise, I am grateful for much help and patience. Specific thanks go to these people, in no particular order: Ed Latham and his son Dan, Robert Van Nostrand, John and Ann Wickham, Claes Cassel, Sal Iacono, Tony Tiska, Pete Corwith, Mark Miloski, Douglas Corwin, Louis Gallo, Joe Birk, Alex Hargrave, Pat and Peter Lenz, Richard Miller, Vincent J. Daley, John Rempe, Calvin Lester, Paul Flagg, Lyle Wells, David Mudd, Phil McSweeney, Ray Halsey, Richard Hendrickson, Rich Harbich, Gertrude McCombe, Dave Relyea, H. Butler Flower, Neil Tully, Bill Pell, Ken Kurkowski, John Mulhall, Kevin DeVries, Wanda Mead, Richard Weir, and Ken Gall.

Many others from a variety of fields gave much needed advice and counsel. Thanks to Nach Waxman, Bill Sanok, Jeff Kassner, Charles Light; writers, cooks, and good friends Alice Ross and Libby Hillman; restaurateurs Karen Frame Pancake of Peche Mignon, Nicola Zanghi of Restaurant Zanghi, Maria and Guy Reuge of Mirabelle, and Jean Arondel of The American Hotel. At Harry N. Abrams Publishers, Eric Himmel, Pam Harwood, and Ruth Peltason deserve thanks for their support of this project. And at *Newsday,* Stan Asimov and Phyllis Singer worked hard to let this book happen; again, much thanks. Also, I am very grateful to Marie Bianco, Sylvia Carter, Bea Lewis, Alice Maenza, Eileen McDermott, and Herbie Wheeler at *Newsday* for their help and understanding. To J. Michael Dombroski, many thanks for making this book such a pleasure to create. And to Jules and Marjorie Bond, a hearty thank you for advice and support.

Index